THE MAGIC
OF
NEW ISHTAR POWER

AL G. MANNING

PARKER PUBLISHING COMPANY, INC.
WEST NYACK, NEW YORK

© 1977 by

Parker Publishing Company, Inc.

West Nyack, New York

All rights reserved. No part of this book may be reproduced in any form or by any means, without permission in writing from the publisher.

Library of Congress Cataloging in Publication Data

```
Manning, Al G
    The magic of new Ishtar power.

    1.  Success.   2.  Occult sciences.   I.  Title.
BJ1611.2.M33        131'.32      77-4502
ISBN 0-13-545137-X
```

Printed in the United States of America

Dedication

To the wonderful people who have inspired and assisted me in bringing this book to fruition.

Especially those from the spirit world: Ishtar, Isis, Marduk, Bast, Osiris, Thoth, Ra, Nergal, Prof. Reinhardt, Wild Eagle, Karakassa and all the rest.

And in their earthly bodies, Fay, Harriet, Sandra, Sue and all the members of E.S.P. Laboratory throughout the world.

Other Books by Al. G. Manning

Helping Yourself with ESP

Helping Yourself with Psycho-Cosmic Power

Helping Yourself with White Witchcraft

The Miracle of Universal Psychic Power: How to Pyramid Your Way to Prosperity

Miracle Spiritology

How This Book Can Help You

Magic, in the sense that we will use it, is accurately defined as *causing change in accordance with your will*. The magic I offer you here is so powerful, yet so simple to use, that it continues to amaze everyone who encounters it—even as it brings their fondest hopes and dreams into magnificent reality. With just the touch of your finger to a point of the star we will print for you in our first chapter, you will be in full contact with all the power and help you need to accomplish your most difficult tasks and achieve your most cherished goals! And just as flipping the switch turns on your electric light, so your simple touch will turn on the power for YOU.

What You Can Accomplish with the Magic in This Book

Your first introduction to Ishtar will put you into working contact with the POWER TO ACHIEVE _____. Go ahead and fill in the blank (mentally, not by writing in the book), and it will be yours. It works like magic, because by our definition above it IS magic. Let's take a quick look at what the magic has already done for others—and you can expect it to do for you also.

From the preliminary work in Chapter 1, Ralph H., who had just been laid off from his job, touched the magic star and in less than a week he had a new job at 10% BETTER wages. And for a quickie, with a knob pulled off and the picture hopelessly blurred, C.A. called out to Ishtar for help to see her favorite program—it worked and the TV has performed perfectly for many months afterwards, too.

Using the magic chakra check-and-cleansing technique of Chapter 2, Cheri J. brought her grades from a bare C average to straight A's so she could get into college. Using the same technique plus a small piece of stone, Harold T. not only eliminated all his asthma symptoms, but got a $175.00/month raise to boot.

By using the simple Ishtar Money/Fertility Rite of Chapter 3, W.H. increased his annual income from less than $10,000.00 to $150,000.000.

With the lovely and enjoyable Ishtar Renewal Rite of Chapter 4, G.F. cured a chronic gastric disturbance in less than a week; H.P. avoided an operation by dissolving a tumor from her throat; and O.N. cured his problem of impotence.

By applying the Ishtar Root Center Breathing Technique of Chapter 5, A.B. found himself being approached for sex by his wife for the first time in 15 years. And with the marvelous Ishtar Rite, *The Power of Positive Sensuality,* YOU can easily bring out the sensuousness in ANYONE.

Using the Ishtar Psychic Blockbuster technique of Chapter 6, Roger reversed the psychic attack and turned a long string of really tragic events into a richer, fuller, more prosperous life for himself and his family.

With this much, we have touched just a fraction of the power of only the first quarter of the book! It gets better and more powerful for YOU with each succeeding chapter! There is no way that mere words can convince you of the great power that eagerly awaits your direction to turn on giant faucets of riches, love, health, fame and power for you; or how fantastically easy it is to make it all work for you. But work it will! Let me give you a brief idea of how I came to know Ishtar and the other super spirit beings who work with him to help you. At least this may help you to understand the magnitude of the tangible power and help that Ishtar offers YOU through this book.

We Meet Ishtar—He Helps Us

Several years ago a powerful spirit came to our evening class at E.S.P. Laboratory and telepathically asked for the use of my body in the trance state. His goodness was so apparent that I proferred my body without hesitation. The entity announced that his name is ISHTAR and said that he would proceed to charge the aura of everyone present with a very special energy that he called THE POWER TO ACHIEVE. When he was finished, he challenged us to use his special energy in the week to come and report back at the next weekly meeting.

On the purely personal level, I was able to report honestly that on two separate occasions that week, a group of tasks I had expected to take me eight hours or more to accomplish somehow got completed in something less than two hours, and with *excellent* quality to the work. My wife reported receiving specific help in finding misplaced articles simply by asking aloud, "Ishtar, please tell me where I put...." Others who had experienced that first "dose" of Ishtar Energy reported similar help, so we eagerly accepted this Ishtar as a regular member of our band of spirit helpers. And his help got stronger and stronger—bringing us ever more wonderful results.

Let's pause here to agree that in the ancient Babylonian "Mythology" there was a female deity—goddess of fertility and battle—who was called Ishtar. The Arabian version of this same deity was a male god called Athtar. But let's not try to split hairs. My approach is to accept the personality and his chosen name in exactly the same way that I have accepted quite a few of my Spanish-speaking friends who just happened to be named Jesus. And in keeping with our E.S.P. Lab motto: RESULTS, let's borrow a pet saying from our football friends and say, THEY PAY OFF ON THE SCOREBOARD—the challenge is to get YOUR results, then you can call Ishtar anything you like, but I'm sure it will be something like Mr. Wonderful.

What the Power Can Do for You

Regardless of any present handicap (physical, mental or financial deficiency) that is apparently holding you back, YOU CAN USE THE ISHTAR POWER TO TAKE CHARGE OF YOUR LIFE EXPRESSION AND MAKE IT THE HEALTHY, SUCCESSFUL, OPULENT LIFE OF YOUR WILDEST DREAMS. Just to understand the simple beauty of our world and your magnificent place in it that is part of the explanation of the Ishtar Power would make this book worth thousands of dollars to you. But that is only the first of the natural benefits as you learn to use Ishtar Power to be the dynamic, successful being that you have always been in your wildest fantasies. When you have taken the simple steps to put yourself in tune with this power, you will look on the comic strip idea of Superman as a sloppy piker—you could handle the likes of him blindfolded with one arm in a sling! And indeed, as you use the easy techniques of each chapter, you will have the happy sensation of being a WINNER, EVERY TIME.

ISHTAR POWER is not concerned with your ethnic or religious background or the color of your skin, but the *quality* of your AURA. This power can as easily make you a multi-millionaire as you can earn the modest price of this book—whatever "miracle" YOU need to make your life a magnificent joy and pleasure awaits you in the proper uses of ISHTAR POWER. If you will but read and APPLY these easy principles, the true command of your life and all that affects it belongs to you. Back to paying off on the scoreboard, let's wrap up this section by saying simply, READ ON AND WIN!

Al G. Manning

CONTENTS

HOW THIS BOOK CAN HELP YOU 7

1. ISHTAR: YOUR PERSONAL POWER TO ACHIEVE ANYTHING 17

Historical manifestations of your new power to achieve... Your personal meeting with Ishtar... How to improve your contact with Ishtar Power to insure ever better results... Ishtar's power symbol, the eight-pointed star... The eight power points of the Star of Ishtar and how they are important to you... How to use Ishtar's eight-pointed power symbol to bring irresistible power into your life... What you can expect in the way of results... How to carry the power with you in the Ishtar Power Medallion

2. LET ISHTAR POWER SWEEP AWAY THE OBSTACLES TO YOUR SUCCESS 29

How the eight power transformer personalities work through your seven chakras... Correlation of Ishtar Power to astrology, music, color and psychic energy... How to check your psychic centers for blocks... Quickie chants to clear the blocks in your psychic centers... How to use gemstone energy to clear and enhance the psychic centers for greater personal power... How to call in a surge of omnipotent power to control any situation

CONTENTS

3. FOCUS ISHTAR POWER TO BRING A BIG BOOST TO YOUR FINANCES 41

The money rectangle—4 is the number of manifestation... Getting better acquainted with the money-energy transformer personalities... You form the fifth point and turn it into the pentagram of infinite wealth... Enhancing the money pentagram chant with color and gemstone energy... The ancient Ishtar Money/Fertility Rite... How to use the Ishtar Money/Fertility Rite to attain super prosperity

4. COMMAND ISHTAR POWER TO GET A FAST LIFT FOR YOUR VITALITY, HEALTH AND ZEST FOR LIFE 52

How to build personal reaction and response patterns that insure your perfect health... The health pentagram—the five lower chakras are your key to vibrant health... How to use the Ishtar Renewal Rite to return your body's health to perfection... How to use the Ishtar Renewal Rite to help a friend or loved one... Using the Ishtar Renewal Rite chant as a healing amulet... Using gemstones to help with special health problems

5. HOW TO APPLY ISHTAR ENERGY TO BRING A BIG BOOST TO YOUR LOVE LIFE 64

Sex appeal is 20% physical and 80% aura... Simple techniques to add sex appeal and charisma to your aura... The sensually powerful Ishtar version of the Root Center Breathing Exercise... Gaining the irresistible Ishtar smile and eye twinkle as a happy "fall-out"... The subtle, but strong power of scent... Using the Power of Positive Sensuality... How to use your aura to bring out the sensuality in other people... How Positive Sensuality put the life back into a 30-year-old marriage

6. ISHTAR ENERGY FOR CLEARING AWAY SECRET PSYCHIC ATTACK AND/OR OBSESSING ENTITIES 76

Paraphrasing Teddy Roosevelt: Walk softly and carry a big psychic stick... How to build and activate your own

CONTENTS

6. ISHTAR ENERGY FOR CLEARING AWAY SECRET PSYCHIC ATTACK AND/OR OBSESSING ENTITIES (Continued)

big psychic stick... What to expect in the way of help from your big psychic stick... How to practice Psychic Ecology to avoid secret psychic attack... How to recognize psychic attack before it has time to harm you... The Ishtar Psychic Blockbuster for the really tough psychic problems... 15 years of terrible obsession and haunting ended by the Ishtar Blockbuster

7. HARNESS YOUR ISHTAR ENERGY TO OVERCOME FEELINGS OF FUTILITY OR USELESSNESS AND ADD RICH NEW MEANING TO YOUR LIFE 88

You are no longer "on your own" (how to meet your Spirit Lover)... How to work with Ishtar's power and your Spirit Lover to find fresh creativity and challenge... Begin with high expectations... The Ishtar/Marduk Laser Power for burning your way out of life's traps... Do you have a special mission in this life?... How to attract the material and psychic help you need to achieve your mission or goal... How to find new dimensions of experience that make every moment of your life rewarding and fun

8. USING ISHTAR ENERGY TO BECOME A TRULY "SUPER" BEING 99

The secret of becoming a super new you... How to get your body, mind and emotions to work in harmony with your spiritual self and produce super new effectiveness for you... Courting the muse of creativity to bring through a gripping novel or major new invention... How to do your best work while your physical body is "asleep"... Ways to make the body alignment/dream exercise even more effective

9. GENERATE FINANCIAL WINDFALLS AND WIN AT GAMBLING AND CONTESTS— WITH ISHTAR ENERGY 110

Overcoming the "worthiness block"... How to become a consistent winner... The "Monopoly Money" technique... How to win in contests and lotteries... The Ishtar

9. GENERATE FINANCIAL WINDFALLS AND WIN AT GAMBLING AND CONTESTS— WITH ISHTAR ENERGY (Continued)

permanent thoughtform for continuing financial windfalls... How to consolidate and multiply your gains

10. HOW TO DRAW ON ISHTAR POWER FOR SPECIAL HELP IN BUSINESS OR TO GET A NEW JOB OR PROMOTION 121

How to use Ishtar's gift of the Power to Achieve to get ahead in business... The Ishtar Business Fertility Rite for super business improvement... Job hunting is easy with the Ishtar Job Attracting Fertility Rite... Open your doors of opportunity with the Ishtar Job Expanding and Promotion Rite... Retired or handicapped, but need extra income?

11. ISHTAR MAGIC FOR SPECIAL HELP IN STUBBORN HEALTH PROBLEMS 132

The Ishtar Unifying Rite for health... Special gemstone applications to heal or eliminate stubborn problems... How to make Ishtar Amulets for healing... Putting it all together to win the big ones... How to build a perfect figure—the Ishtar Body-Shaping Program... A note about where to get your gemstones

12. LET ISHTAR POWER OVERCOME THE TOUGHEST CASES OF LONELINESS, LACK OF LOVE, OR LACK OF RESPECT AND PRESTIGE 143

A look at yourself through the eyes of the world... How to use the Ishtar Attract-Friendship Program... Your right to loving companionship... The Ishtar Mating Call Rite... Developing the bearing and attitude that command respect... How to charge your aura with the energy that commands respect... The Ishtar Take-Charge Rite to control any life situation

CONTENTS

13. HOW TO USE ISHTAR POWER TO BRING YOURSELF GOOD LUCK AND THE "CHARMED LIFE" **155**

Psychic Magnetism, a small force operating constantly, can move the highest mountain (how to set your "Good Fortune" magnetism effectively)... Timing—how to make it work for you "The Chakra Check for Acceptance"... The Ishtar Metaphysics of the charmed life... How to earn a reputation of being lucky for yourself and others by your very presence... How to make sure that your good fortune will continue forever

14. SUMMON ISHTAR POWER TO SEE INTO AND CONTROL YOUR FUTURE **164**

A working picture of what makes your future... The Ishtar Future Viewing Rite—for a look ahead... When you see a big hole in the road—steer around it... Group Karma (war, depression, natural disasters, etc.) and how to turn its effects to your advantage... Harnessing the Ishtar Vector Rite to change the future... Using the Ishtar Vector Rite to increase the price of a stock in the market

15. LET ISHTAR AND THOTH HELP YOU ACHIEVE CONTROLLED OUT-OF-THE-BODY EXPERIENCES **175**

The natural separation from your physical body—usually called sleep... How to program yourself to remember your dreams and unplanned out-of-the-body excursions... Degrees of projection, astral and mental—the Shortcut Ishtar Exercise for Mental Projection... How to generate a fully conscious astral (or out-of-the-body) projection... Troubleshooting your astral projection exercise (what to do if you seem unable to get out)

16. TROUBLESHOOTING WITH ISHTAR— THE POWER OF POSITIVE STUPIDITY **186**

Your Master's view of the fundamentals... Applying the principles of timing to your work... How to increase the power of your magical rites by harnessing the Babylonian

16. TROUBLESHOOTING WITH ISHTAR—
THE POWER OF
POSITIVE STUPIDITY *(Continued)*

Planetary Hours System... Combining the power of positive stupidity with the planetary hours system for ever more effective magical work

17. NOW LET ISHTAR OPEN THE DOOR TO YOUR HIGHER POWERS 197

Passing your test of fear... Passing your test of love... Now comes your biggie, the test of power... How to pass your test of power... The rewards of passing all three tests

18. ISHTAR PYRAMONIX: DISCOVER AND WORK THE GLITTERING GOLD MINE OF THE PAST................................. 206

Mental projection to view past events... Picking your landmarks for a good look at the wonders of the world's distant past... Mining the creative ideas of the ancients... Another popular application—a look at your own past lives... Can we look forward too?

19. EXOTIC APPLICATIONS OF ISHTAR POWER 216

Another free gift for you—a source of great extra power... More magnificent applications of the Ishtar Multi-star Sheet... Special Ishtar gadgetry for even more power... Need still more power? There are ways... The most exotic power of all, back to the fundamentals

20. HOW TO MAKE ISHTAR A PARTNER IN YOUR PERMANENTLY VICTORIOUS LIFE 224

Putting it all together as a super love affair with life... What should Ishtar get out of all this?... Now, the fertilizer for the soil that produces your good and growth... The chain reaction of love and friendship... A parting word of friendship

CHAPTER 1

Ishtar: Your Personal Power to Achieve Anything

There are persistent legends of earthly civilizations, now buried beneath the silt of time, whose culture and technology far exceeded that of our present material excellence. Recent archeological discoveries have added much fuel to the fires of our curiosity—ancient Babylonian batteries that must have provided electrical energy to something—a bas-relief quite clearly depicting Television and its coaxial cables in ancient Egyptian artifacts—old Hindu scriptures speaking of flying machines used to frighten the elephants of opposing armies—of course the growing interest in pyramid power—and you will no doubt think of several more examples you have read about recently.

For the last 2,000 or more years, mankind has been so deeply immersed in a psychic, spiritual and intellectual dark age that most of these discoveries would not have been recognized at all without the technological advances of the last few decades for a fresh frame of reference. It will take many more discoveries to bring re-enlightenment to the world, but the time for *your* personal enlightenment is now at hand, and it is the purpose of this book to bring it through for you, and to bring you wealth, love, health and a brand new mastery of your life as the happy byproduct! You will find the process easy and rewarding from the very beginning—what could be more wonderful than to be shown the convenient handles and push buttons by which you can reshape your life to do, to be, and to have, all the things you have always wanted? We are ready to introduce you to your enlightenment and PERSONAL POWER TO ACHIEVE, but we need to set the mood and flavor for you with a few brief sentences of historical perspective.

Historical Manifestations of Your New Power to Achieve

The legend of the *Deluge* or Flood is found literally everywhere in the most ancient tablets, scriptures and folklore of the planet. A mighty civilization grew up and flourished by virtue of a special "extra" oneness and cooperation with Nature and her life forces. Then Man forgot what had brought his greatness and so strayed from his *oneness,* with the result that the tremendous technological manifestations of the age went for naught and were swallowed up forever by the sea. But traces of the grandeur of old were brought forward by the Ishtar Power into the magnificent civilizations of Sumer, Babylon, Assyria and Arabia well before the dawn of the "golden age" of ancient Egypt. Of course not as much is known of the pre-Egyptian civilizations as about the ones that came later, but we do know that each one waxed into magnificence while in tune with its magic, then waned and was destroyed as the magic left and the people were dependent only on the puny intellect and ego of their political leaders. Since our founding fathers were powerful occultists (see the face of your dollar bill, for instance), we can easily envision a similar fate for ourselves.

To avoid the downfall that history projects for us—and as a bit of happy "fallout" make our lives richer, fuller, more meaningful and abundant—it is clear that we must regain the magic of old. But I assure you that the REAL MAGIC is already your personal heritage. You have lived the magic in lives past and can easily re-kindle it in the present. And as you lift your own life to happy magnificence, you will be lifting your country and indeed the whole world with you. It is for this purpose that I now introduce you to a very special spirit entity who chooses to be called ISHTAR.

Your Personal Meeting with Ishtar

In the "How This Book Can Help You" section, I told you of my own first meeting with Ishtar and his ability to use the printed

ISHTAR: YOUR PERSONAL POWER TO ACHIEVE ANYTHING

word as a special point of contact with people. Now we will demonstrate it for you. As you read these words, the contact is being made, and the spirit of Ishtar is standing close behind you. Be especially aware of the skin area around the back of your neck. You should begin to feel slightly "goose pimply" there or "all over" in a few moments: then speak aloud just his name, Ishtar; and feel a gentle surge of extra energy flow into your aura and down your spine. Then take this introductory meeting as a perfect time to talk over your most pressing problem(s) and invite Ishtar's guidance and help. Know that the presence is there with you and that your spoken words are heard by Ishtar. If you immediately get fresh insights or mental pictures, do pay attention and *apply* the suggestions. But if you seem to get no specific directions or comments, just go about your normal routine with the extra zest and confidence that come from certain knowledge that you have the Ishtar Power working to bring you surprisingly wonderful solutions without any special action on your part.

Ishtar has a way of getting your attention with very happy initial results. For instance, here is Ralph H.'s experience. Ralph had just been laid off from his job. When he felt his first meeting with Ishtar, he asked for help in finding a new job, and in less than a week he was employed again. Here was his happy comment:

> The new job is better in all ways than my old one. Not only is my salary a good 10% better, but the people are friendlier and the working conditions are much more enjoyable. Thanks for introducing me to Ishtar.

Judy G. had just found a "lump on my body" and was quite frightened about it. During her meeting with Ishtar, she felt the urge to get pencil and paper. On a small sheet, she wrote, "Ishtar, please help me by removing this lump and its cause." She held the paper between her hands for a few minutes and felt Ishtar charging it with energy. Then she "pinned it to my undergarment where the lump was," and in just four days the lump had disappeared, never to return.

Irma N. was concerned not for herself but for her daughter. So she asked for Ishtar's help at almost her first sitting. Here is her comment:

> My contact with Ishtar really paid off. My daughter needed a job so badly and now has one paying $150.00 more a month than we anticipated. Isn't he glorious?"

How to Improve Your Contact with Ishtar Power to Insure Ever Better Results

There is an old Mantra Yoga technique which has been used for centuries to contact beings from the higher spiritual realms. A slight variation of this process will prove to be a highly effective tool to strengthen your Ishtar contact. In the ancient tradition you are given a two-syllable word as your "personal mantra" which you chant aloud a few times to get the feel of the sound of it. After which, you spend 15 minutes once or twice a day silently chanting your mantra—hearing the mantra "inside" your head. You are told that your mind may wander during your chanting sessions, but each time you realize it, just re-focus your attention on the sound you are reproducing in your head. Now let's give you Ishtar's two variations that will indeed make this a potent tool, bringing you the relaxation of the meditational process with tremendously helpful side benefits.

For this exercise forget any other mantra that has been given to you and use the word ISHTAR. Sit, or lay your body down comfortably and speak the mantra aloud a few times until you have the sound of it nicely inside your head, then remain silent, mentally chanting again and again, ISHTAR, ISHTAR, ISHTAR, with rhythm and harmony. Now it has been truly said that in an exercise of this type, your mind is very apt to wander, but with the Ishtar mantra you will find that the wandering is itself most constructive. Focus as intently as possible on simply repeating the mantra. Then when your mind has wandered, instead of just bringing it back, pause to notice the idea that distracted you—you will find that about 90% of the time the distracting idea is a creative solution to the problem uppermost in your mind at the time you started the exercise.

Martha C. found the basic Ishtar mantra chant very helpful. There is her report:

> I didn't realize I had anything in particular on my mind as I sat down for my newly scheduled 10-minute Ishtar chanting session. But I had only been hearing the chant inside my head for a couple of minutes when I realized that my mind had wandered. My attention seemed focused in the back corner of a drawer of my dresser. Suddenly it seemed imperative

ISHTAR: YOUR PERSONAL POWER TO ACHIEVE ANYTHING

that I get up and look there. Sure enough, way back in the corner was a very valuable ring I had somehow misplaced several weeks before. I thought I had really lost it. You can be sure that I resumed my Ishtar chanting session with a big thank you to Ishtar for the special help.

Michael W. had quite a different report:

> I knew I was quite frustrated with a problem that had followed me home from work. It was about that time, so I sat down to do my Ishtar chanting in hopes it would help me relax and calm down. After a few minutes I realized I had forgotten about the chanting and was mentally reviewing a circuit diagram. There almost circled in red was the error in my circuitry that had caused my frustration to follow me home. I grabbed a piece of paper and scribbled the solution to be sure it didn't get away. Then the rest of the chanting session was relaxing beyond anything I have ever experienced. My special thanks to Ishtar, and to you, Al, for introducing me.

Let me add a personal comment from the early stages of the specific research for this book. I often set about my basic problem-solving by lying on my office couch using this same Ishtar chanting technique. Very quickly, my mind would be distracted by the solution. But I generally wanted more material than came at any one time, so I would continue the chanting, trying to hold the flow of ideas in my memory until I was ready to get to my typewriter. But it didn't work that way. I would get a prod, almost like being poked with a stick, that said, in effect, "Go write this down so you won't forget it. Afterwards I will give you the next step." All through my personal Ishtar work, I have found Ishtar's emphasis to be on my *Doing the Task at Hand* that I already know how to do—when that is completed and I am *really* "stuck," the next input will come right away. I want to interject this idea strongly here, so you will understand more of the flavor and attitude of the wonderfully helpful friend, Ishtar.

Ishtar's Power Symbol—The Eight-Pointed Star

Figure 1 shows the Ishtar Power Symbol as it should be used on your altar. Figure 2 presents the same symbol, reversed for use as a medallion. Note first that it is in the shape of the eight-pointed star which has been the classic symbol of Ishtar since it came into this age from the pre-deluge culture. The tridents and center triangle stem from the original concept of the Trinity which came forward from the same pre-flood times as the Moon, Sun and Morning Star (Venus). While the Moon and Sun are the major figures, it is the Morning Star, Ishtar, which is responsible for the manifestation of all—hence we find the legendary Ishtar bringing the power of both fertility and winning one's battles. And though the Star of Ishtar Power Symbol gives the prominent points to Moon and Sun, it is through the junior member, Ishtar, that the power is transformed into that which is most usable by man. When you have both the feeling and flavor of the Star of Ishtar working for you, you will find that nothing can be denied you.

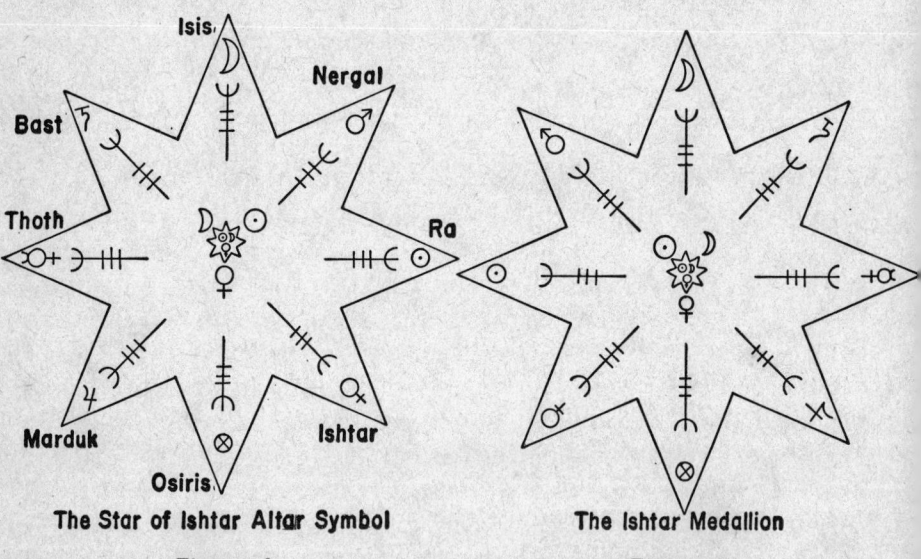

Figure 1 — The Star of Ishtar Altar Symbol

Figure 2 — The Ishtar Medallion

Let's work on the flavor first to quiet the misgivings of subliminal prejudice and make this magnificent power system acceptable to you. We will be using the names of the basic luminaries of our solar system and relating them to the Egyptian or Babylonian names of their corresponding deities. But this is NOT to be confused with religion. Regardless of your chosen religion (or lack of one), these power transformer personalities will deliver for you when you learn to simply push their "on buttons." In the setting of the early post-Deluge civilizations, electricity, gasoline, light bulbs and television also would have been deified—but you use each of these every day with no thought of it being "against your religion", and the same will be true of your use of the Ishtar Power if you will just take the time to understand it.

We can assert with completely acceptable scientific accurac. that the luminaries of our solar system are indeed radiating and/or reflecting ENERGY which reaches and can materially affect life on earth. The personalities who will enjoy using the old deities' names can best be understood as TRANSFORMERS (just like an electrical transformer) who convert the raw energy into a form most useful to you. We might give them letters or numbers instead, but the *personal* name is part of the flavor—all my plants and machines have names, too; my car is George, my motorcycle is Shorty, my favorite office plant is Leroy—and there is an extra rapport generated when you call them by name. You will understand much more of the value of this flavor and rapport as our work progresses and your mound of personal RESULTS grows ever larger.

The Eight Power Points of the Star of Ishtar and How They Are Important to You

We will begin at the top of Figure 1 and consider the points by traveling in the direction of the East, thence around to touch each point. Remember that when worn, the Star of Ishtar will face the other way, so that Figure 2 presented here is like a mirror image of Figure 1.

The top point, the North, is dedicated to the Moon. The energy transformer personality associated with Moon Energy uses the old Egyptian name, Isis. We are all familiar with the Moon's effect on tides and growing crops, but Isis will wonderfully personalize this energy for you. If you have read my previous book, *Miracle Spirituality,** you are already somewhat familiar with Isis, Ra, Osiris and Thoth, but in this work you will get to know them much better.

The Northeast point is dedicated to Mars. This energy transformer personality uses the name Nergal, and will bring you much extra physical energy and vitality when your contact is perfected.

---

* Prentice-Hall, Inc. (Englewood Cliffs, N.J., 1975).

The East point is dedicated to the Sun. This energy transformer personality uses the Egyptian name, Ra, and will bring you much extra mental power along with the special power of *will*. From him you will learn that clarity of thought is a key ingredient of truly effective *will power*.

The Southeast point is dedicated to Venus. This energy transformer personality uses the Babylonian name, Ishtar, and will indeed bring you all the fertility and victory associated with the legendary Ishtar. Yes, this is the powerful helper we have grown to know and love through his work with us at E.S.P. Lab.

The South point is dedicated to the earth. This energy transformer personality uses the Egyptian name Osiris, and is a source of love and prosperity to us all. All the gifts of the abundance of NATURE are brought to us by the work of this good friend.

The Southwest point is dedicated to Jupiter. This energy transformer personality uses the Babylonian name, Marduk, and is associated with the energies of healing, prosperity and creativity.

The West point is dedicated to Mercury. This energy transformer personality uses the Egyptian name, Thoth, and is associated with the energies of communication, both by verbal and written means and all psychic phenomena such as telepathic communication between "humans" and/or "spirit" beings.

The final point is the Northwest which is dedicated to Saturn. The energy transformer personality uses the Egyptian name, Bast, and is associated with spiritual power. Saturn, through Bast, is the great teacher of us all—the way-shower of life as it should be lived to the highest spiritual expression.

Note also that the symbol of the eight tridents is an ancient symbol of universal and irresistible power.

How to Use Ishtar's Eight-Pointed Power Symbol to Bring Irresistible Power into Your Life

Draw the Figure 1 version of the Ishtar Power Symbol to use for your altar-type ritual work. The Figure 2 version is the way it should look if you make it into a medallion to be worn. Whether or not you choose to use the medallion version, the altar version should be prepared as a major aid to getting better "plugged in" to the tremendous power that is now becoming available to you.

ISHTAR: YOUR PERSONAL POWER TO ACHIEVE ANYTHING 25

Warning: do not deface the figures in your book. If you have trouble drawing your altar Star, write me, Al Manning, % E.S.P. Laboratory, 7559 Santa Monica Blvd., Los Angeles, Ca., 90046, and I will be delighted to send you a *free* drawing of the Altar Star that is just the right size for your altar work.

If you are familiar with my previous books, you have already set aside an occult working place or "altar" where you do your meditation, chanting and ritual work. For those not familiar with it, let me suggest that a small dressing table (or perhaps a telephone table) be set aside in an alcove or corner of your bedroom or den. Minimum pieces of equipment for this work place would be two candle holders, a makeshift incense burner and a candle snuffer (a jigger will do if you use it carefully). Your personal taste and esthetic sense will take care of all the rest of the decorations or lack of them.

Take your Ishtar Power Symbol to your altar area and set it up with the East point toward the East, etc. It is best to be able to sit facing the East yourself, but the second choice would be to face North. Light your candles and incense (just consider it an occult tradition for now and we will explain more of the why later), then place the tips of three fingers of your left hand on the center of the eight-pointed symbol and say aloud, "Ishtar, I thank you for putting me in touch with these great power sources of all time."

Leave your left hand in position, and with your right index finger touch the point dedicated to Isis (the North), and say aloud, "Isis, Isis, Isis, thank you for your love, friendship and help."

Move your right index finger to touch the point dedicated to Nergal (Northeast) and say aloud, "Nergal, Nergal, Nergal, thank you for your love, friendship and help." Continue by moving your right index finger to the points of Ra, Ishtar, Osiris, Marduk, Thoth and Bast in turn, finishing with, "Bast, Bast, Bast, thank you for your love, friendship and help."

Then relax and thank your friends for the help you have recognized since your last session, and talk over current problems with them as time and your inclination dictate. During the touching of the eight points or shortly after, you will often feel gentle surges of energy sending shivers of power up or down your spine—or the soft touch of a spirit hand somewhere on your body. But the physical manifestations at your altar are quite unimportant; just feel your aura being charged with power and judge the result by the magnificent manifestations of the power in your life expression itself.

What You Can Expect in the Way of Results

Regardless of how long you may have been studying metaphysics and/or the occult, this exercise will carry you into a fresh "honeymoon" period with the spirit world. You will find the whole world treating you as someone special indeed, and the "fallout" of problem solving, healing and good fortune will prove to be magnificent at the very least.

S.K. had this to report:

> Last week a friend fixed our car as a birthday present and my boss gave me a 20¢-an-hour raise. I have been wondering for a time what Ishtar's power to achieve is. I started using Ishtar's star when I found it combated fatigue—then I found that questions I asked while touching the star were answered—but I didn't seem to see any improvement in my efficiency or ability. But now I understand better—all the little things I want are delivered to me by this person or that in my daily routine. I don't seem to have to do anything but want them. Wow! That's some power Ishtar distributes.

It had been a stormy romance at best. They had broken up several times with no communication at all between them for weeks, then a few tentative moves on Roberta's part had finally reached Jim again and the roller coaster started over. But the last time seemed really permanent to Roberta unless she could get some powerful outside help. So she turned to her newly-drawn Ishtar Power Symbol. Let's continue the story in her words:

> I felt I should not be the one to make the first move this time, but he had never given any hint of getting back together in all the other times we had broken up. I went to my altar and after touching the eight power spots, I asked for help, "Ishtar and friends, please bring Jim back to me with love in his heart and marriage on his mind." Next I made the medallion version of the Ishtar Star, and on the back I carefully wrote the same request. I pinned the paper medallion to my bra, right over my heart and wore it all the time, also repeating my request with the power-point touching ritual at my altar morning and evening. On the afternoon of the third day, Jim called and asked if he could come over. I said OK. He arrived carrying a box of candy and he had been in the house less than five minutes when he asked me to marry him! We were married in

exactly one week—it's wonderful. I really feel that Ishtar can do ANYTHING!

On the instant help level, let's look at this report from G.W., a widow in her early 70's living alone:

> I pulled a muscle in my right thumb yesterday and it was very painful. This morning I could barely move my thumb and it looked like it would be a very painful day just doing the bare survival necessities. I want to my altar area and went through the touching of the eight power points of the Ishtar Power Star, asking for help at each one. My thumb was healed immediately! It turned out to be a glorious day with many extra happy accomplishments.

How To Carry the Power with You in the Ishtar Power Medallion

In Figure 2, I presented the Ishtar Power Symbol in the medallion version. Roberta's feedback in the last section gave us a hint of the potential, and it is well to be sure that you have the Ishtar Power with you at all times. I personally wear a small sterling silver version, but you can do almost as much with a simple drawing (or tracing) of Figure 2. **The medallion is activated at your altar.** Do the touching of the points of your altar version, and when you are finished, transfer the power to your medallion by touching it in the same sequence. Then pin it inside your shirt or blouse (or carry it in a pocket above the waist), and whenever you need to call on the energy, just put your left hand over the medallion and think, "Ishtar, please help *now*."

C.A. had just finished her Ishtar Power Medallion when she had a special chance to try out its effectiveness. She reported:

> For several days the TV had been blurred and the audio very weak. On last Monday it got so bad you couldn't enjoy the picture at all. I tried to adjust the vertical hold on the back and the knob came out in my hand. I placed both hands over my Ishtar medallion, explained the problem and asked him to fix the TV. He did! Within seconds the picture cleared up. The set has never operated better, either audio or video, and the vertical hold knob is still in my desk drawer. ISHTAR FIXED MY TV!!!

A student found this his perfect help. V.O. had this happy report:

> I made the president's honor roll, Summa Cum Laude, thanks to my contact with Ishtar. I am never without my Ishtar Power Medallion and the special effectiveness it brings me.

Let's wrap our introduction to *your* magnificent Ishtar Power with this quickie report from L.B.:

> I am starting a new and wonderful position which is an increase and an upgrade for me. I earned it by my new super effectiveness that I have gained by constantly staying in touch with Ishtar's help through my Power Medallion.

CHAPTER POINTS TO REMEMBER

1. The Ishtar Power has been known and used by highly successful people, beginning before the catastrophe of legend and scripture known as the Deluge or Flood. It brings a special magic that is best described as a love affair with all life, and can easily manifest your fondest desires.

2. Enjoy your personal meeting with Ishtar which is so easily accomplished by entering into the spirit of the introduction process. There is always a bit of special help for you that comes as part of the introduction.

3. Use the basic Ishtar chant to deepen and strengthen your Ishtar Power contact.

4. Trace or draw the Ishtar Power Symbol for your altar, and use it to meet the seven other power transformer personalities associated with Ishtar. As you get to know them, you will find their omnipotent help always available to you.

5. You can maintain your power contact by using the simple ritual of touching the eight points of the power symbol twice daily while using the greeting chant for each power transformer personality.

6. Draw or trace the Ishtar Power Symbol Medallion and wear or carry it regularly to take a strong tie to Ishtar's help with you everywhere. The tangible results in your life expression will quickly prove its value to you.

CHAPTER 2

Let Ishtar Power Sweep Away the Obstacles to Your Success

The wonderful feeling of fresh victory is the best possible tool to produce more and greater triumphs. Do use the work of Chapter 1 and let Ishtar get your interested attention by bringing you many victories, so we can use that glorious feeling to make you an ever more successful WINNER. To insure that YOU constantly grow more wonderfully into the win column, we must combine an increasing sense of personal worthiness with a better understanding of the mechanics of the Ishtar Power and how it can be used to sweep away any obstacles to your ever more wonderful success. The first step is to understand how the eight power transformer personalities relate to your own seven Chakras or psychic energy centers.

How the Eight Power Transformer Personalities Work Through Your Seven Chakras

Nergal focuses the bright red energy associated with the Martian influences into your aura through your root chakra, the psychic center located at the base of your spine. Yes, this is the seat of the sex drive, but it also brings us our physical vitality and that special attractiveness to other beings most often called animal magnetism. A blockage of the normal energy flow through this center will manifest in your life as lethargy, that run-down feeling, or an "unexplainable" lack of ability to influence other people positively.

Ra focuses the brilliant orange energy associated with the sun's influences into your aura through your spleen chakra (this is a slight misnomer since the chakra is not located in the area of the physical spleen, but is along the spine about half way between the root chakra and your solar plexus—I use the term because it is an old convention with much inner meaning that we will seek to unfold later). This is the energy that brings you clear, sharp thinking with well developed purpose and a strong will. A blockage of this normal energy flow will show up as fuzzy thinking, confusion, or lack of resolve that lets people "walk all over you."

Ishtar focuses the bright yellow energy associated with the Venusian influences into your aura through your solar plexus chakra, the psychic center located just behind your physical solar plexus. This is the energy that brings your intuitional faculties to effectiveness, provides your sense of timing and poise, and instills your sense of aspiration to something better which lends richness and meaning to life. A blockage of this energy flow manifests as feelings of being cut-off or left out of life, depression, or lack of personal meaning and purpose.

Osiris focuses the gorgeous green energy of the earth into your aura through your heart chakra, the psychic center located along the spine just behind your physical heart. This is the energy that promotes growth, love, givingness, enthusiasm and prosperity. A blockage in this energy flow manifests as loneliness, lack of money and the frustration of "not getting anywhere".

Marduk focuses the electric blue energy associated with Jupiterian influences into your aura through your throat chakra, the psychic center located just behind the thyroid gland, slightly below the voice box. This is the energy of change, creativity and the breaking up of thoughtform causes of physical or mental ills. We will learn to use the Marduk energy in healing work, but it is important right now to be sure that you provide outlets for your natural creative drives. A blockage of this energy flow will make you feel stifled and/or may cause a flare-up in any chronic ailment.

Thoth focuses the indigo (very deep blue) energy associated with the mercurial influences into your aura through your brow chakra, the psychic center located just behind the center of your forehead. This is the energy of communication whether by psychic or physical means. It is a vital factor in maintaining the cooperation of all the other energy transformer personalities, as well as one's normal contact with the spirit beings in your own "band." A blockage of this energy flow manifests as a general lack of ability to communicate as well as inability to get help from your spirit band and the energy transformer personalities.

Bast focuses the violet energy associated with the great teacher symbolized by Saturn into your aura through your crown chakra, the psychic center just below the "soft spot" area of your head from when you were a baby. The keynote of this energy is purification and the learning or digesting of the spiritual lesson(s) of any situation. A blockage of the normal flow of this energy will cause "everything" to go wrong for you—the feeling of being kicked by your own child and bitten by your own dog, but clearing the block brings the spiritual power to succeed.

Isis is associated with the white light of the Moon or the red-violet of the union of the crown and root chakras. This is the synthesizing energy transformer personality, able to bring you the energy to clear blocks in any chakra, plus extra power from "outside" the spectrum of your bodily functions. There are no blocks to this energy, but it takes a well balanced cooperation with Ishtar to bring it fully into your life expression.

Correlation of the Ishtar Power to Astrology, Music, Color and Psychic Energy

In my introduction I commented that this book will wrap up all my six previously published books into one super-system. Here is the real beginning. On the personal level, I struggled for years seeking the simple correlations which Ishtar so naturally presents here. In Chapter 2 of my *Miracle of Universal Psychic Power*,* I presented as much of the correlation as I then understood. Now it is my special pleasure to complete it for you below:

Psychic Center (chakra)	Energy Transformer Personality	Luminary	Color of Light	Musical Note	Governed Area of Human Manifestation
Root	Nergal	Mars	Red	Middle C	Physical vitality, healing, material power, personal magnetism, sex drive

* Prentice-Hall, Inc. (Englewood Cliffs, N.J., 1974).

Psychic Center (chakra)	Energy Transformer Personality	Luminary	Color of Light	Musical Note	Governed Area of Human Manifestation
Spleen	Ra	Sun	Orange	D	Mental clarity, positive will, intellect, power of logical thought
Solar Plexus	Ishtar	Venus	Yellow	E	Key to energy transformation for practical use, aspiration, intuition, effectiveness
Heart	Osiris	Earth	Green	F	Love, givingness, growth, prosperity, wealth
Throat	Marduk	Jupiter	Blue	G	Creativity, controlled change, healing, thoughtform control
Brow	Thoth	Mercury	Indigo	A	Communication in all forms, psychic ability, spirit contact, mediumship
Crown	Bast	Saturn	Violet	B	Spiritual power, lessons understood, fulfillment
Risen Kundalini	Isis	Moon	Red-Violet or White	High C	Enlightenment, Cosmic consciousness, Total Oneness, Satori, Samadhi

How to Check Your Psychic Centers for Blocks

In the beginning, a brief contemplation of the areas of lack in your life may be all that is necessary to point out the chakras that are weak or blocked, but it is our theme to bring you the healthy, abundant life, so we will need ways to check your centers to clean them up BEFORE there is the slightest negative manifestation in your life experience.

My last book *Miracle Spiritology* gives a good method for checking the psychic center energy flow, but now we have a new tool to make it easier—your Ishtar Power Star Symbol on your altar. By holding the palm of one hand about ½ inch above the Ishtar Power star, you should notice a subtle but very real flow of energy. Don't dismiss this as the "heat from your hand," it is a wonderfully useful flow of energy. Now try the same thing with your other hand. Most people will notice a consistently stronger

LET ISHTAR POWER SWEEP AWAY OBSTACLES   33

flow to one hand than to the other. For convenience we will label the hand that feels the most energy your *receiving hand;* thus the other will be labeled your *sending hand*. We must pause to note that about 5% of the population will feel just about equal energy flows with either hand. If you are one of these, your hands are interchangeable, so you can use the one that seems most natural to you for the work. When you are finished experimenting with the energy flow and have designated the sending and receiving hands, we are ready to check the psychic centers themselves.

Place your sending hand, palm down, on the Ishtar Power Star and leave it there to bring in extra energy as you check the centers. Now bring your receiving hand palm to within about ½ inch of the center of your forehead, and feel the energy flow much as you felt it when you approached the Ishtar Star. Because there is no hair or clothing to get in the way, this is the easiest center to feel any time. When you are used to the sensation, move your hand to the point near the front of your head that used to be your "soft spot" and feel that energy flow. Continue to feel the energy flow from your throat, heart, solar plexus, spleen and root centers, and mentally note any differences in the feel of the flow. Since a weaker than normal flow of energy through any one center is a danger signal of present or future problems, the sooner we spot and cure a blockage, the smoother and more comfortable will be our life expression.

Quickie Chants to Clear the Blocks in Your Psychic Centers

Most blocks will respond to a quickie method of chanting that asks the power transformer personality for help. Move your sending hand to the point of the power star corresponding with the personality concerned with the weak chakra and ask: (e.g.) "Nergal, Nergal, Nergal, please bring me extra energy to break the block in your chakra." Repeat the chant over and over while holding your receiving hand near the center to feel the response. When you get the energy flow, the block is dissolved and the problem it represents should simply fade away.

Charles G. was experiencing the "embarrassment of occasional impotence," and was naturally quite upset about it. It came as no surprise to him when he checked his chakras and found almost no flow from his root center. Let him continue:

> When I found that my root center was not flowing, I moved my sending hand to Nergal's point on my altar Power Star and began the chant, "Nergal, Nergal, Nergal, please bring me the extra energy to dissolve my root center block and bring it back to a healthy, vigorous flow." I repeated the chant this way for almost 10 minutes before I noticed anything like a significant response. When the energy started to flow, I continued the chant for another 10 minutes just to be sure. Next day when I checked my centers, the root center was delivering very well, and I am happy to report that I have lots of vitality and am once more as virile as I was in my early twenties. For a man of 67 this is a truly magnificent rejuvenation.

Cheri J. was a high school student struggling to keep her grades high enough to enter a good college, but it was seemingly a losing battle. When Cheri checked her chakras, she found two that seemed quite weak, the spleen and brow. Beginning with the lower center, as it is most often best to do, she worked with the Ra point to clear her spleen, then the Thoth point to clear her brow center. Let Cheri finish her own story:

> I found that I had to clean out both centers just about once a week to keep in good shape, but it has worked wonderfully well for me. Believe it or not, I got straight A's to finish my last semester of high school, and I have all A's except one B in my freshman semester at college. Ishtar and his friends are wonderful.

For several years John H. had made a good living as a free lance writer. Then he "went into a slump" and in one month's time had four rejections of articles and "no good ideas at all." When he checked his chakras he found no energy flow through his solar plexus. He put his whole sending hand over the Ishtar point of his altar star and chanted, "Ishtar, Ishtar, Ishtar, please help me clear this solar plexus energy block so I can write well again!" After about 5 minutes, he felt the energy begin to come out of his solar plexus into his receiving hand, and very soon he had an idea of how to revise one of the rejected articles to make it a real winner. He went right to work on that one, and as he finished it, the idea came to fix the next one. As John said, "Everything fell nicely back into place and now with a feeling of a special partnership with Ishtar I am much more successful than ever before."

Henry K. was what he described as "middle aged" and settled in his home life and his job. He had reconciled himself to the spot in lower middle management as "as high as I was going to get." Then Henry checked his chakras and found a distinct weakness in the heart chakra. He didn't really expect much change, but Henry figured that "on general principles" he should try to clear the block. He worked with the Osiris energy from his altar power star, chanting, "Osiris, Osiris, Osiris, please send me extra energy to clear the block in your chakra." There was some response the first night, but it took a full week of 15-minute sessions to get a steady flow. Let Henry finish the story:

> The Monday morning after I cleared my heart chakra block, I was called into the big boss' office. He told me that I had been selected for promotion and my future with the company is bright indeed—I'm to be next in line for a Vice-Presidency!

How to Use Gemstone Energy to Clear and Enhance the Psychic Centers for Greater Personal Power

"What if I can't clear a blocked chakra with the quickie chants?" This is a valid question often posed by the serious student. Let's borrow from and adapt the work of my book, *Miracle Spiritology*, for the next step. In that book I gave a listing of the chakras and the gemstones normally most useful in positively stimulating them. I will repeat it now with some additions based upon our most recent experience:

ROOT CENTER — Red Jasper, Coral, Iron Pyrite, Garnet, Ruby Tourmaline

SPLEEN CENTER — Carnelian, Topaz, Agate, Tiger Eye, Quartz (clear).

SOLAR PLEXUS — Onyx, Marble, Gypsum, Pearl, Opal, Goldstone

HEART CENTER — Emerald, Jade, Chrysocolla, Green Adventurine, Beryl, Turquoise

THROAT CENTER — Lapis Lazuli, Azurite, Sapphire, Blue Adventurine, Blue Agate, or any of the Root Center Stones

BROW CENTER — Bloodstone, Moonstone, Zircon, Jet, or any of the Spleen Center Stones

CROWN CENTER — Amethyst, Rhodocrosite, Amber, Fire Agate, or any of the Solar Plexus Stones.

Notice that for each chakra there are very inexpensive stones available to help you—small tumbled stones work very well, and should come in the price range of a dollar or two at the most. Where possible, select your stone(s) by passing your receiving hand over a group of the chosen kind of stones and picking out the one(s) that give you the best feeling of a powerful, but comfortable energy flow. In the work we did in *Miracle Spiritology*, the primary method of harnessing a stone's energy was to physically tape it to the skin area in front of the chakra, and this is still a very potent way to do it. The alternative now is to carry the stone(s) in a handy pocket or purse, and fondle it with your receiving hand periodically during the day while mentally asking for help from the related Energy Transformer Personality. This should bring you positive results more swiftly and certainly than using the quickie chants by themselves.

Harold T. was an asthma sufferer. When he checked his chakras for weakness, he discovered that his throat center was giving almost no energy flow. He tried the quickie chants for two weeks with very little progress, so he decided that more power was in order. Here is his report:

> I have always admired blue agate, so I bought a nice one to use as a boost to helping Marduk clear my throat center block. I wear it taped to my throat center when I go to bed, and I carry it in my left-hand pants pocket so I can reach it easily with my receiving hand during the day. My asthma symptoms decreased from the first time I held the stone and chanted to Marduk for help. I have been completely off all medication for six months now. At the slightest hint of asthma symptoms, I reach into my pocket and grasp the blue agate while thinking, "Marduk, please help keep my throat chakra clear." It is a wonderful feeling to be free from the symptoms AND the medications. And as a happy bit of fallout, I've been so much more effective on my job that I got a promotion and a $175.00/month raise.

LET ISHTAR POWER SWEEP AWAY OBSTACLES

Ted G. had this to report:

> I felt completely out of it—nobody seemed to pay any attention to me at all, and my love life was at an all time low (I hadn't had a date in six months and there seemed to be no prospects). When I checked my chakras, I seemed able to get no noticeable energy flow from my root center I tried to open the chakra with a series of quickie chants to Nergal, but there was still no energy flow—so out I went to find a piece of red jasper. Arriving home with it, I could find no convenient way to fasten it to my root center, so I held it in my receiving hand with my thumb as I put my sending hand on the altar star and chanted to Nergal, while monitoring the chakra with my receiving hand (still holding the red jasper). In about five minutes there was a significant improvement in the root center energy flow. I kept the stone with me and touched it often during the next day—and the results were astounding! People who had regularly ignored me seemed to actually make a big, friendly fuss over me, and one casual acquaintance invited me to dinner, saying he had a cute cousin he wanted me to meet. Let's summarize the rest by saying I got promoted on my job and I'm dating four lovely girls all the time. My only problem is to decide if I want to settle down to married life or keep on as a debonair man about town. It's wonderful, and I keep remembering the cause so I won't lose it.

How to Call in a Surge of Omnipotent Power to Control Any Situation

Your basic Ishtar Power Star on your altar is a magnificent source of energy and help, but naturally it is not all that portable. In Chapter 1 we also discussed a medallion version which can be worn under the clothing or outside as a decoration. These power stars used in the power hook-up ritual will keep you extra effective, productive and full of personal magnetism, but there are still those times when it is highly desirable to bring your auric forces to a super peak of power—either to handle a big emergency or to win quickly in a confrontation or tense situation. For this purpose I want to give you the basic Pentagram Ritual evolved out of the work we did in *Miracle Spiritology*. This is the way I use it myself.

Picture a five-pointed star with its top touching the center of your forehead, one point touching each of your shoulder tips, and the other two points touching the points of your hip bones. Now trace the pentagram with me with your right hand: first touch the center of your forehead, now move your hand to your left hip point, next to your right shoulder tip, then your left shoulder tip, next your right hip point, and finally return your hand to the center of your forehead in completion of the figure. As a practical matter, you will find yourself touching these key points with the three center fingers of your right hand as you work. There is so much power to the pentagram ritual that just describing the complete figure with your right hand in this manner will bring a degree of immediate extra power, but of course we have much more to add.

Let us describe the figure again, this time adding aloud the simple salutation of the name of the related power transformer personality. Go through it with me, touching the point and speaking the personality's name this way: Ishtar (forehead), Bast (left hip), Isis (right shoulder), Osiris (left shoulder), Thoth (right hip), Ra (the completed figure by touching the forehead again). The good occultist or magician will recognize that performing this simple ritual actually establishes an immediate line of communication. Therefore, we need only use it effectively. In dealing with the power transformer personalities in this way, it is most effective not to ask for help, but to give thanks for the help you KNOW is already given and will manifest as needed.

Let me stay on the personal level to explain that I start any and all of my daily ritual work with this simple pentagram ritual. You can easily visualize me touching the appropriate points as I speak aloud, "Ishtar, Bast, Isis, Osiris, Thoth, Mighty Ra, Thank you for your love and friendship, your help, protection, effectiveness and prosperity. So mote it be." If you are seated at your altar, your left hand resting on the Ishtar Power Star will add much to your efforts. If you are anywhere else and are wearing the Ishtar Power Medallion, put your left hand on it as you go through the pentagram. Otherwise your left hand should be placed over Ishtar's chakra (solar plexus). This speedy little power ritual can be done anywhere and anytime you feel the need for extra help—it never wears out, but improves with use. You can also derive almost as much power from going through the whole thing just mentally if you are some place where doing the motions and speaking aloud would cause embarrassment. The beauty and power of this linking of the Ishtar Power Star of eight points with the classic Pentagram bring truly magnificent help.

LET ISHTAR POWER SWEEP AWAY OBSTACLES

H.N. reported:

> I was running late on my way to the airport when I realized I was stuck on the freeway. All four lanes had stopped completely and it began to look like I would miss my plane. This was clearly a time when I could use the pentagram ritual in my car in perfect safety. I went through the ritual like this: "Ishtar, Bast, Isis, Osiris, Thoth, Mighty Ra, thank you for your love and friendship, your help, protection, effectiveness and prosperity—and please help me through this traffic so I can make my plane." Within about 10 seconds, only MY lane began to move and somehow I got past the tie-up and boarded the plane with five minutes to spare. For all I know, the other three lanes are still sitting there full of stopped cars. You can be sure I said lots of thank you's to Ishtar and company.

Mary A. had supplemented her husband's income as a "hobby time" real estate sales person for several years. She was generally the one who handled small rentals and small properties. On a quiet Sunday afternoon Mary found herself alone in the real estate office with "nothing much to do", so she tried the Ishtar Pentagram Ritual to "stir things up a bit." Here is her report:

> Happiness is being the big winner! Alone in the office I used the Ishtar Pentagram Ritual and Chant this way: "Ishtar, Bast, Isis, Osiris, Thoth, Mighty Ra, thank you for your love and friendship, your help, protection, effectiveness and prosperity—and please send me a buyer for one of our big listings." I did it several times, probably to keep from doing the last bit of filing that was left for me. In about 15 minutes a gentleman walked casually into the office and I showed him a $150,000.00 piece of property, AND WROTE UP HIS OFFER all within about an hour's time. The deal sailed through escrow with no problems and closed yesterday. I'm especially elated because my biggest sale EVER before this one was a house that went for $29,500.00! Ishtar sure makes a great business partner!

J.S. was called "on the carpet" in the big boss' office and was in the process of being accused of a "horrendous booboo" that would most assuredly "get me not only fired but blacklisted as far as a reference goes." In the presence of the "bigwigs" he couldn't very well go through the motions and chanting, but he kept going over the ritual in his mind as he mentally asked Ishtar for help. Suddenly the big boss broke off right in the middle of a sentence with, "Wait a minute! . . . . ." The boss left the room with J's supervisor and returned in a few minutes to offer J. an apology, a pat on the back and a modest raise. J. never found out the whole story, but as he says, "It's really none of my business. Ishtar saved the day and my place is to accept with thanks."

CHAPTER POINTS TO REMEMBER

1. Since the eight power transformer personalities deliver their helpful energies to you through your chakras or psychic centers, you can check for blocks in the energy flow by sensing the energy flow of each chakra in turn.

2. Determine your receiving hand by the Ishtar Power Symbol test, then use it to check the flow of your chakras.

3. When you find a block or sluggish flow of energy in a center, immediately use the quickie chant to improve your contact with the related energy transformer personality and bring the energy flow back to the normal positive condition.

4. If one or more chakras fail to respond to the quickie chant work, select an appropriate gemstone to hold for the clearing process and/or wear attached to the weak chakra.

5. Practice the Ishtar Pentagram Ritual and Chant to have a powerful source of immediate help for any emergency or "tight" situation.

CHAPTER 3

Focus Ishtar Power to Bring a Big Boost to Your Finances

There is a special magic to the feeling of prosperity—we have all felt it at least once, and for that moment we knew that the world was ours just for accepting it. But all too often the "hot streak" fades away as quickly as it began and we rejoin the ranks of the "want" or "need more" group. Occultists, Metaphysicians and Magicians strive mightily with their favorite techniques, but have you yet met one who says he has too much money? It is the purpose of this chapter to put you in touch with the power to produce a permanent "hot streak" that will provide you with at least more money than you need, and for those who use the power well, as much as you want.

The Money Rectangle—4 Is the Number of Manifestation

It is a basic law of physics that a solid object can have no less than four sides. We find the same idea expressed in the alchemical and astrological postulation of the four elements, *fire, air, water, earth*. And for fans of numerology, you will remember that 4 is the number of physical manifestation. But for our purposes it is best to think of the number 4 embodied in the four sides of a rectangle the size and shape of a dollar (or hundred, etc.) bill.

To easily understand this section, I suggest that you draw yourself a pretty Ishtar Power Symbol which would just fit into a circle seven inches in diameter. Use the altar symbol format because you will leave it set up in a quiet place to work for you 24 hours of every day. Set your power star up properly with the Isis point to the north and the Ra point to the east. Now lay a dollar bill (or larger denomination if it appeals to you) across your power star from east to west, with the top of the picture's head facing north. You will notice that it covers the symbols of Ra (east) and Thoth (west). Going clockwise (which is the direction of creation) from the east, you will find the closest points to the dollar bill are those of Ishtar, Marduk, Bast and Nergal, and they are the energy transformer personalities whose combined energy will bring you financial abundance.

Now just to get a good feel for it, put your sending hand over your solar plexus and hold your receiving hand just above the dollar bill that is resting on the power star. Feel the Ishtar energy flowing up through the currency, literally filling your aura with the essence of money. Just that tiny bit of application can bring you fast results, as Joan Z. enthusiastically reported:

> I made the seven-inch Ishtar Power Altar Star and put a $5 bill on it as you suggested. I enjoyed the feeling of the essence of money, and when I finished I sort of forgot about it. But I got up from my altar with the urge to clean out a section of my closet. As I puttered around with it I noticed an old purse and decided to throw it away, but before I did I looked inside and found $50 in it. I have no idea if or when I put the money there, so it was just like a gift from heaven. I said a happy thank you to Ishtar, you can be sure.

Charlie B. reported a very helpful initial result, too:

> It couldn't have been more than 15 minutes after my first time of feeling the money energy flow to my hand from the dollar bill on my altar star when the phone rang. It was a sort of long-lost friend asking if it would be all right for him to come over and pay me back the $100 he borrowed from me three years ago. Honestly, I had mentally written that hundred bucks off as a bad debt long before, but it was nice to get it and even nicer to renew an old friendship and sort of restore one's faith in human nature.

Getting Better Acquainted with the Money-Energy Transformer Personalities

To insure a complete and permanent hook-up with the money energy, it is worthwhile to pause here to develop a better contact with the money-energy transformer personalities. Naturally, the better we know each other, the stronger will be our contact. We will begin by coming clockwise from the north point of your Ishtar Power Altar Star, to the first money-energy source, Nergal. Touch Nergal's spot on your star as we contemplate the beauty of his bright red root center energy. We know that this is the energy of physical vitality, the drive for procreation and therefore the source of your sex appeal, and it is the regenerative part of the healing force as well. This is the source of raw courage and the natural drive to make a success of yourself, but alone this energy would make you overbearing, arrogant and totally without respect for the rights of others. Thus, to be useful but not destructive, your Nergal energy must be balanced by the energy from the personality of the opposite point, Marduk.

Touch Marduk's point on your Star now as we soak up a better understanding of his role in your life. Where the Nergal energy is the drive toward acquisitiveness, the Marduk energy is the Jupiter blue of distribution, givingness. Thus Marduk maintains a free flow of good into and through your life, and works constantly to break up blocks that would cause stagnation—for instance accumulating your money in a tin box instead of using it for enjoyment or to make more money will bring out the slashing side of Marduk's energy and create a turmoil that will get the money flowing again. Thus the secret of working well with Marduk is to recognize the difference between a comfortable surplus and a stagnating accumulation—it fits the metaphysical idea of "never save for a rainy day, because that is to pray for trouble. Instead save for a happy day or a big opportunity, because that is to pray for increasing good and happiness." Marduk is also the bringer of the energy of creative activity, so to get along well with him you should cooperate in finding happy, creative outlets for your talents.

Now touch Ishtar's point on your Star as we soak up more understanding of the second pair of money energy personalities. I often think of Ishtar as the great door opener. This is the key to entering the realm of positive achievement. The energy he calls the POWER TO ACHIEVE is rich in intuition and a sense of timing, but it is also an aspiration to better living and a flowing force that goes ahead of you to smooth the way and get those whom you will meet into a receptive mood for you. Keep in mind that Ishtar's basic response to you is to your desire to make something better of yourself and all who are closely associated with you. But we must also be aware of the ancient occult saying, "The fruits of success turn to ashes in your mouth." And it is true that Ishtar's help alone would have a strong tendency to bring hollow victory after hollow victory. Thus we need the balance of the opposite point of your Star, Bast.

Touch Bast's point of your Star now as we seek a closer relationship to this most interesting personality. It is no accident that Bast is associated with both Saturn, the great task master and teacher, and the cat which is the most independent of all domestic animals (remember that legally you can own a dog, but you merely *harbor* a cat). Bast provides your drive for spiritual growth and psychological independence that will allow you to digest and enjoy the material and physical gains provided by the other three personalities. This is obviously the comfortable energy that allows you to say NO to an unreasonable demand on your time or resources, and in general keeps you wonderfully spiritually minded without the weakness of being used by others.

Let these fresh insights seep into the inner recesses of your being to help generate ever more positive and complete contacts with the money energy personalities as we turn now to the methods of turning the money rectangle into the pentagram of financial manifestation for YOU.

You Form the Fifth Point and Turn it into the
Pentagram of Infinite Wealth

Although 4 is the number of material manifestation, we need the motive power of the number 5 to bring the riches through to you. We closed Chapter 2 with a basic pentagram ritual that has been used primarily for protection for eons. Many have tried to use it also for a prosperity ritual, but have had little in the way of results because they were calling on the wrong set of energy transformer personalities. But you have now met the right personalities, so we have but to slightly adapt the Chapter 2 pentagram ritual to make it the money ritual that can bring you literally infinite wealth.

We will assume that you are comfortably seated in front of your Ishtar Altar Star and have your sample of currency properly placed. Begin by holding your receiving hand just above the Altar Star, and feel it soaking up the energy and essence of money. Let your receiving hand remain in that position (it's okay to let the tips of your fingers rest on the Star to keep your arm from getting tired.). As you raise your sending hand to the center of your forehead, speak aloud the name, Ishtar. Move your sending hand to your left hip point and speak the name, Marduk. Move your sending hand to your right shoulder and speak the name, Bast. Move your sending hand to your left shoulder point and speak the name, Nergal. Move your sending hand to your right hip point and speak the word, Prosperity (or money). Then return your sending hand to the center of your forehead to close the figure, as you speak the words, For (your name), until you feel that it is finished and your word has become the LAW OF THE UNIVERSE. Then close by saying, "Thank you, and so mote it be."

It works wonders, as S.N. reports:

> I needed a $150,000 loan to keep from losing my business. I had applied to 10 different banks and insurance companies and had been turned down by each of them. My back was really to the wall. In desperation I used the Money Pentagram Ritual and instead of the word prosperity or money, I said, "$150,000 for S.," using the ritual over and over again. I must have sat there for 45 minutes making the pentagram and speaking the words. Then I felt it was finished. All I can say is I needed a financial miracle and I received it. The next morning at work, I got a call from one of the bankers who had turned me down. He said his loan committee had reconsidered and decided to go along with me. I thank you and all the prayer partners at E.S.P. laboratory. My business was saved!

O.L. tried a different approach and won. Here is her report.

> I set up my Ishtar Altar Star with a $10 bill and put my lottery ticket on top. I used the pentagram ritual with the

words, "Ishtar, Marduk, Bast, Nergal, Lottery Winner, for O.," and it worked! I chanted for about 15 minutes until I felt it was accomplished, and I came up a winner. I'm sending a tithe to say thanks to our spirit friends and the Lab.

B.F. made a bit of a deal with Ishtar, and here is his report:

Promised Ishtar 10% for the Lab if I won at the races. Then I did the money pentagram ritual. For the first time in a long time I was a winner—came home with $990 more than I went with. Thanks to Ishtar, and here is my $99 check for the Lab.

Enhancing the Money Pentagram Chant with Color and Gemstone Energy

During the times that you are using the Ishtar Money Pentagram Ritual, it is important to maintain a high level of awareness and effectiveness—you never know where your good is coming from and should be alert to make the most of your opportunities. Regular checking of the energy flow, particularly of the four key money chakras, and enhancing of their energy flow will help to bring you maximum results. Most of us can quite easily wear a gemstone to stimulate the solar plexus and throat chakras (I generally wear a topaz on my own solar plexus and often a pet piece of lapis lazuli on my throat chakra), but there are practical difficulties to wearing a stone on either your root chakra or the crown chakra. Here we can compensate by wearing bright red colors for the root, and violet or purple colors for the crown chakra. Your ingenuity and personal taste will help you devise special ways of your own to bring the power to a very effective level.

C.J. had this to report:

I had been using the basic Ishtar Star Money Ritual for about a week with very little success. It seemed that my key money chakras would plug back up almost as soon as I finished the ritual, and each time I started I had to really struggle to get any energy flow. So I dropped in on a little rock shop in our neighborhood and bought myself four pretty stones, a red jasper, a topaz, a blue agate and an amethyst. It was probably the best $6.00 I've ever spent in my life. As soon as I got home I went to my altar and permanently taped the topaz to my solar plexus and the blue agate to my throat chakra. And for the exercise itself, I put the red jasper on Nergal's point of the Altar Star and the amethyst on Bast's point. This time the ritual seemed to bring a much better reponse from all my chakras, and since then, by carrying the stones I can't comfortably wear and wearing lots of reds and purples, I can feel the power really working for me.

As to results, I am an insurance salesman, and I'm happy to announce that starting a week into the month, I still finished last month with the best sales record of any month in my life, and so far this month I'm running better than 10% ahead of even that! It really helps to learn the tricks of the trade—this time I mean the use of the Ishtar energies. My thanks to Ishtar and to you, Al, for the beautiful introduction and the excellent instruction.

The Ancient Ishtar Money/Fertility Rite

Before man's society became so technologically complex, our utter dependence upon the produce of the soil was much more obvious. Modern man uses machines to plow, plant, fertilize and harvest his crops (almost totally out of sight and mind of the city dwelling consumer), but all of this would be wasted expense without the cooperation of Nature. Even with his marvelous technological expertise, man still finds himself vulnerable to drought, flood, "pests" and other often unknown drains on the productivity of his growing crops. And if nothing else, the city dweller certainly suffers from the resultant higher prices for his food and clothing. All of this has been a way to prepare you to look empathetically upon a mental picture of ancient man, without benefit of modern technology, performing ritual copulation in his growing fields quite literally to "give the plants the idea" that reproduction is their purpose.

NO, I'm not going to try to lure you and your mate out into some corn field in the nude to perform ritual sex. But we can understand a lot more of the power of sympathetic magic as we recognize that moods and urges are indeed transmitted by something akin to electrical induction. Let me state categorically that when the ancient rites of ritual copulation were performed in the fields, the crops indeed did grow better and yield more produce! And our purpose here is to learn to achieve the same result, and find a greater enjoyment of life itself in the process. We all remember Freud's emphasis on the negative consequences of repressed sexuality, but perhaps it took the generation of flower children to prepare us for an updated version of Norman Vincent Peale's *Power of Positive Thinking*.* We might stick with the same terminology and call this the OMNIPOTENT POWER OF POSITIVE SEXUALITY.

Modern Psychology recognizes everything from overpowered cars to fancy clothes and gourmet foods as overt expressions of sexuality. These physical things may be enjoyable of themselves, but the truly omnipotent power of positive sexuality resides in the more subtle world of imagination and the chakra energies. In my *Miracle of Universal Psychic Power* (page 104), I gave a special bit of raw power in a thing I called the "Root Center Breathing Exercise." Its purpose in that context was to make every living creature you meet respond to you in a more friendly and a more loving manner. You will not object to that sort of happy fallout from the Ishtar Money/Fertility Rite, I'm sure, but this has the primary purpose of making you RICH. It is useful to warm up with that basic root center exercise in preparation for the complete fertility rite. Here is an abbreviated version that will work well as a starter:

Take a deep breath, pushing it way down into the deepest parts of your diaphragm. Then hold it as you *will* and *image* the extra energy of the breath directed all the way down to your root chakra, then flowing out the chakra as a surge of bright red energy that curves down, then up and around, completing a great sphere of the red energy all around the outer edges of your aura, and re-entering your body through your crown center. When it feels necessary, let out your breath and take another one as deep or deeper, but keep the image of the bright red glowing and flowing in your aura. Five or six minutes of this should have you feeling full of pep and indeed mildly "turned on." Then you are ready for the new power.

How to Use the Ishtar Money/Fertility Rite to Attain Super Prosperity

The theme of this fertility rite is your astral participation in a very special bit of love making. You will happily join the energy

---

*Norman Vincent Peale, *The Power of Positive Thinking* (Englewood Cliffs, N.J.: Prentice-Hall, Inc. 1954: 39th Printing).

FOCUS ISHTAR POWER FOR A BOOST TO YOUR FINANCES

transformer personalities in producing the astral unions which promote the full flow of riches into your personal experience. You have been working with the bright red Nergal energy, now lift it up to your Solar Plexus as a love offering to Ishtar (do it in your imagination at first, but a little practice will demonstrate an ever growing reality to each step). Feel the union of the red and the yellow so fully that the bright orange of Ra is synthesized in the joy of it—let your emotions participate in the full feelings of mutual love and union. When "it is done", lift Ishtar's bright yellow energy up as a love offering to Marduk, and participate in the joyous union that synthesizes the green of Osiris. When you have shared that loving union and are ready, lift the electric blue of Marduk up as a love offering to Bast and share in the beautiful emotions that synthesize the bright indigo of Thoth.

Now if we were working for an ecstatic spiritual experience, we would float on off into the mystical realms to commune with a happy oneness with the universe—and you may want to do that from time to time because it is a magnificent experience. But our purpose at this point is to use the energy on the practical material level, so there is one more step. Bring the brilliant violet energy of Bast back to your root center to complete the loving with Nergal and feel it synthesize the glorious White of Isis.

Now recognize that you have completed the most powerful creative circle of energy in the universe, and continue to live the loving unions agains and again as you chant:

> "Nergal, Ishtar, Marduk, Bast, our loving union's here at last.
> Ishtar, Marduk, Bast, Nergal, feel the power drawing circle.
> Manifest so naturally, and bring great riches straight to me.
> Marduk, Bast, Nergal, Ishtar, make me a point in this great star.
> Bast, Nergal, Ishtar, Marduk, together now great things we'll do.
> With money piled so high you see, that we can use it wondrously.
> Our purpose true, indeed must be to make a winner out of me."

After you get the rhythm and feel of the chant, it is most effective when used with your receiving hand resting on your Ishtar Altar Star and your sending hand moving to touch each chakra as the energy transformer personality is called by name. The chant should be used from three to 21 times or until you feel that it is a completed project. Then it is reasonable and proper to sit quietly and talk over specific goals with your four power sources, asking for guidance and specific help. Be sure to thank them for their help, and invite them to go with you as you leave your altar to apply the new power to your practical goals and tasks.

R.S., a young engineer had been having a very mediocre career in the aerospace and communications industries. After being laid off from the third job in four years, he decided to go into business for himself. He developed a couple of simple products to market and also "hung out a shingle" as a consultant. After a few months he was "making it, but only because my wife had a good job and was carrying more than half of our household expenses." Let's look at his report:

> Al, I was pretty frustrated at my lack of financial progress, so I was ready to try just about anything. Your Ishtar work certainly sounded appealing, and I got a good feeling when I used the Altar Star. So I decided to try the Ishtar Money/Fertility Rite. The root center breathing part was simple enough, but I had to do the energy union bit mostly in my imagination—for the first few days. I allocated one-half hour a night and resolved to give it two weeks to do something for me. Now let me say that up until this time, my biggest day of total orders was right at $200. Then on the fifth day of using the fertility rite, my mail and phone orders totaled a magnificent $2,036! And the change has held up! Almost over night, my business increased to better than 10 times the dollar volume it had been doing. Suddenly I have a whole new wonderful set of problems, like where to invest my money and how to use income averaging and all sorts of methods to cut down my income tax. I have shortened the fertility rite to take only about 10 minutes a night, but I suspect that I will do it for the rest of my life—it's the best time I can possibly spend to stay happily prosperous!

W.H. is an "amateur chemist" who had struggled for three years to gather the equipment to make and market a common product by a new and exceptionally inexpensive process he had conceived. During the whole three years he had had no success or encouragement at all, and he was quite ready to "try anything." Here is his report:

> I used the Ishtar Money/Fertility Rite, and after the first session I felt so good that I talked over the process and the

equipment and financing problems with those wonderful energy transformer personalities. We had a nice chat (of course I did all the talking), and I came away with a good feeling that they would help. The very next day, a man who had already turned me down twice called me up and said he had been thinking about me last night and decided to let me have the equipment I needed at no money down with very easy payments. The results are indeed magnificent. Let's put it this way—I got started in the second half of the year and still *netted* $70,000. Considering that I have never made as much as $10,000 in a whole year before, you get the idea. And next year with a full year's operation I expect to make more than $150,000 net before taxes. As you can imagine, I do the fertility rite quite often now, mostly to say thank you to the energy transformer personalities.

CHAPTER POINTS TO REMEMBER

1. 4 is the number of physical manifestation. The rectangle of a dollar bill is an excellent example for our work.

2. Draw a neat Ishtar Altar Power Star just seven inches in diameter, and set it up with the Isis point to the north. Then place a dollar bill across the star so that the picture's head faces the north. Hold your receiving hand over the star and feel your aura soaking up the ESSENCE OF MONEY.

3. Take the trouble to experiment and get better acquainted with Nergal, Ishtar, Marduk, and Bast. They are the energy transformer personalities directly connected to your personal prosperity and money supply.

4. You next learn to make yourself the fifth point, thus turning the money rectangle into a money pentagram to bring riches to you in abundance.

5. Use the money pentagram ritual often, and enhance the related psychic centers by direct application of gemstones and/or wearing chakra stimulating colors.

6. Ancient fertility rites were meant to give the plants and nature spirits the idea that their purpose is reproduction—they are intrinsically good in nature and THEY WORK.

7. The Ishtar Money/Fertility Rite will work for you—use it to bring abundance and super prosperity into your life permanently.

CHAPTER 4

Command Ishtar Power to Get a Fast Lift for Your Vitality, Health and Zest for Life

It is quite appropriate to begin this chapter by paraphrasing one of the classic pronouncements of the U.S. Surgeon General by saying: CAUTION: LIVING IN THE UNITED STATES MAY BE HAZARDOUS TO YOUR HEALTH. Certainly the economic, sociological and emotional pressures that we confront in modern society cause our physical and emotional bodies amounts of psychological stress undreamed of by our forefathers. Science tells us that stress is a bigger killer than either guns or automobiles! But not for everybody! Some people seem to thrive on pressure, although it literally kills others. Let's show *you* how to thrive on today's problems and handle them with ever increasing vitality and zest, right here and now.

How to Build Personal Reaction and Response Patterns that Insure Your Perfect Health

It is extremely important to recognize that your growing rapport with the energy transformer personalities adds power and effectiveness to your every thought and action. And that is wonderful! But the power that we gain brings with it new sets of responsibilities for its intelligent use. Nowhere in life is this more evident than in the special area of physical health and emotional well being. A quick review of the "fundamentals" will help to set the stage for our new ways to attain and keep perfect health—surely the first steps to health are to quit thinking and *feeling* the things that make us sick. In each of my first three books I presented a "Table of Mental Poisons and Their Symptoms," making minor additions and changes until the last printing in my *Helping Yourself with Psycho-Cosmic Power.** I was surprised at how few changes I wanted to make to present it here—perhaps the most significant one is in the title. Let's look at it now as a table of mental/emotional poisons and their symptoms.

Poison Mental/Emotional Patterns	Resulting Symptoms
1. Resentment, Bitterness, Hatred (or psychic attack)	Skin rash, boils, acne, blood disorders, cancer, allergies, heart trouble, stiff joints, arthritis, rheumatism, stomach trouble.
2. Confusion, Frustration, Anger	Common cold, pneumonia, tuberlosis, emphysema; disorders of the respiratory tract, asthma; eye, ear, nose and throat trouble.
3. Anxiety, Impatience, Greed, Repression	High blood pressure, migraine headaches, ulcers, nearsightedness, hard of hearing, heart attacks.
4. Cynicism, Pessimism, Defeatism	Low blood pressure, anemia, polio, diabetes, leprosy, low income, kidney disorders, aching backs.
5. Revulsion, Fear, Guilt	Accidents, cancer, personal failure, impotence, poverty, poor sex, "tired blood".
6. Antagonism, Inferiority, Introversion	Allergies, recurring headaches, lack of friends, heart murmur, accident prone.

---

* Prentice-Hall, Inc. (Englewood Cliffs, N.J., 1968)

Obviously, a tiny bit of one of these mental/emotional poisons will not manifest as the worst symptom on its list for you overnight. But the better you get at producing positive effects deliberately, the better you become at producing negative effects when you slip and wallow in emotional poisons. Thus our path to perfect health, vitality and zest for life, does clearly begin with a bit of mental/emotional housecleaning. Remember that regardless of how justified your anger or resentment may be, YOU CAN'T AFFORD THE EFFECT IN YOUR LIFE, so you must release it and go on to happier things. I will not belabor this with a whole program of getting rid of your guilt, resentment, etc.,—I've done that in previous books (like *Helping Yourself with Psycho-Cosmic Power*). Let's just let this section stand as a word to the wise and a place to start if you find it necessary to trouble-shoot your positive work. One thing I can guarantee you—every time you seem to get a negative effect from your positive work, it is because a poison listed above was present in too great a quantity.

The Health Pentagram—the Five Lower Chakras Are Your Key to Vibrant Health

Just as 4 is the number of physical manifestation, so 5 is the number of movement and dynamics—and health is clearly a dynamic situation, perpetuated only as we are able to direct the forces of change in a positive manner. Thus, it is easy to understand that the five lower chakras must work in smooth cooperation to restore or maintain your vibrant health. Let's first relate the energy transformer personalities to the *Table of Mental/Emotional poisons and Their Symptoms* for a better handle on the functioning of your physical/emotional/mental organism.

Nergal's bright red center is attacked and restricted by feelings of revulsion, guilt, inferiority and many forms of fear. Keep it clear to ensure your high energy level and attractiveness to others.

Ra's brilliant orange center is attacked and blocked by resentment, bitterness, hatred and anger. Keep this one clear to assure your mental effectiveness.

COMMAND ISHTAR POWER FOR VITALITY AND HEALTH 55

Ishtar's lovely yellow center is rendered ineffective by confusion, frustration and anxiety. Keep this one clear to enjoy the power of intuition and fun emotions.

Osiris' lush green center loses its natural power when you are suffering from cynicism, pessimism, defeatism and introversion. Keep this one clear to ensure a steady flow of nourishment and sustenance from the Infinite.

Marduk's electric blue center is hampered by antagonism, impatience, greed and any kind of repression. Keep this one clear to assure your creativity and protection from negative thought-forms (yours and others').

We have already learned the value of checking the energy flow of your chakras with your receiving hand. Now when you notice a restricted flow in one or more centers, you will have a better idea of the negative mental/emotional patterns that are the cause. Recognize that there are two distinct parts to a permanent healing—first, you must unplug any blocked centers and get the energy flowing in balance and harmony through all five health centers—and second, you must take all necessary steps to keep from plugging them up again. And if you do healing work for others as we will suggest in a later part of this chapter, the key to lasting success is that you spot the blocked centers, clean them out, then give your patient a homework assignment to drop the poisonous mental/emotional patterns that are the true cause of the malady.

We should take note that as you are doing the work of healing for yourself, there will be occasions when an old guilt or resentment will seem to pop into your mind. This must be considered as a direct communication from your subconscious beingness revealing at least part of the mental/emotional pattern behind the health problem. At that point your only choice is to respond to the subconscious appeal for help and burn away the negative pattern. However most of the poisons will be naturally burned away as you practice the simple ritual we will present next, the conversion of the pentagram into your perfect health mechanism by the Ishtar Renewal Rite.

How to Use the Ishtar Renewal Rite to Return Your Body's Health to Perfection

Just as the renewal of the life of the land in spring was the time for the ancient fertility rites, so any physical renewal process logically begins with the revitalization and harnessing of the root center energy. Thus, we naturally begin this exercise with the root center breathing, just as we presented it to you to begin the Ishtar Money/Fertility Rite. When you have the bright red Nergal energy flowing at a peak of power, you are ready to begin the Ishtar Renewal Rite.

This time our aim is to make your perfect health the extra point that converts your normal body energy pentagram into the hexagram of perfect health. In the Money/Fertility Rite we sought to synthesize the colors between the alternate centers as we lifted our energy, but this time we will take the pure energy and let it maintain its purity. Begin by lifting the root center energy to your solar plexus, offering it as a gift of love to Ishtar. Feel the happy surge of extra bright yellow energy as the gift is accepted, and lift the yellow to your throat center as a gift of love to Marduk. Feel the powerful surge of bright blue energy as this gift is accepted, and carry it to your spleen center as a gift of love to Ra. Now feel the powerful surge of brilliant orange energy as the gift is accepted, and carry it to your heart as a gift of love to Osiris. Feel the wonderful surge of lush green energy as this gift is accepted, and return it to your root center as a gift of love to Nergal.

During the Renewal Rite, your receiving hand should be resting on your Ishtar Altar Star or alternately on your Ishtar Medallion. Your sending hand should be moved from center to center as you move the energy and chant:

"Nergal's red to Ishtar bring, Your loving praises I do sing.
Ishtar yellow to Marduk now, with love to you, good friend, I bow.
Marduk's blue to Ra deliver, power so strong it makes me quiver.
Ra's bright orange to Osiris flows, the health within me grows and grows.
Osiris' green to Nergal, neat, the hexagram is now complete.

And health throughout my body thrills, eliminating all its
  ills.
Making me a wondrous sight, a temple of the Living Light."

Repeat the process at least three times, and as many as it takes for you to feel that the energy is flowing with omnipotent power so your renewal is complete.

The results are more than excellent for those who enter into the spirit of the Rite. G.F. had this to report:

> For many years I had been suffering from a chronic digestive disturbance that seemed to get progressively worse. I was getting more and more afraid that the doctors would give me a major operation and remove a whole bunch of my digestive organs. Then I tried the Ishtar Renewal Rite. I decided that a fair test would be to perform it each morning and evening for a month, but by the end of the first week I was feeling wonderful, and NOT experiencing digestive troubles. It has been three months now without a flare-up, where before I had five or six painful gastric attacks a week! By the way, I am continuing to use the Ishtar Renewal Rite every day because it makes me feel 20 years younger and just full of fun and energy.

Even against a deadline, the Renewal Rite proved effective for H.P. She had a tumor in her throat near the thyroid gland. Her doctor told her that an operation was necessary, but agreed to examine her again in one week to make a final decision about scheduling surgery. Here is her report:

> Doc only gave me a week's reprieve from the operation, but the thought of being cut on bugs me no end, so I decided to try an intensive use of the Ishtar Renewal Rite. I started getting up 15 minutes early to do my chanting and energy moving first thing in the morning. I did it again before dinner (as soon as I got home from work), and a third time at bedtime. As you can imagine, I was motivated enough never to miss one of my planned sessions, including an extra one just before I left to see my Doc. He was a pretty amazed cat! In just that week, all trace of the tumor (I started to say MY tumor, but that would be wrong thinking) was gone. NO OPERATION! Just a Doctor with a puzzled expression on his face. Our Ishtar is wonderful!

O.N. had this expecially happy report:

> I had reached the point where I was afraid to do any teasing or preliminary love making because I was afraid it might develop into a bedroom scene and I would fail again. Anybody who's experienced this can fully understand how completely it takes the color and fun out of living. I tried doctors and even some of those wild ads in the sex-oriented magazines, but nothing helped. I was looking ahead at a very empty and unexciting set of advancing years. Then I began using the Ishtar Renewal Rite at bedtime, not so much with hope but as kind of a last resort. On the morning of the fourth day of using the Rite I awoke in a state of potency. This hadn't happened to me for five or six years! At the beginning of the third week, I decided to take a chance on it and had the most enjoyable experience I can remember. Now I am once more a full-fledged male member of society, but perhaps with a deeper appreciation of my sexuality than most. To say that the Ishtar Renewal Rite is a permanent part of my daily routine is clearly an understatement, but I can think of no better words to describe the situation.

How to Use the Ishtar Renewal Rite to Help a Friend or Loved One

For many of us the powerful renewal of our own physical body would be something of a hollow victory without the ability to bring similar rejuvenation to your life partner or someone else who is close to you. Of course the best way to share your new found vitality and health would be to get that special loved one to join you and perform the Renewal Rite in the happy atmosphere of a tenderly shared experience. But we must learn to handle life as it is, and all too often the person you want to help may have strong prejudices against "occult work," or simply feel it is too "silly and worthless" to be bothered. Or your special person may be too far away to join you. And these may be exactly the cases where your desire to help is strongest, but with Ishtar Power there is ALWAYS a way. It is quite natural and very effective to use the principles of sympathetic magic to bring the renewal to the person in need.

The best thing to use to establish the psychic contact is a

snapshot of the person to be helped. Alternately, a handwriting sample, a lock of hair, a keepsake or a sketch (drawn from memory) of the person will serve quite well. It is best to set up a second Ishtar Altar Star and place the snapshot or its substitute on the Star just as you have done for yourself on your own Altar Star. When you are ready, begin by following the occult maxim that may seem to violate the normal rules of politeness: ALWAYS WORK FOR *YOURSELF* FIRST. It is only *after* you bring your own beingness to a peak of power and effectiveness that you can expect to do good work for another. So perform the renewal rite for yourself just as we did it in the prior section. Then place your *sending* hand on the picture of your loved one on the altar star and use your *receiving* hand to touch your chakras, as you repeat the Renewal Rite and in the chant substitute "we" for "I" and the person's name or the appropriate personal pronoun for "me."

There should be NO feeling of depleting your own energy in this way. Recognize that you are working with an INFINITE supply of energy and are letting your own chakras act simply as focusing points to carry an ample portion of your infinite supply to achieve the renewal. And EXPECT to get very happy results, while in fact making yourself even healthier and *more* full of vitality.

How well should it work? Let R.O. tell us. Here is her report:

> The doctors had told us not to expect my sister to return home from the hospital alive. I deliberately did not listen to the medical details—sick and not expected to live was enough of a challenge to me. I rushed home and made an Ishtar Altar Star for my sister and put her picture on it, placing the whole thing on my altar next to my own altar star. I knew I needed strengthening so of course I did the Renewal Rite for myself first, then I switched hands and worked it on her for about 15 minutes before I felt I had done enough for one time. Then I planned my schedule so I could do the renewal rite for both of us four times a day. I knew I was doing some good, but honestly, even I was surprised when my sister was released from the hospital in just two weeks! Yes, there were several more weeks of recuperation, but she is again active, ALIVE and quite well. The doctors still have no explanation, but I do—chalk up another win for Ishtar!

John T. had been happily married for 35 years when his wife had a stroke that left her left leg completely paralyzed. It was quite a shock for both of them because they had always lived a physically active life. After over a year of physical therapy there had been essentially no improvement. Then John encountered the Ishtar Renewal Rite. He talked it over with his wife and persuaded her to join him regularly in the exercise. Here is his report:

> I decided that if doing the Renewal Rite together was good, then my doing it for her while she was working with me would be even better. So I would prepare by doing the Rite for myself, then wheeling my wife in and working on her picture while she did the Rite with me. It was not an overnight victory, but after the first week she was actually able to move her big toe! This was all the encouragement we needed. In four weeks she could wiggle all her toes and flex her ankle. In eight weeks she was walking with a cane. Then last evening, just 12 weeks after we started the renewal rite, she walked around the block with me, UNAIDED. By the way, I'm feeling better physically than at any time since I was in my 20's. That Ishtar Energy is powerful stuff!

Using the Ishtar Renewal Chant as a Healing Amulet

Where the physical problem is local in nature, direct application of the Ishtar renewal energy by way of a simple amulet can materially speed the healing process. For this purpose, a small piece of paper with the Ishtar Renewal Rite chant written on it in your own handwriting can serve admirably. Write out the chant and take it to your altar. Go through the Ishtar Renewal Rite in the normal manner, and when you feel it is finished, take the paper between your hands and repeat the chant three more times to charge the paper with the renewal energy. Then put the paper as close as possible to the afflicted area and wear it regularly. For maximum power, repeat the Renewal Rite once a day and recharge the paper each time.

G.Y. reported on this one:

> I had a sore on my leg that just wouldn't heal properly. I had tried all sorts of things, and my doctor had made several suggestions, none of which worked. I was afraid he was about to diagnose it as skin cancer, so I decided to try the amulet idea with the Ishtar Renewal Rite. I charged up my handwritten amulet after the Rite and attached it to my leg, just

above the sore, with a tiny piece of tape. I kept the amulet charged and in place except for my shower times, and I thought I felt it helping. Sure enough, in four days the sore was noticeably smaller, and in just three weeks it was healed. In another week the pinkness of the new skin had faded into the natural color and the sore is gone completely!

M.P. reported:

I have suffered for several years from arthritis in the fingers of my right hand. Unfortunately, the doctor recommended Bufferin and offered no other help. When I tried the Ishtar Renewal Rite, I did seem to get some relief, but there was obviously a long way to go. Then I tried making the amulet on paper and charging it with the energy of the Ishtar Renewal Rite. The very first night I used it on my hands I got relief. My fingers felt better than they had for several years. Of course, I continued to wear the amulet at night and charge it with fresh energy daily. After three weeks, my fingers were as good as new, so I discontinued wearing the amulet. It seems that once a month or thereabouts I get a hint that the old condition is trying to return. Then, at night I charge up my old paper amulet and put it in place on my hand, and the next morning all the symptioms are gone. When I was a child we had an expression "glory beat a pancake." I feel in that mood as I paraphrase it to say, "Glory be to Ishtar!"

Using Gemstones to Help with Special Health Problems

Let's pause to remind you that the smooth, balanced flow of energy through the five lower chakras is the essence of the maintenance of perfect health. When you check the energy flow of the centers with your receiving hand, if one or two are weak, there is nothing like an appropriate gemstone to bring the chakra outputs into balance. Or if you have an astrological chart which indicates an afflicted planet, take this as a clue and apply a gemstone to the corresponding chakra to achieve the natural balance that nature may otherwise deny you. Refer to the list of gemstones and the astrological correspondences as given in Chapter 2 at any time when a problem seems not to be responding to our other treatments. Also, a gemstone may be charged with the Ishtar Renewal Energy and used as an amulet. Sometimes this combination of gemstone energy and the Ishtar Renewal amulet will win where everything else seems to have failed.

A.H. had this to report on the gemstone work:

> I knew that I was under serious psychic attack which took the form of exruciating pains in my feet. The doctors assured my that there was no physical cause, so I tried the Ishtar Renewal ritual and the Ishtar Chant amulet inside my shoe, and there was some relief, but far from enough. I recognized that the basic attack was through my solar plexus, so I selected three small pieces of marble and charged them up during my next Renewal ritual. And it was a real godsend! Every time I feel the pain beginning to start, I put a piece of the marble on my solar plexus and one piece on each foot, and I can literally feel the attack being warded off. My feet are pain free for the first time in 19 months! Another victory for Ishtar power!

N.O. had suffered from chronic digestive disorders for several years. His almost constant complaint was a burning feeling in the stomach. Here is his report:

> When I checked my five health chakras, I found a decided weakness in the spleen center. I admit that I had harbored a few strong resentments for several years, and I realized that the stomach problems did start right about the time of the situations I resented. But there is a gap between theory and practice—I couldn't seem to lose the negative feelings. After two weeks I realized that I felt as much resentment as before, so more help was needed. I got a nice flat carnelian to attach to my spleen center, then I did the chanting to charge up the stone and a piece of paper to use as the ISHTAR CHANT AMULET. After the charging ceremony (at bedtime), I taped the carnelian in place on my lower abdomen and also taped the paper amulet on my stomach right over the place that seemed to be the seat of the pain. That night I slept well, without the usual waking up in pain. And to my amazement, I woke up in the morning with all traces of the burning gone. I still wear the stone and paper amulet at night just for "safety," but six weeks have gone by without any sign of pain. After six years of almost constant suffering that is a MIRACLE!

CHAPTER POINTS TO REMEMBER

1. As you become more effective in your Ishtar work, your strongly negative thoughts and emotions tend to become more effective also. Thus, it is ever more important to lessen and eliminate the mental/emotional poisons. This form of psychic ecology will insure your ever more vibrant health.

2. Your 5 lower chakras are your key to perfect health—there are two parts to any successful healing—first, to unplug any blocked centers—second, to maintain a full and balanced energy flow through the centers.

3. Use the Ishtar Renewal Rite to enhance the chakra energy flow and help your body renew itself all the way to perfect health.

4. You can use the Ishtar Renewal Rite to bring healing and fresh life to a friend or loved one by applying the principles of sympathetic magic to a picture or handwriting sample of the person you wish to help.

5. The Ishtar Renewal Chant can be written on a piece of paper and used as a powerful healing amulet.

6. The use of gemstones to bolster the chakra energy flow, particularly in combination with the paper Ishtar Renewal Chant Amulet, can bring victory where everything else seems to have failed.

CHAPTER 5

How to Apply Ishtar Energy to Bring a Big Boost to Your Love Life

What makes a super-star, like a Marilyn Monroe, John Wayne, Brigitte Bardot or Elvis Presley? And wouldn't you like to have "tons" of that elusive quality doing all manner of good things for you? Words like *charisma, sex appeal, animal magnetism, oomph,* and *it* have been used to describe that special something which sets a few individuals apart as "super desirable," and literally guarantees their success. Whether or not it suits your fancy to become a super sex symbol, the quality that produces it is latent within YOU, and we will show you many, many other advantages to be derived from it. Let's take a closer look at the quality to understand better how to bring it out in YOU.

Sex Appeal Is 20% Physical and 80% Aura

It was said of Marilyn Monroe that she would look sexy clad in a potato sack, and to prove the point someone finally did get her to pose in one, and the natural Monroe charisma showed excitingly through. Do you fully realize that YOU have an inexhaustible source of that same charisma, just aching to express through you and make you a fantastically desirable person to all who come within range of your special charm? But what is it? And how shall you harness it?

We must recognize that sexual attractiveness may seem to start with the physical, but a good 80% of it comes into play in the subtle, often subliminal, energy field that is generally called your AURA. When your aura is giving off the special Ishtar Charismatic Energy, literally everyone who comes within 10 feet of you will feel titillated, excited and indeed "turned on" about YOU. To get a working handle on this, we must face life exactly as it is and not waste our time with the wrong kinds of thought projection. Let me illustrate with a true story that happened to a good friend of mine.

Charlie came to me one day to complain that his occult work had backfired. He said:

> Al, I was lying on the couch pretending to read a book. As you know I've been having trouble getting my wife to participate in the sex act with me, so I was trying to avoid a fight, yet still get some loving by seducing her psychically. I kept projecting a strong thought to her that she would want to take me to bed right then. Now, you know that she doesn't believe in the occult at all, but right in the middle of my thought projection she got up, stomped her foot, glared at me and shouted, "You're not going to make a sex machine out of me!" and stomped out of the room.

I couldn't resist a chuckle as I replied, "But, Charlie, you were working on the wrong end." Then we had a discussion about appealing to the three lower chakras of Nergal, Ra and Ishtar, *before* sending the triggering thought to Thoth's brow chakra. With the redirection of the psychic effort, Charlie happily reported a wholesome, satisfying sex life again, in just a few weeks.

For this work, I will assume that you are skilled at the physical part of "putting your best foot forward," so we will direct our attention and effort to the subliminal 80% of your attractiveness.

Simple Techniques to Add Sex Appeal and Charisma to Your Aura

We can learn a lot by considering the courtship and mating process as demonstrated in nature. The process of attracting a mate ranges from the fierce battles for supremacy staged by competing bulls (as well as everything from seals to moose to apes), through fancy plumage and strutting dances (best demonstrated by the peacock), to exciting scents emitted by one member of a species to attract the opposite sex. But these are only the things man has observed with his limited five senses, and they still fall into the 20% physical side of the process. Whether it be insect, bird, animal or human, the *real* interface with the environment is through the respective auras of the beings, thus through the psychic centers or chakras where it is translated into the urges and feelings that keep all creatures motivated (or stirred up).

In the animal world, of course, the procreative urge is accepted as natural in and of itself, and blatant sexuality is the order of the day. But mankind has evolved a degree of sophistication which considers too great an extreme of language, dress or action as "coarse," "gross," or "lack of breeding." Thus, even a substantial part of the 20% of sexuality that is physical is denied us, and we must rely more completely on our auric emanations to be successful. But complaining about it will get us nowhere, we must recognize life AS IT IS, and play the game to win. I assure you that you have all the tools you need to be INFINITELY DESIRABLE!

In Chapters 3 and 4, we used the technique of the "root center breathing exercise," but here this powerful tool really comes into its fullest potential. Before we go into the full power of the Ishtar version of the root center breathing exercise, let's look at a few simple techniques that should become immediate habits for you. Most of us can remember the experience of reaching out to light someone else's cigarette, and having the person touch your hand as if to steady the lighter or match. Do you also remember the feeling of slight surprise and gentle pleasantness from the unexpected touch? We can state this as a very useful rule for you: *Any tiny, socially acceptable touch transmits vast amounts of auric energy to positively influence the person you touch. And tiny acts of special consideration generate wonderfully positive responses.*

In both cases, a degree of finesse and subtlty are necessary to stay out of the "coarse" category, but there are literally millions of completely "acceptable" touches that can add great zest to the courtship/friendship process. The offered hand or touch on the arm as if to help another when she is arising from a sofa or chair, the touch of the arm as you gently offer to help carry a package, or the subtle touching of any parts of the body as you stand close to a desirable person. Most persons will purr if you gently rub their necks or shoulders while standing behind them—and EVERY TOUCH imparts the influential power of your aura.

HOW TO APPLY ISHTAR ENERGY TO YOUR LOVE LIFE

especially if it is well "turned on" by use of the Ishtar version of the root center breathing exercise.

The Sensually Powerful Ishtar Version of the Root Center Breathing Exercise

The full union and sharing of experience by two human beings ultimately require the harmonious blending of the energies of all seven chakras, but the beginning is clearly based on the two key centers which we associate with Nergal and Ishtar—Nergal for sheer physical attraction and Ishtar for the emotional power to overcome any mental or psychological reservations. It is a good idea to conclude your morning ritual at your Ishtar Altar Star with this exercise, if for no other reason than to insure friendly treatment wherever you go during the day.

If you are seated facing east with your altar star properly oriented, you will find that you can reach out with your left hand and touch the Nergal point with the ring finger, and the Ishtar point with your thumb, while the palm of your hand rests over the center of the star. With your hand in this position, ask, "Ishtar, and Nergal, please add your special power to my root center breathing work." Then take a very deep breath through your nose, physically striving to pull the air as deeply into your lower back area as possible. Mentally push the prana or life energy of the breath out your root center while you are holding your breath and picture the bright red energy curving down, then out and around, to re-enter your body through your crown center and surround you in a field of the powerful red energy. See the energy still flowing as you exhale and say aloud, "I am infinitely attractive and desirable to all beings." Then take a fresh deep breath and repeat the process. Repeat it at least three, and preferably nine, times until you are sure that the red sphere is bright and strong and will last all day. Then any time during the day when you feel the need for extra desirability, you can take a deep breath and repeat the process mentally—no one need know what you are doing, but the special influence will reach out and indeed make all who come near you especially friendly and attentive. Understand that this is a completely safe exercise because it promotes *cooperation*, so even if you find it necessary to say, "No thank you," to a "proposition," your desires will be respected in a friendly manner.

The way the whole world treats you is the proper report card on the effectiveness of your use of the exercise. A typical report reads like this one from Molly S.:

> It seems as if the world is a wonderful paradise since I started regular use of the Ishtar Version of the Root Center Breathing Exercise. I can hardly approach a closed door without someone rushing to hold it open for me! Other drivers invariably defer to me with unbelievable courtesy. My job, which used to seem like a rat race, has become a totally fun pastime with my boss and coworkers bending way over backwards to be cooperative and helpful. And AM I IN DEMAND SOCIALLY!! I never realized how many interesting places there are to go with so many nice people.

Or perhaps more directly in point is this report from A.B.:

> We have been married for 22 years, and there was what one might call a typical cooling of physical ardor as the years passed. Then, this Sunday morning I tried the Ishtar Root Center Breathing at my alter. It felt so good I must have sat there doing it for 20 minutes when I was most pleasantly interrupted. I swear to you that it has been at least 15 years since my wife directly approached me for sex—until Sunday morning! It turned into a super day, sort of like a honeymoon only better because we really know and appreciate each other already. The best part is I KNOW what caused it! And you can be sure I'll use the exercise regularly.

Gaining the Irresistible Ishtar Smile and Eye-Twinkle as a Happy "Fallout"

Remember the old teaser, "Always smile, it makes your adversary wonder what you're up to?" We can do much better than that with just a bit of extra understanding of what the Ishtar version of the root center breathing exercise is doing for you! There is always a slightly mischievous smile and a twinkle to your eye when you know a happy secret. And indeed you have a happy secret as you watch the positive effects of your root center exercise powered aura! It works this easily: Simply be aware of the new power of your aura, and enjoy watching it get people's attention directed to you so very positively. Every time you see it begin to work, it will naturally bring a bright smile to your face and a twinkle to your eye, and these outward expressions of happiness will spur your associates to be even more wonderful in their response and treatment of you. And a little practice by smiling and twinkling at your own face in the mirror will let you see the extra power to be gained by letting your good humor and good nature show on your face.

C.R. had this report on the process:

> I guess I used to be a bit forbidding or grumpy looking to other people, but I'm pleased to report that it's much different now. I began using the Ishtar root center breathing thing a few weeks ago, and I was pleasantly surprised at the change in the way people approached me. But it was just two weeks ago today that I let the idea of the "I know something good" smile sink in. I looked in the mirror and realized that I had been in the habit of almost scowling as my "normal" look. I practiced letting a fun smile out, and realized that it did wonders for my appearance. Then I tried at work, and honestly in just two weeks I have learned that my old behind-the-scenes nickname of "Grumpy" has been changed to "Smiley"! It may not sound like much to you, but it has opened up a whole new social life for me, and three of the lovely young girls in the office who used to ignore me now make it a point to stop at my desk to tease me or just exchange pleasantries. If I were 20 years younger, I might date one of them. Come to think of it, I may anyway!

The Subtle, but Strong Power of Scent

Flowers use odors to attract the bees who are essential for the cross-pollination of the plant's reproductive process, and many animals use odors to attract their mates. In the world of man, the perfume industry has been with us since long before the industrial revolution, and witches and magicians have used odors for countless centuries to attract the nature spirits and otherwise enhance their attractiveness. Since our sense of smell is the most subliminal of the five "normal" senses, its effects on the emotions are not well understood scientifically, but the ladies know instinctively that the "right" odor helps greatly to set them apart from the rest as "somebody special." And regardless of your sex, you will find that the use of the right perfume oil has a tremendous effect on your own mood, and also on the mood of the people who come close to you.

But to the uninitiated, the world of perfume is a maze—what scent shall you choose, and how does one use it to the best advantage? Here we can rely on the basic idea that *you want to be most attractive to those people who like and enjoy many of the same things that you do,* so the scents that "do the most for you" are clearly the ones that will have the most attractive effect on the people who will be most important to you. But where should you go to choose your scent? The perfume counter of your favorite department store is all right, but you can do much better if there is an "occult shop" nearby which caters to the local magicians, witches, etc. Here the essential oils are sold in wide variety at prices ranging from $1 to $3 per dram—and a dram of essential oil will last for a very long time!

Smell as many of the different scents as possible—take your time and notice which ones really make you feel sensuous. Try to do your shopping when you are in a very vivacious or happy mood, since that is the mood you want to bring out in the people you attract. If you have trouble making the final selection, take two or three different ones and experiment, or even mix them. Then make part of your morning ritual the application of your specially chosen oil to your brow, throat and heart chakras as well as a goodly dab behind each ear (yes, this goes for the men, too, it in no way detracts from your masculinity to smell attractive).

At E.S.P. Lab we have a tiny Occult Shop that features my favorite scents in its oils. My personal favorite is a mixture I call "power oil," so I was especially delighted with this report from B.H.:

> I had experimented with your Ishtar Root Center Breathing Exercise and the results were quite gratifying. But it was not until I started wearing the Power Oil with it that the really magnificent results began. On the third day of the Power oil, Breathing Exercise combination, a friend introduced me to the man of my dreams! It was a three-weeks courtship, and we were married a month ago. It has been BETTER than anything I ever dreamed of, and I know I have the tools to keep it that way always.

Using the Power of Positive Sensuality

In the fertility rite in Chapter 3, I mentioned the Power of Positive Sexuality and the tangible benefits from its application. Now let's broaden it a bit with the term POSITIVE SENSUALITY and let it bring you even greater good. One of the drawbacks to so-called modern civilization is the "Victorian" remnant of psuedo-morality that requires denial and/or repression of the sensual/animal nature that is indeed an important part of our evolutionary heritage. Let's face it honestly, YOU LIVE IN AN ANIMAL BODY WHICH HAS ALL OF THE NORMAL ANIMAL DESIRES AND DRIVES, and your body is entitled to its gratifications *equally* with your mental, emotional and spiritual natures. I have heard many a GOOD salesman say, "If you can just get your prospect to break bread with you, you're 90% of the way to your sale," and the idea is sound. The sharing of food is part of the social aspect of mutual satisfaction of the animal nature and it indeed does create a bond of trust.

The theme here is simple. Gratification of the natural animal desires of your body brings a sense of well being that adds power to your aura. No, I'm not suggesting that you become purely animal—that would be as far out of balance as to deny the animal nature in favor of that great intangible called spirituality. But the true balance that gives you real auric power comes from giving something like "equal time" to each of the four major aspects of your nature. And again, since the Victorian ethic taught such a stringent denial of the animal nature, a comfortable emancipation from its shackles can produce an extra shot of power to your aura that will materially add to the mystique of your "very special person" new personality.

Sensuality suggests a much broader field than mere sexuality—it involves rich enjoyment of all of the inputs of your five senses, and indeed a special extra feeling of oneness with nature and all of her creatures. The sensual being delights in the tiny intimacies of touching, in the enjoyment of exotic flavors and the music of the night whether it be in the city or the country. In this sense we might equate sensuality with being more fully ALIVE, and with enjoying every second of it!

Now how shall you go about becoming more fully alive? Let's suggest that you set a sort of mental alarm clock to remind you to pause for a few seconds every half hour to simply note and enjoy the physical sensations around you. If you are involved in a "dull" or routine task, you can still notice the sensation of the tools you are using, or the music of the machine you are running. A good machine operator for instance, will always be at least subliminally aware of the rhythmic noises it makes, and will become instantly alert to any changes in pattern. It is just in this way that we can train ourselves to notice the small variations in the life around us and so enjoy it all the more—and one nice bit of fallout from your growing sensuality will be increasing psychic awareness as well.

How to Use Your Aura to Bring Out the Sensuality in Other People

When your sensuality is shared, the extra quality of livingness and enjoyment for both of you is always something much more than the simple sum of two individual experiences. It automatically builds bonds of love and friendship that are more real and wonderful than the "ordinary" world even imagines in its wildest dreams. It will brighten up any relationship, and has rescued many a sagging marriage. The trick of sharing is to mount a coordinated "attack" on your object, focusing the auric energy while engaging in provocative but tasteful, sensual suggestions or discussion.

To focus the sensual power of your aura, quietly picture yourself again seated at your altar star with your left hand touching the Nergal and Ishtar points as we did in the Ishtar version of the root center breathing exercise. Take your deep diaphragmatic breath and *will* the red energy to flow out to form your bright red sphere, just as before. Then as you exhale, picture a shaft of the bright red energy flowing from you to directly stimulate the objects's root center as you speak (aloud or mentally, depending on the circumstances), "I am infinitely desirable and attractive to (your object's name), and he (or she) responds to me very positively now." This is a good exercise to practice while driving or riding to meet the person who is (at least temporarily) the object of your focused sensuality. Then employ the verbal/physical suggestion and stimulation directly—share the touch of a flower or a soft garment, or perhaps the hand or arm of your object. And call attention to the sensuousness of the touch, then continue by finding several other sensuous objects to share in a stimulating manner—and indeed as you feel your own life force more aroused and vivid you can feel it having the identical effect on your object both from the physical sensations and from the bright red shaft you sent to the other's root center as you were on the way.

Let's review the obvious ground rules: *subtlety* and the smooth approach are what will make the application of your positive sensuality work exceedingly well for you. We must never cross the line labeled "crass" or "gross," but the true sensualist would never stray in that direction, anyway. By its very nature, sensuality is the special extra enjoyment of the subtleties, tenderness and infinitie tiny variations that make you more fully alive. And *alive* and keenly *aware* are the opposites of *crass* and *gross*. But this in no way limits one's ability to be firmly aggressive when the situation required it, and it will make you a more passionate rather than less passionate lover. Perhaps we can best explain this part by sharing a very special feedback report.

How Positive Sensuality Put the Life Back Into a 30-Year-Old Marriage

They were married when each was 19 and had been through the "family raising" stage together, with no more than the usual inter-personal problems. But they had grown in different directions. Bob was busy with his sales career, always meeting and entertaining new people, while Mary had been the rock of the house and the liaison with the school, P.T.A. and even the Little League. After 30 years, the children were grown and gone, and they each seemed to have their own world with very little in common with each other, yet no real reason to break up. Mary turned to the occult in hopes of finding some sort of meaning to her "drab" life, and soon got into our Ishtar work. Let her continue from her own viewpoint:

> At first I tried the root center breathing on Bob, but if it helped he must have used it for somebody else. Our sex life

was down to once or twice a month in a more or less mechanical manner—and I finally realized how 30 years worth of bad habits and tired shortcuts had built a deep moat between us. I know then that it could take many weeks of rebuilding and applied sensuality to bridge our marriage gap, but it would be worth it.

I made a list of sensuous things I could share with Bob, including ideas like running my fingers gently through his hair, rubbing neck and shoulders, and refusing to settle for the very married peck that had too long ago replaced a passionate kiss. I worked on my appearance, the condition of the house, and tried to pay special attention to a more varied and sensuous menu. And I even practiced gracefully getting in his way so there would have to be some contact as he passed me at various placed in the house. All this and as many spontaneous little things as possible, combined with the Ishtar root center breathing and the red shaft I shot at his root center each time I was sure he was on his way home, and HE BEGAN TO RESPOND. Within only three weeks from the time I began my all out effort, our home life had returned almost to the honeymoon stage, and it has stayed that way for three whole months! You can be sure I will be on my guard to keep us from slipping back into the old bad habits. Married life is wonderful again.

Doug S. applied his positive sensuality in a different but equally effective manner. Here is his interesting report:

I am a salesman and so am constantly called upon to positively influence people. When I began to experiment with your ideas of positive sensuality, I very quickly learned that when I got "turned on" sexually, I had a much easier time closing my sales. On the day I want to tell you about, I had an appointment to have my teeth cleaned early in the morning. Let me hasten to assure you that the hygienist who did the work was quite a plain girl and not at all attractive to me (I thought). But in her chair, I was facing the other way and she had a gentle touch which took some of the anxiety out of her work. Then my earlier self-training in positive sensuality alerted me to the fact that as she worked on my teeth, her "tummy" kept very pleasantly coming into contact with my arm. I recognized a special form of intimacy in this, and before the hour was up I was really turned on.

I decided to take that wonderful feeling with me in my aura to my first sales call—and it resulted in an order 10 times bigger than any I had ever received from that customer. And on the way to my next stop, I kept remembering that friendly "tummy" and let the feeling charge me up again. And again the order was at least five times the amount I had hoped for! I'm now working on ways to rekindle that turned-on feeling in my aura at will. A guy can make more in one day turned on than in a whole week of plodding!

CHAPTER POINTS TO REMEMBER

1. Sex appeal is 80% what goes on in your aura—when you want to influence another person positively, be sure you are appealing to the right end—only the lower three chakras are involved with the basic sexual influence.

2. You can use the Ishtar version of the root center breathing exercise to greatly improve your attractiveness and desirability to all beings. It makes the whole world treat you like a super special person.

3. A brighter smile and special twinkle to your eye will come as the natural "fallout" of observing the effect of your Ishtar root center breathing exercise on others—there is a very happy feeling to the simple knowing that you can use your aura to cause all people to be especially nice to you.

4. Use the subliminal power of odor to enhance your powerful new aura also.

5. Sensuality is a great strengthener of your aura and therefore of your attractiveness. Practice the POWER OF POSITIVE SENSUALITY and it will add much to your overall desirability.

6. Learn the tricks to bring out the positive sensuality in all the other people you meet—it is good practice and will build your ability to handle any situation and put life back into even the deadest relationships.

CHAPTER 6

Ishtar Energy for Clearing Away Secret Psychic Attack and/or Obsessing Entities

The "normal" American Citizen would no doubt respond to the suggestion that black magic and secret psychic attack are rampant in our country today with "Hogwash," or some unprintable expletive suggesting doubt. But regardless of the general public's belief, these things go on in this country in great proliferation. And don't brush this one off with an, "It can't happen here." YOU HAVE TOO MUCH TO LOSE! One tends to open a chapter like this with a question such as, "Had a run of bad luck lately?" Or an opening focus on some similar symptom of psychic attack— and we will give you lost of new tools to handle it, but let's put the emphasis where it belongs, on PREVENTION.

Paraphrasing Teddy Roosevelt: Walk Softly and Carry a Big Psychic Stick

Within the literature of our time, two very interesting men are reported to have said essentially the same thing in quite different ways. Teddy Roosevelt's, "Walk softly and carry a big stick," carries the oft-quoted words of Jesus, "Turn the other cheek," to the modern world's better understanding. Neither man was a coward or shirker of responsiblity, yet, they certainly stressed the approach of meeting the world in an outwardly mild and conciliatory manner. But the essential that is too often overlooked, particularly in the Biblical quotation, is that this is intended to be the action of an individual (or country) who is "dealing from *strength*." And it is quite true that a very strong person can properly be a bit more patient and understanding with those who seek to take advantage than can one who suffers from weakness. It is the specific purpose of this chapter to give you the tools and power sufficient to allow you to comfortably function in a mellow manner because you KNOW YOU HAVE ALL THE STRENGTH NECESSARY TO WIN UNDER ANY CIRCUMSTANCES.

Let's begin by reviewing the strengths you have already gained by the introduction to the working power of Ishtar and the related power transformer personalities. You have felt the touch of Ishtar's energy and most probably the touch of this and several other of the energy personalities—SO YOU KNOW THAT YOU ARE NO LONGER ON YOUR OWN! You have felt the Ishtar energies clean out your chakras and enhance your finances, health and love life; and you KNOW that this has barely scratched the surface of the potential help that is constantly available to you. How can you describe this except as a position of STRENGTH!

You have a good enough feel for the help of Ishtar and the others that you know you can work your way out of just about any mess with enough time. But there are those emergencies which require a quick boost of something "extra." Then it would be most useful to have handy a sort of psychic electric poker to frighten away or stun a would-be psychic or even a physical attacker. When we met Marduk, we spoke only of his Jupiterian side, the expansive givingness of success, but he has another side that the astrologers would associate with the cutting energy of Uranus. And it is to this Uranian energy of Marduk that we now turn to forge your very special psychic poker.

How to Build and Activate Your Own Big Psychic Stick

If you were ever around a prankster when you were about junior high school age, you must have encountered the cigar box rigged with an old Ford ignition coil, four small batteries, a push button switch and a length of wire. When you touched the unsuspecting victim with the wire, nothing happened until you pushed the switch, then he shrieked with the shock of enough voltage to fire a spark plug. And wouldn't it be a nice touch to have one of these rigged on the psychic level to defend you when you really need it? We will procede to build yours together now.

Your own throat chakra will be the firing point of the powerful cutting energy of Marduk, that you will have programmed to stimulate positive thoughtforms and entities, and to destroy negative thoughtforms and/or drive away negative entities or people. It will take about 15 minutes to build your system the first time, so prepare a comfortable place and choose a time when you can have a full 15 minutes of uninterrupted privacy. The only tools required which are not already attached to your body are your Ishtar Altar Star and a felt-tipped marking pen (any color of your choice). Take them to your chosen place at your appointed time and sit or lie down as comfortably as possible. First touch your left index finger with your left thumb to see where the touching happens naturally, and mark the place with your felt pen—in effect you are drawing the switch or button which activates the system. Draw just a dot or as elaborate and artistic a button as suits your personal taste, but recognize that this is the designated trigger to "fire" your system.

Next, place your left index finger on the Ishtar point of your Altar Star and your left thumb on the Marduk point, with the palm of your hand basically over the center of the star. With your right hand, cover your throat chakra, again in as comfortable a position as possible. Adjust and arrange your body and hands so that you can remain in this position for the full 15 minutes without generating any distracting muscular discomfort. Then take a very deep diaphragmatic breath, and as you slowly exhale, say: "Ishtar and Marduk, thank you for your gift of effectiveness and sparking electric-like power to perfect my psychic protection apparatus. Let the energy be carefully programmed to disperse and destroy the negative while it stimulates and enhances the positive. Thus, I can fire it without hesitation knowing I am adding to the total good in the world with each use." Continue the deep breathing and speaking the affirmation for the full 15 minutes, or longer until you KNOW that IT IS FINISHED.

During the building period, you will sometimes experience sharp tingling in one or both hands as the energy is programmed and stored for your future use. And of course it is a good idea to keep your system at a peak of power by re-charging it each morning at your altar—touch the star as above, take one deep breath and repeat the affirmation one time, and you should feel the system "charged and ready." To fire it, mentally focus your throat chakra on the thoughtform or person disturbing you, and firmly press the firing button on your left index finger with your left thumb. It is not necessary to keep the button drawn on your finger—you did it once and you *know* it is always there—keep it ALWAYS READY. Then be "quick on the trigger," follow that often-teased-about "rule" of the old West, "Shoot first and then ask questions!" Or as I would say, "When in doubt, fire your psychic poker. It will help you to quickly tell the good guys from the negatives!"

What to Expect In the Way of Help From Your Big Psychic Stick

As is the case with most psychic techniques, the Psychic Big Stick improves with attention and regular use. This feedback report from O.P. will help you understand:

> I work in the most confused department of a very confused business (or is that what everyone thinks?) Over the three years I've worked here, I've tried many techniques to cope with the confusion, but it almost always won, leaving me a heap of nerves at the end of the day. Your Marduk/Ishtar psychic poker idea sounded like a helpful potential solution, so I tried it. I spent close to a half hour building my idea of the system and charging it with effectiveness and Marduk's slashing energy. I had hoped to write you the next day to tell you it was a smashing success, but it wasn't quite that easy. I stared firing my throat chakra energy as I entered the door of the building, and fired it at least every 15 minutes all day. I felt that it had helped some, and I wasn't quite such a mess at the end of the day—but it didn't seem to be something I could write enthusiastically about either. So I re-charged my system at my altar both that evening and the next morning, and resolved to hit it harder the next day. And again I felt there was some improvement. To make it brief, I seemed to get a little improvement each day, until the end of about a 30-day period when I could say, YES, I really have something to write Al about.

But this letter was triggered by yesterday's happy surprise. I was called into the big boss' office, complimented on the way my work has improved over the last 30 days, given a $100/month raise and promised a promotion when next there is an opening. For a guy who has gone three years in almost mortal fear of losing his miserable job, THAT IS PROGRESS! And the nicest part is I have a new confidence in my ability not just to cope, but to HANDLE the problems as they come along. I'll never forget to use my Marduk/Ishtar poker!

A lover "scorned" sometimes uses the black arts to gain revenge. This was happening to Mike D., but he had the presence of mind and the tools to break the negative "spell" before it could do any serious damage. Let's hear the story from him:

Martha was a torrid lover, but when I realized she was far too possessive for me, I decided to break off with her. That's when the trouble started. I cut my finger in a freak accident, had my first flat tire in years, dented the fender of the car, and had numerous smaller mishaps like I couldn't seem to pick up a glass without dropping it—all within the space of just three days! Suddenly I wondered if a bookcase had to fall on me to make me realize I was under psychic attack. I had experimented with the Marduk/Ishtar psychic poker idea, but had let it slide because I thought I'd never need it. But now I rushed to my altar to rebuild it, and began using it immediately. When I pushed the firing button the first time, I could almost hear a crackling sound as the Marduk energy fought with the negative energy. It took almost a week of firing my Marduk energy every 10 or 15 minutes while awake and setting lots of extra protection at bedtime until I felt sure the mess was cleaned up. I just didn't realize the necessity of that Ishtar/Marduk poker idea before, but you can be sure I will use it regularly from now on. And I'm happy to say that my life is back to a happy normal with no more psychic attack caused accidents.

Rodney P. is very thankful that he did his homework on this one. Here is his report:

I was out later than normal and it was pitch dark in the parking lot. Suddenly I was looking down the barrel of a gun and hearing the command, "Hands up!" As I raised my hands I instinctively put my left thumb on the Marduk firing button. I'm not sure what happened, but the gunman suddenly looked scared to death. He turned and ran. I didn't wait to see anything, I just got in my car and drove away FAST. And as I gunned the motor, you can be sure I said a special thank you to Marduk and Ishtar *out loud.*

How to Practice Psychic Ecology to Avoid Secret Psychic Attack

Now that you have your "big stick," it is well to pause to reconsider the first half of the phrase: "Walk softly." We might have heard this said in many other ways, as, "Don't take excess advantage of a good thing," but in all cases the idea is the same—it would be poor policy to ride roughshod over other people just because your psychic poker is doing a good job of cleaning up your psychic mess. Quite the contrary, your new position of strength provides the comfortable base to make your life much richer and fuller by the practice of what I like to call *psychic ecology.* The idea of ecology applies equally to the psychic and the physical, except that the physical is more outwardly demanding because the results of the pollution of our rivers, lakes, oceans and air is obvious to even the grossest of human beings. But you should understand clearly that *the creation of negative thoughtforms pollutes the psychic atmosphere just as surely as automobile exhaust fumes pollute the air.* And any thought that you give life by the process of FEELING strongly about it takes life as a new thoughtform!

This brings us to the natural way to EARN maximum cooperation from Ishtar, Marduk and all the other positive psychic forces. That is *to so live your life that you generate the minimum of negative responses from other people, and the maximum of positive responses; and that you strive to adopt the most positive attitude toward all beings and circumstances in your personal experience.* Combine this approach with liberal use of your Marduk/Ishtar psychic poker to break up existing negative psychic patterns and you have become an active psychic ecologist. The results may not always be spectacular or immediate, but they are certain to build a wonderful new life for you as your practice of psychic ecology extends over the weeks and months to come.

P.H. had this to report:

Your discourse on psychic ecology caused me to do a bit of introspection and realize that I was unwittingly being a bit of a stinker in several areas of my life. My first resolution was to clean the cyncism out of my approach to my husband and children, then to be more outgoing and friendly to my social friends. And each bit of change brought its own reward of new peace of mind! As I changed, my husband became more attentive and the children actaully started to cooperate with me! Each time I bit my tongue and reworded a potentially caustic remark to something friendly, I swear I felt a kind of psychic pat on the head from Marduk—and my Marduk/Ishtar psychic poker began to find extra energy to help my positive thoughtforms instead of just defending me from negative ones.

Looking back over these last six months, I honestly don't understand how I could have so constantly wallowed in the psychic filth I used to generate for myself and others. Life has taken on a new richness, and the momentary setbacks have become humorous anecdotes instead of cause for ranting and raving. I suspect that my change saved my marriage—I hadn't realized how shaky it must have been. But now I'm entering a new life of FUN AND GROWTH AND HAPPINESS, thanks to the persevering practice of psychic ecology. Do tell everyone how wonderful it is!

How to Recognize Psychic Attack
Before It Has Time to Harm You

One very happy side effect of your practice of psychic ecology will be an ever growing degree of *relaxed awareness*—you will *notice* subtle changes in the psychic atmosphere and in moods, both your own and others. Here we must recognize a very thin line between paranoia and practical psychic self defense. It would be equally disastrous to interpret every tiny circumstance as serious psychic attack as to ignore a real warning that strong defensive measures are necessary. But we do have that happy Marduk/Ishtar psychic power—whenever you are in doubt, push the firing button; at worst you'll give a bit of stimulus to the positive thoughtforms around you.

Still without turning into paranoiacs, let's list a few basic indications of a negative psychic atmosphere that requires special measures to insure your continued well being:

1) A sudden shift of mood from positive to feeling antagonistic or defeatist.
2) An apparent shift of the mood of others toward you from friendly to hostile.
3) Any unusual tendency to be clumsy or drop things.
4) Any strange urge to do something spiteful or hurtful to another.
5) More than one sloppy (or worse) accident in any three-day period.
6) Any reasonable feeling of being blocked from your good or trapped in a negative situation, even when you have done your best.
7) Any series of happenings that feel like the beginning of a string of "bad luck."
8) Any normally unexplainable drop off in your business or other regular income.
9) Being ignored or slighted by more than one acquaintance who normally acts friendly toward you (again within a three-day period).
10) A sudden flare up of a chronic bodily ailment, any unusual or unexplainable pains or a lack of energy and that "draggy" feeling.
11) Objects mysteriously out of place around the house and/or small things of yours apparently lost or misplaced—or poltergeist phenomena such as objects flying around the room or falling to the floor for no physical reason.

Whenever you notice one of the potential symptoms of psychic attack, push your Marduk/Ishtar psychic poker button and expect things to clear up at once. If the symptoms continue, use the basic pentagram ritual for protection as we gave it near the end of Chapter 2. The combination of the psychic poker and basic pentagram ritual can be supplemented with the uncrossing ritual from my book, *Helping Yourself with White Witchcraft** or the psychic defense work from my *Miracle of Universal Power*. If the

---
*Prentice-Hall Inc. (Englewood Cliffs, N.j., 1972)

symptoms still persist, the ISHTAR PSYCHIC BLOCK-BUSTER, which I will present next, is clearly called for.

The Ishtar Psychic Blockbuster for the Really Tough Psychic Problems

There is a very ancient Babylonian ritual for breaking up obsession, possession, curses, and all forms of psychic attack. Ishtar brings it forward for us in what he calls a simplified and modernized version that retains all the power of the ancient way with even greater help as you work in friendly cooperation with Ishtar and Marduk. Until now, we have tried to make all of the work such that it would attract little attention even if done with others in the next room, but this one will require a few extra tools and an extra bit of preparation. However, if you ever find it necessary, the extra work will prove well worth your effort.

Ideally your preparation would include procuring a small charcoal brazier (a hibachi is excellent for this) and a few pieces of charcoal, an onion, a date and a candle wick. Because of the burning charcoal, it is best to perform this ritual in your kitchen, outdoors, or perhaps in your garage. Choose your location and time to insure the best possible privacy and the fewest interruptions—we live in the real world, and no matter how carefully you try to avoid it, there will sometimes be interruptions during your ritual work. If you allow yourself to react negatively at such times, you will do more harm than good to yourself with the work. The RIGHT way to handle an intrusion is to answer the question patiently or do what is necessary to politely get rid of the person or animal who has disturbed you, then go right back to the ritual and begin where you left off. This is good advice for any form of ritual or meditation work, but it is *essential* for this project.

When you are ready, take your tools and supplies to your chosen place and build a small but well-burning charcoal fire in your brazier. Orient your altar star with Isis' point facing North as always very near the brazier. Begin the ritual itself by holding your receiving hand over the Altar Star as you say, "Thank you, Ishtar, for your help in making this powerful contact." Then with the index finger of your sending hand, touch each point of the star as you speak the name of the Energy Transformer Personality, thus: "Isis, Nergal, Ra, Ishtar, Osiris, Marduk, Thoth, Bast, thank you for your love and friendship, your help, protection, effectiveness and prosperity. So mote it be."

Then pick up the onion and begin peeling off layers of it with your hands and throwing them into the fire as you repeat over and over: "Let all curses and any forms of psychic control over me be peeled off and burned away like this onion."

When the onion is all in the fire, pick up the date and begin to tear it apart quite violently, throwing the tiny pieces into the fire as you repeat over and over: "Let all curses and any forms of psychic control over me be wrenched apart like this date."

When the pieces of date are all in the fire, throw the pit in also and pick up the candlewick. As you carefully and fully untwine the wick, repeat over and over: "Let all curses and any forms of psychic control over me be untwined," throw it into the fire and repeat three or more times: "By the power of my will, reinforced by all the power of Isis, Nergal, Ra, Ishtar, Osiris, Marduk, Thoth and Bast, all curses and any forms of psychic control over me are broken and destroyed forevermore."

Complete the ritual by again touching the points of your Altar Star with the index finger of your sending hand as you say: "Isis, Nergal, Ra, Ishtar, Osiris, Marduk, Thoth, Bast, thank you for your love and friendship, your help, protection, effectiveness and prosperity. So mote it be." Then wait until the ashes in your brazier are cool before you dump them in the trash, or preferably bury them in your flower bed.

Fifteen Years of Terrible Obsession and Haunting Ended by the Ishtar Blockbuster

Mary Y. married when she was very young and it turned out to be a miserable situation. Her husband was a real "stinker," calling her names and cursing her in public and always carrying on a "bunch of psychological warfare." After 20 years of this misery, her husband died and Mary quite rightly breathed a sigh of relief. But the respite was short indeed. About the third day after his death the husband reappeared in spirit form to continue his abuse of her. He managed to break small items around the house, especially when she had friends in, and the abusive presence followed her everywhere. To say he scared away all her friends would be an understatement, and the abusive language was with her "every night." Mary naturally sought help of a psychic nature, but for 15 years the misery continued—all her attempts at exorcism and all those who tried to help her failed. She felt doomed, but never gave up trying to rid herself of this nuisance. Finally, she learned of the Ishtar Blockbuster ritual and decided to use it. Here is her report:

> To say thank you seems so little for the wonderful relief I feel. I gathered the materials and performed the Ishtar Blockbuster ritual on the night of the full moon (this was when he seemed to be able to get at me the most). When the ritual was over, I felt at peace and had an uninterrupted night's sleep for the first time in 15 years! Just to be sure I repeated the Blockbuster for six more nights. It has been three months now and there has not been a peep out of him. I feel it is safe to say that I am FREE AT LAST! Again my heartfelt thanks.

Roger was a $35,000 a year executive, successful, prosperous and happy by his own standards. Then he had a brief affair with a young lady. He found out later that when he broke off with her she went straight to a voodoo practitioner and had a path-blocking ceremony done to him. Suddenly there was a corporate "raid" and Roger lost his job in the shuffle. Then his wife went to the hospital for major surgery, and his biggest investment turned sour. Roger had to put his big house up for what he called a "distress sale," and wound up in a small apartment, still without a job. Finally Roger realized he was under psychic attack, but his first attempts at uncrossing seemed to do no good at all. So he turned to the Ishtar Blockbuster Ritual. Here is his report:

> I gathered my materials and determined to do the Ishtar Blockbusting thing every day until I was sure I had won. After just the first ritual, I felt better—as if some sort of a weight had been lifted from my shoulders. On the third day, my wife was released from the hospital (much earlier than I had expected) pronounced cured. During the weeks out of a job I had sent out many resumes, but had not even one nibble. But on the fifth day of my ritual work I got TWO calls for job interviews, AND THREE MORE on the next day. To be brief, I stopped the ritual work after the ninth day because I knew I had won. Believe it or not I wound up with a better-paying job with a better future potential than the one I had lost. The insurance paid more of my wife's medical expenses than I had

expected. My new job required relocation and I got a fantastic buy on a house we like better than the one I had to unload. And the investment I thought had died suddenly came to life and started to pay dividends plus some return of capital. The storm is over and it is beautiful here on the bright side. I hope I never need that ritual again, but you can be sure I'll never forget it.

CHAPTER POINTS TO REMEMBER

1. Recognize the wisdom of the advice to walk softly and carry a big psychic stick.

2. Build and use your own psychic poker to keep the psychic atmosphere around you clear and wholesome.

3. Psychic ecology, the practice of keeping your psychic surroundings clean and fresh, will keep you from most of the "normal" psychic attack problems.

4. Avoid paranoia of course, but be constantly alert for the symptoms of psychic attack, and use your psychic poker to break it up before it has a chance to harm you.

5. When you are under serious psychic attack and the regular methods of defense seem to fail, use the Ishtar Psychic Blockbuster to free yourself.

CHAPTER 7

Harness Your Ishtar Energy to Overcome Feelings of Futility or Uselessness and Add Rich New Meaning to Your Life

We all have those occasional days of questioning—"Why am I not getting anywhere?", "What's the use?" or, "Why bother, the undertaker and tax man will get it all anyway?" If we use those times positively to challenge our "ruts" and seek fresh inspiration they can be of great value to us. But sometimes the answers we give ourselves are more discouraging than the questions. Be careful of this, or a pensive day can turn into a miserable several months. And with your growing familiarity with the Ishtar Power, discouragement is no longer necessary. You can and should be happily growing from victory to glorious victory. The work of our first six chapters should have already convinced you that:

You Are No Longer "On Your Own"
(How to Meet Your Spirit Lover)

Your contact with Ishtar and the other Energy Transformer Personalities has clearly demonstrated that there can be tangible help to YOU from the unseen side of life. Your every use of any of the many forms of the Ishtar Power acquaints you more fully with the reality of beings without physical bodies. I trust that you are fortunate enough not to have suffered an experience like that of Mary Y. in our previous chapter, but this too reminds us of the reality of non-physical beings. Let me hasten to assure you that there are many, many, more positive and helpful non-physical beings than negative ones—indeed, much more so than we find in beings who do still inhabit physical bodies! And with your psychic protection work well mastered, it will be not only safe but MOST rewarding to set about meeting and working with more non-physical beings. The best and quickest way to deepen the reality for you is to put you into closer contact with the wonderful spirit being I like to describe as your SPIRIT LOVER. This is most often a being who was actually a physical lover of yours in some previous lifetime, but we'll leave that for the two of you to work out together.

Let's head right to your altar star and set about making this happy introduction. Affairs of the heart belong naturally to Osiris, so after your normal greeting to all points of the altar star, place your index finger on the Ishtar point and let your hand rest comfortably on the star with your thumb touching the Osiris point. Take a nice deep breath and relax to add power and comfort to your aura, then ask aloud: "Ishtar and Osiris, I am ready to work closely with my Spirit Lover. Please put us into happy contact now." Repeat the request three times with your hand still placed on the altar star, then sit quietly in relaxed but happy anticipation. The words of an old song come quickly to mind here: "And when you touch me and there's fire in every finger....." You WILL feel the loving touch of your spirit lover within three minutes! And it will probably send a shiver from your neck all the way to the base of your spine—it's a truly wonderful and enjoyable sensation, sometimes very subtle, but on special occasions so strong that you will shake all over with the JOY of it.

Take care to note the pleasant sensation because it will come to you often in relaxed or even troubled moments. For years I have felt the loving touch myself quite regularly while driving home from work or even in the middle of an important Board of Directors Meeting! I can assure you that it gives richer meaning to life ALL BY ITSELF. But this is only the happy beginning. Your Spirit Lover is intensely interested in your growth, material progress, and general well being. This lovely person is quite without jealousy and is simply devoted to inspiring your life—including helping you find a lover in a physical body or improving your relationship with your present spouse as part of helping you to enjoy your life more fully. Repeat the introductory exercise as often as necessary to get a solid feeling that the contact is well established.

How to Work with Ishtar's Power and Your Spirit Lover to Find Fresh Creativity and Challenge

The vast majority of our problems are really good for us as challenges to stimulate our creativity and thus our growth. When we adopt the attitude of acceptance of the challenge to be creative, the array of problems we have been facing can be very rapidly diminished, leaving only a few key lessons to be learned to find the "paradise on earth" of our dreams. And who could possibly be the most help in stimulating you to find the creative solutions you need? Obviously it is that special being we now call your Spirit Lover. And there is no better way to deepen this wonderful relationship than to cooperate in the happy enrichment of your whole life.

After a week or two of just enjoying each other to deepen the happy relationship, it's time to start to work together in earnest. Begin by preparing a list of goals to achieve and problems to overcome. Take your time at it, and mentally or aloud invite your Spirit Lover to add to the list. Then watch for the little ideas that will pop into your head, often with a gentle caress that by now should be unmistakably the special touch of your Spirit Lover. One of the questions for the list should be, "What is my Spirit Lover's name?" The answer to this one should pop through to you very easily, and it's good to have something besides just "lover" to call this special one. You will find some solutions occurring to you even before you feel that your list is pretty comprehensive, and of course it is proper and even necessary to proceed to handle those at once. But when your list is ready, do take it to your altar star and specifically invite the help of Ishtar and your Spirit Lover.

Begin with High Expectations

Open the session by touching all points of your star, greeting each energy transformer personality as usual. Then call aloud to your Spirit Lover, inviting a big hug to announce the presence. Next announce that your list of problems and goals is ready, and read it aloud. Invite both their guidance and tangible help, then sit quietly in relaxed meditation to give them a chance to reach you with helpful ideas. Regularly talk over your progress at your altar star during one of your daily sessions—and it will be a good idea to keep score; you should be amazed at your rapid progress.

D.H. had been out of a job for 13 months when she took her list to the altar star and asked for help from Ishtar and her Spirit Lover. Somehow there was a feeling of help at last. Let her tell the rest:

> The next morning after my first real session with my problem list and the Ishtar/Spirit Lover combination, I bumped into an old acquaintance in the grocery store. She said, "Hey, did you get a job yet?" When I answered, "not yet," she told me about an opening in the office of a friend of hers. I called as soon as I got home and was given an appointment for an interview that same afternoon. I had to wait three days for the final decision, BUT I GOT THE JOB! And at more money than I had hoped, too! I started last week and they are just wonderful to work with. This is the first victory for the Ishtar/Spirit Lover combination, but I KNOW there will be many more.

Bill K. had a small retail business that had slowed down to the point where he felt he was working for something like a "negative 30¢ an hour." So Number 1 on Bill's list was, "How can I build up my business?" Bill had this to report:

> When I first invited Charlene (my Spirit Lover) to participate in making my list of goals, the help started. She easily understood the pressure of the dying business and how it was detracting from my whole life experience. The first idea came as a tricky window display that is a real eye-catcher. Then came a way to rearrange the place (ingeniously easy, as it turned out) and make room for some smart looking high-markup new items. And she worked on me—everytime a customer came in I could feel Charlene giving my aura a shot of extra energy to make me more friendly and helpful. There were many more smaller things, too, and business began to get better right away. In just three months we went from a bare break-even to a healthy profit situation. I enjoy going to work now, it has become a real pleasure to serve my nice customers—and I have been approached to open a branch.

The rest of my life is improving equally well. Starting to work with my Spirit Lover and Ishtar is clearly the best thing that ever happened to me.

The Ishtar/Marduk Laser Power for Burning Your Way out of Life's Traps

Even with all the good going for you and the loving help of your personal Spirit Lover, you may find that you have worked your way into what seems like one of life's inescapable traps. I like to think that if so, it happened before you learned to use the Ishtar power and work with your Spirit Lover. But you could also ignore the good spirit advice and demand that Ishtar help you make a big mistake—and if you are insistent enough, you'll get the help. Either way, say you find yourself in an "impossible" marriage, a "hopeless" financial mess, a "no future" job, or all three! What do you do? In my limited private counseling work, I all too often encounter the typical situation of a problem so defined by the "patient" that it clearly has no solution. Naturally, the first step should be to carefully re-examine all the assumptions and parameters of the problem to be sure you're not overlooking a simple solution. But if, say three days of serious meditation turn up no help, then the Ishtar/Marduk Laser Power is your only way out.

We met the slashing power of Marduk and harnessed it for your psychic poker in our last chapter. That is a good use for psychic ecology, but we need to use it in a somewhat different way to dissolve a set of limiting conditions. For an analogy think of the old Buck Rogers comic strip and his disintegrator ray gun. Combine this with the two inert liquids that mix to become the strength of an epoxy glue (again analogy), and we create the Ishtar/Marduk Laser that is indeed capable of burning your way out of any set of conditions. When you focus them together on a condition, they will act just like the Buck Rogers disintegrator ray and burn away the limiting condition.

The "how to" remains simple. Go to your altar star and after the normal greeting to all the energy transformer personalities, put your index finger on the Ishtar point and your thumb on the Marduk point with your hand resting comfortably on the center of the star. Visualize the limiting condition squarely in front of you and project a ray of Ishtar's *power to achieve* from your solar plexus and a ray of Marduk's *slashing energy* from your Throat Center to meet and become a laser-disintegrator ray, right in the center of the condition. ENJOY the happy feeling of the limitation being literally destroyed—burned up and swept away to nothingness by the combined power of the two rays. If you can picture the system still turned on as you go back to your daily routine, all the better, but at least repeat the process every evening (and morning if you have a chance) until you break through into glorious victory.

Typical of reports on the Ishtar/Marduk Laser power is this one from F.S.:

> I had been stuck in the same job for 12 years, and there was no future because for reasons I never understood the President and major stockholder literally hated my guts. Over the years I had periodically sent out resumes seeking to find a position with a future in another company, but I never even got a nibble. It would be a great understatement to say it was a very frustrating 12 years.
>
> When I encountered the Ishtar/Marduk Laser idea, I wasn't quite sure whether to focus it on the President or on the situation, but I decided to avoid any guilt if something should happen to him and focused simply on the limiting condition. I pictured the rays meeting at my desk which seemed to be the symbol of my frustrations. It took exactly 10 days to work! And the soltuion was indeed amazing. I was called into the President's office totally unexpectedly. He began by apologizing for his treatment of me for the last 12 years. He said he finally realized that subconsciously he had associated me with the man who ran off with his first wife, because we looked alike. He announced a significant promotion for me that carries a major raise in salary. Ishtar and Marduk really came through for me, and it's nice to finally understand why that man seemed to hate me. I think we are about to become really good friends. It's all wonderful!

It was almost the classic triangle. Diane was the "other woman," and Walter's wife steadfastly refused to agree to a divorce, although she would give him none of the normal personal privileges of a husband. Walter suggested that Diane join him in using the Ishtar/Marduk Laser approach. They agreed that the image of the old wedding certificate would be a logical focal point for the work, and they worked together as often as possible and individually every day. This one took 35 days. Walter's wife met another man, there was a whirlwind courtship and suddenly, it was the wife asking Walter for a divorce. In this setting of cooperation the divorce arrangements went smoothly. Walter and Diane are happily married now, as they would say, "Thanks to Ishtar and Marduk!"

Do You Have a Special Mission in This Life?

It is important to recognize that the paramount mission for each of us in life is to learn and evolve enough to become a true master of our own destiny. Thus, we have plenty to work on at all times, but it is also quite true that you may have accepted one or more special assignments before you took your first breath in your present physical body. It is to this probability that we now properly address our attention. The special assignment or mission generally announces itself to you with a deep-seated restlessness, or as Bob Blake once so aptly put it as Barretta, "When you can't sleep, it must mean you have something to do."

Sometimes with the restlessness comes a "strange" urge to accomplish, but all too often it manifests just as a general dissatisfaction with your life as it is. Thus, the first task is always to begin at your altar star with the greeting to all energy transformer personalities. Then greet your Spirit Lover and invite that one's special participation. Now put your ring finger on the Ishtar point and let your thumb rest on the Thoth point of the star and inquire aloud: "Good friends, please tell me as clearly as possible what task I must perform or goal I must reach to relieve this restlessness." Repeat the request three times, then sit in relaxed silence. The initial goal should be to relax so completely that you drift into a deep reverie or even a short nap. Expect to be brought quickly back to your normal waking alertness by a shiver-producing pat or hug from your Spirit Lover when the right idea has been implanted in your mind. The reverie idea is the key here—we must get the waking consciousness far enough out of the way for the spirit guidance to reach you. It may take several evening sessions or even several weeks, but perseverance will definitely bring you the needed guidance.

The spirit solutions vary widely with individual development and the areas in which we may be out of balance. For a busy business man the answer came, "Work to bring out the loving side of your nature by giving more attention to your wife and family." To a young pre-law student came the suggestion, "You are a born healer, medicine is the career you should follow." A 35-year-old playboy-bachelor heard, "It is time to learn the lessons of responsiblity and shared love. Choose a mate and raise a family." Many a complacent housewife has heard, "You need the lesson of greater independence. Get at least a part-time job to broaden your field of experience." A middle-aged lady received this response: "Go and become a healing missionary to the Navajo Indians." Or you may get a strong desire to build a bridge or building, or to embark on some form of "preaching the Gospel."

It is extremely important to keep your balance at the time of receiving your spirit guidance. In most cases it will not be something you can merely drop everything and do! Getting the urge and direction is a good first step, but it must be understood just that way. The NEXT step is the one which requires real practicality and dedication.

How to Attract the Material and Psychic Help You Need to Achieve Your Mission or Goal

Particularly if the spirit guidance has a religious or ministerial flavor (but often in other callings also), the student's inclination is to assume that "spirit said do it, so I have to do it now." And disaster is the normal result. We must remind ourselves of the important truth that *Even Spirit Guidance is Not a Substitute for Judgment and Practicality!* Indeed I urge my students to be skeptics at these times—my favorite line is to respond to a spirit suggestion which is obviously beyond one's present financial means with, "I'd love to do it, just as soon as you (spirit) put your money where your mouth is." Another way to say this is that the economics of the market place may not be perfect, but it is an excellent way to eliminate a product, service or teaching that nobody wants. The world will not *subsidize* you, BUT if you work in intelligent cooperation with your spirit guidance and the energy transformer personalities, you can always find the means to achieve a meaningful goal—and always the means to fulfill any sort of special mission that is truly yours.

This is the time to treat your spirit friends as business partners. Sit in "conference" and divide the task or goal up into as many tiny individual steps as possible. Invite spirit's help as well as guidance in the financing, and go one step at a time. When the funds are available to complete one step, do it, then work towards the next. Many of the major corporate giants of our age had their beginnings in the garage workshop, or even the bathroom of the founder. Success can come only if you start from where you are with what you have available in equipment, funds, energy, etc. Indeed YOUR "MISSION" may be to build a "new age" corporate giant which is totally conscious of and responsible for its effect on the environment as well as the providing of good jobs and working conditions for its people—and all the other ideals we are slowly coming to picture. But you can achieve it ONLY if you have the humility to start with what you have, combined with the vision to see the big goal clearly and strive enthusiastically toward it.

Don R. Built a Successful Counseling Service

Don R. had been "kicking around in the spiritualist movement" for years. He had completed an ordination program in one of the movements but had been unable to do much with it. When Don asked about his "mission," he again very clearly felt the call to spiritual service. And like most of us, he longed to do "just that" without the economic responsibilities of providing a reasonable living for himself and his family. At the "conference" with his spirit guidance, he received the blunt suggestion, "Start in your spare time with what you have at hand." Don then got the idea of turning his living room into a tiny chapel for church services, so he put a small ad in several local "throw away" papers announcing Sunday Services.

As Don would say, "My little flock started with three people and grew painfully slowly, but it did grow." All of the donations from the church services and the slowly growing demand for Don's personal counseling went carefully into a savings account in the church name. After about a year and a half there was enough money in the account to sponsor what turned out to be a successful "psychic adventure night" in a nearby high school auditorium. This became a regular quarterly event for the group and helped it grow much faster. By now, Don's living room was overcrowded for every service (he had expanded to Sunday and Wednesday), but since all the money from the services and counseling had accumulated in the church savings account, there was enough to rent a small building nearby, and by cutting corners, to equip it to seat 90 people. It took Don seven years to build his organization to the point that it could "afford" to pay for his services, but now things are just as Don dreamed when he started. His full efforts are devoted to the spiritual service he longed for at the beginning, and the church group he built is strong and growing. As Don explains it:

> Perseverance, dedication and regular conferences with my spirit guidance paid off. Many times my impatience almost had me jumping the gun and quitting my job too soon, but although I complained to my spirit people, I also listened when they told me to hang on a while longer. Now I am enjoying just the life of happy service to my fellow beings that I dreamed of that long seven years ago.

But don't think the results can't come fast here, too! This is the way it worked for Bill B.: Bill graduated from college at the "wrong time," and was working for about $3/hour as a helper in a small machine shop. Bill's request at his spirit conference was simply, "Please lead me to a job that will use my education and provide challenge and opportunity for growth." Right in the middle of the session, he got a strong urge to go get the classified section of his newspaper. A clear thought "popped" into his head that "a company needs you to straighten out a mess that's right up your alley." The paper seemed almost to open itself, and an ad almost leaped up at him. He answered by phone, got a quick appointment for an interview and was hired "on the spot at almost twice my machine shop salary." Then, with the Ishtar effectiveness and Spirit-Lover guidance he became a "fair haired boy" in the new company, with promotions and salary advances that "doubled my income at least once a year for the next three years."

How to Find New Dimensions of Experience That Make Every Moment of Your Life Rewarding and Fun

The work of this chapter barely gives you the first glimmer of the fresh, new life that is waiting to open up to you as you add the growing relationship with your Spirit Lover to the ever improving power of your contact with the energy transformer personalities. It may take a bit of time to realize that your Spirit Lover is *always* close by to share ideas, give you a friendly hug, or bring an "expert" from the spirit world to help you solve even the toughest of technical problems. The challenge is simple—give your Spirit Lover enough attention to fully establish the REALITY of the contact and the relationship in your "normal," reasoning mind. Then help it grow up into a power for good and accomplishment for you that is presently quite beyond your wildest imaginings. Life will be ever more rewarding as you fully part the "Veil" and enter into a whole extra set of relationships with the fascinating beings of the "spirit world." We will work to develop this theme in the next chapter and others that follow.

CHAPTER POINTS TO REMEMBER

1. As you use the Ishtar Power to achieve ever more glorious victories in your life, the reality of beings in the "unseen world" should be apparent to you and you are ready to meet other beings who will also be of great help to you.

2. Use the exercise to meet your Spirit Lover and realize that you are never again left strictly alone or "on your own." Loving spirit help is with you ALWAYS.

3. Let the Ishtar/Spirit Lover combination lead you to a fresh creativity that brings inspired and effective solutions to all your problems.

4. Whether you need it immediately or not, get used to the Ishtar/Marduk Laser Power for burning your way out of life's traps. You need never feel trapped again; this is a positive and effective way out of any limiting situation.

5. A feeling of deep seated restlessness means that YOU HAVE SOMETHING TO DO. Use the exercise to discover your special mission or calling in life and find contentment.

6. Spirit Guidance is NOT a substitute for good judgment and practicality. If the task is big, demand that spirit "put its money where its mouth is" and follow the guidance to the accomplishment of your life tasks.

CHAPTER 8

Using Ishtar Energy to Become a Truly "Super" Being

What does it take to become a "super" being? And do you realize that you are well on your way to becoming one with the Ishtar work you have done already? Psychologists generally assert that the average human being uses something less than 10% of his (or her) potential. With a very minimum of effort you can literally double your present degree of awareness, perception, intuition and reasoning power! Still, you may find it comfortable to maintain the outward "you" as sort of a "Clark Kent" disguise in order to avoid frightening your friends and family—the nice part is you won't need a telephone booth in which to change costumes; you will know and act in an unobtrusive but super-effective manner.

The Secret of Becoming a Super New You

Let's begin by remembering your six most recent costly mistakes. What caused each one? The answer will usually be "my emotions got away," or "my mind just wandered off," or a combination of the two. Or, as I so often hear in my counseling work when a marriage is at a breaking point, "It must have been karmic, I couldn't have been stupid enough to marry a person I have so little in common with!" Then there was the case of the lady who had the dentist WIRE HER JAWS SHUT because that was the only way she could lose weight. All of our self inflicted trouble (and that amounts to about 98% of it comes from a lack of cooperation between the thinking, emotional and spiritual parts of our beingness. We might borrow an expression from the "younger generation" and say, you can be a super being simply by "getting it all together."

For the experimental class which preceeded this book I explained it this way: Upstairs I have a micro-computer system which includes a card reader, line printer and all the goodies. In order to get the card reader to talk intelligently with the rest of the system, there must be a control character in the first field of the card. If the reader gets a card with some other character or a blank in the control field, the computer will throw up its hands and run screaming from the room in utter confusion. So, always before I put a deck of cards in the hopper, I hold them up to the light to be sure I can see the control character punched in all the cards—if I see light through the expected holes, all is well, otherwise I must get rid of the error card to avoid throwing the computer into chaos. And it is quite the same with a human being—if all parts of your beingness are not aligned in cooperation so you can "see the Light," to act is to create chaos and confusion in your life.

Both the Huna of Hawaii and the Theosophy of the well known Madame Blavatsky provide a useful concept of a multiplicity of *selves* or *bodies* which go to make up the wholeness of a single individual, but they also give us the same trap of putting the mental self or body higher on the scale of effectiveness or control than the *emotional* self or body. In both cases we are working (at the practical level) with four forms of beingness, the physical, mental, emotional and spiritual self or body. But let's avoid the trap and state simply that the physical body is controlled by the mental body which is controlled by the emotional body, which in turn is controlled by the casual or spiritual body (called in Huna the "high self"). You can reach the "super being" level of effectiveness only when you have the four bodies lined up in the right order, even as I have to see the Light through the control character punches in my computer cards.

The Light-through-the-cards analogy has much to teach us about "getting it all together." Picture the source of Light as directly above your spiritual body (or high self), but in order to reach and affect the material world in your behalf, it must flow down through your emotional body, then from your emotional body down through your mental body, and only then into your physical body from which point of leverage it can positively change and improve your lot in life. For the "normal" human being, you have been so brainwashed about the superiority of the mind with its scientific methods and such, that your mental body tries to take over the place next to your spiritual body and assert its dominion there. But this is just like turning one of my computer cards upside down—it doesn't work, the whole system goes "tilt." Thus, we remain at that 10% of potential that the psychologists talk about. The trick to doing better is of course to convince your mind that it will be to the great benefit of the whole organism for mind to accept its place on the proper rung of the ladder. Certainly you will not win this all at once, but every tiny bit of acceptance by your mind will bring rich rewards of progress and serve as the spur to more improvement.

How to Get Your Body, Mind and Emotions to Work in Harmony With Your Spiritual Self and Produce Super New Effectiveness for You

Let's paint a quick picture for our understanding. There is a magnificent power shining down on and into your spiritual body as the Light. Your emotional body gently snuggles into place beneath the spiritual body and basks happily in the Light that flows into it. Now because the emotions are relaxed and happy, the mind (mental body) is attracted to its place beneath the emotional body where the Light flows beautifully into it, and completes the circuit of power by flowing on into the physical body itself. You can "check" it by shutting your physical eyes and looking up through the top of your head—when you see the light shining brightly all the way down from the high self into the physical, you know that you're in tune and will be *super effective* as long as you can keep the alignment. Of course if you see little or no Light, you know that your computer cards need a bit of joggling to slip nicely into place. We will go into the "joggling" bit as part of the actual ritual or procedure.

It is quite helpful to set the mood with candles and a good incense at your altar star. Begin with our traditional greeting to each of the eight energy transformer personalities, and invite your

Spirit Lover to join in the exercise. Now run through the picture we painted above. Picture your spiritual self above you, magnificently bathed in pure White Light. Then bring your emotional body to cuddle up in its rightful place just below the high self. Guide the mental body gently into place between the emotional (or astral) body and the physical. When all are in place as best you can seem to do it for the moment, give it the test. Shut your eyes and look up through the top of your head. There should be so much Light inside that you have the urge to open your eyes to "let some of it out!"

If you "see" only darkness or a faint glimmer, the alignment is not complete and the computer card joggling process is indicated. This time we go "backwards" around your altar star. Touch the points as you speak, "Isis, Bast, Thoth, Marduk, Osiris, Ishtar, Ra, Nergal, please help in aligning my emotional, mental and physical bodies with my spiritual body." Repeat the process three times, then again picture your emotional body snuggling into place beneath your spiritual body, and the mental body taking its proper place between the emotional and the physical. Again, shut your eyes and look up for the Light. Keep up the exercise until you see at least a faint glimmer of Light, and work at it regularly until you feel the unity of your beingness and finally experience the fullness of the Light.

The result almost invariably begins with a form of the mystic experience that brings much fresh insight and enlightenment, from which the positive manifestations seem to flow into your life in never ending streams of good. Mark J. had this to report:

> I hadn't realized how hard my mind would fight for its fancied supremacy. When all else failed it, it tried to fill me with doubt, but on the eighth straight night of trying I finally got a bright glimmer, and in two more days I could feel the real alignment of my beingness and began to walk in Light. My high pressure job suddenly became a paradise—I had my solutions started BEFORE anyone else realized a problem! Several people who have owed me money for years paid me back, all within two weeks of my first real alignment with the Light. My wife and kids treat me like a king, and the dissension that always seemed to be in the house is *gone*. I planned a trip to the race track and the night before I dreamed the winners of five races and one exacta—and they all came in, so I came home $900 richer than when I left. And all this seems to be just the happy BEGINNING. In one month I was made

manager of my department at work with a substantial raise. All areas of my life are better and I get up every morning full of happy anticipation of a magnificent day to come. Your terminology is right, I feel like a new "super me!"

Robin W. reported:

With the "card joggling" method, I got a glimmer of Light the very first night I tried the exercise. By the end of the week I was able to align my various bodies with the Light within five minutes of trying. The first tangible result came as insight into my marital problems and a fresh, almost honeymoon-type relationship with my husband of 23 years! Then I learned that I have a sizable inheritance that has been "chasing" me for several years. I got a $10,000 check as my first installment and there seems to be much more to come very shortly. All of my personal relationships with people have been improved "miraculously" to the point that I virtually bound out of bed in the morning because I know the day will be full of pleasantness and fun. I can't understand how I functioned as the mediocre Robin all those years—it's sure nicer to be SUPER ROBIN!

Courting the Muse of Creativity to Bring Through a Gripping Novel or Major New Invention

By this point in our work we can readily understand that the ancient Greek idea of "Courting the Muse" is a valid, if poetic, description of guidance and inspiration through entity or spirit contact. As you practice alignment of your various bodies with your Spirit Lover present, there tends to be a great deal of inspiration and guidance as natural "fallout." But we all would like even more. Everyone dreams of writing the great American novel or inventing the great American gadget, and now the creativity of your dreams is within your easy reach. But let's keep one foot on the ground and remind ourselves that PRACTICAL INSPIRATION AND CREATIVITY come substantially within the areas of your individual training and expertise. For instance, if you flunked third grade English and dropped out, it would be logical to take some basic English courses BEFORE you ask for spirit help in writing a novel. Or if you want to invent a magnificent electronic gadget, be sure you already know a transistor from a diode. In other words, be ready by acquiring at least a glimmering of expertise in the field of your choice. But for most of us, our big dreams naturally follow our training and aptitudes anyway, and it remains only to find the spirit "expert(s)" who will happily participate in enriching mankind through you—and they won't mind at all if you happen to get rich personally in the process!

Once you have experienced even a small degree of success in aligning your various bodies in the Light, the next step is simply to ask your Spirit Lover aloud to introduce you to one or more experts in spirit who are interested in manifesting a project along the lines of your personal inclination. You may be fortunate enough to feel a positive response during the very first session. If so, greet your new collaborator(s) with warmth and friendship, and GO RIGHT TO WORK WITH THEM. On the other hand, your Spirit Lover may need some time to arrange the details on the spirit side. If there is no immediate response to your request for the introduction, just ask your Spirit Lover when you should plan the next session with the expectation of making the requested contact, then KEEP YOUR APPOINTMENT!

Although your "front mind" may still "fight" by suggesting doubt to you, you will find the interchange and dialogue with your spirit "muses" as REAL as the paper on which you will hopefully take notes. You don't have to be tapped on the shoulder or have voices yell into your ear; it is the FLOW OF IDEAS that conclusively proves the practical side of the contact. And that's all that counts: there is no need to "prove" it to the outside world, just accept their opinion that you have suddenly become "brilliant" in your own right and *enjoy* SUCCESS!

A.F. gives us this happy report:

> For just about five years I had been writing short stories and articles and submitting them to all manner of magazines and periodicals, with nothing to show for my efforts but a big drawer full of rejection slips. It took three sessions of asking for my personal muses to get started. Then a short story seemed almost to write itself and I knew that it was of much higher caliber than my works of the past. It was wonderful to get a $150 check for the story, but even more so to see it in print under MY BY-LINE! And of course it was really just the beginning. My muses and I sold a story a month for nine months and NOW I have a contract for publication of my novel!

And you technologically minded people will love this report from G.Y.:

> I had of course read how Nicola Tesla often pictured a completed device so well that he had the individual parts fabricated separately and they went together to work as a new invention the first time. Little did I dream that it could work that way for me, but indeed it DID AND DOES! After I figured out what you meant by aligning the bodies with the Light, the rest was easy. My Spirit Lover was most enthusiastic about bringing me into contact with the experts in my field and they began to communicate with me in pictures and schematics almost at once. I have six patents pending with four of them already licensed for production by a major manufacturer—and I've only scratched the surface! It's very exhilarating to work with the spirit experts in this manner—I'd do it even if it were not so nicely profitable, but I'll admit I like the money, too. My first two devices netted me $15,000 in advance royalties, just to give you an idea.

How to Do Your Best Work While Your Physical Body Is "Asleep"

In a later chapter we will go into full and controlled out-of-the-body work (or astral projection as it is most popularly known), but right now we will consider the practical usefulness of the "spontaneous" out-of-the-body experiences you can expect during periods generally called sleep. A major part of the regenerative value of sleep is produced by at least a partial separation of the emotional (or astral) body from the physical. This allows a more rapid renewal of the energy of the emotional body which we interpret as being "refreshed" by a good night's sleep." During this separation we often tune in on thoughtforms which live in the astral realms, and may play them visually for ourselves in the experience we generally call a "dream." But as you evolve a better understanding of the multiplicity of your nature, you will begin to recognize other "stand-out" experiences as something more than a thoughtform-induced dream—indeed they are *valid out-of-the-body experiences*. These special experiences are of importance both for their potential learning and information gathering content and to prepare you for the time when you may want to leave your body at a specific time to accomplish a specific task.

The "normal" human being remembers only a small fraction of the visual/emotional experiences of an evening of dreaming and/or out-of-the-body traveling. This is true because the mechanism of sleep or astral projection involves a partial decoupling of the mind or mental body from the system so that all the distractions of external noise or wildly churning thoughts are "tuned out" and the rest of the organism can perform its relaxed renewal functions. The alignment of the bodies exercise we presented in this chapter is, by itself, the natural beginning of better recollection and understanding of the dream/out-of-body experiences which are natural to your organism. But just remembering the often incongruous experiences of a typical night's "sleep" is of little practical value. It is the next step, that of programming yourself to perform problem solving or information gathering activities during the sleep periods, that can lead you to indeed "do your best work while your physical body is asleep."

Whether you need a specific question answered, just general guidance, or perhaps a friendly meeting with your Spirit Lover or some other member of your spirit "band," the process is the same. Always take the time first to clearly formulate the question or request. Then write it on a small piece of paper and take it to your altar star just before bedtime. Greet your energy transformer friends in the normal manner, then put your middle finger on the Ishtar point and your thumb on the Thoth point of your star. Ask: "Ishtar and Thoth, please help me." and read your written question (or request) aloud three times. Then fold your paper into a small square about one inch on a side, and use a bit of Scotch Tape to attach the paper to your forehead just over Thoth's brow chakra. Complete any other work you had planned, thank all your friends, and go to bed. Then while you are relaxing to drop off to sleep, keep your attention gently focused on the question itself or your brow chakra.

It is always good policy to keep a pencil and paper where you can reach them without getting out of bed, but during a period of seeking answers while you sleep, it is essential. If you should wake up during the night with an experience or answer fresh in your mind, WRITE IT DOWN right then, otherwise the chances are 10 to 1 that you will have forgotten it by morning. Or if you didn't wake up during the night, take a few minutes when you do wake up to remember anything of importance from the evening's festivities. It's important to keep a relaxed attitude about this part of the work. Don't be bitterly disappointed if you wake up the first morning and can remember nothing of value. Simply resolve to relax better to create a more complete attunement and repeat the exercise that evening. Some will get their answers right away, while for others several evenings may be required, but perserverance is truly its own reward—if you keep at it, you will get results!

The value of perseverance in this part of the work is well illustrated by this report from Joan W.:

> I had always been a special favorite of my uncle, and he had many times told me that he would leave me something very special when he passed on. Then it seemed that it was all talk because he died apparently without leaving a will and with a very nominal estate. But somehow I kept remembering his oft-repeated statement that there was something special for me. I decided to pose the question as part of my practice in body alignment sleep problem solving. The first night I simply asked, "Did Uncle J. leave me something special?" And in the morning I woke up with a clear picture of a bank safe deposit box as my answer. Next evening I asked for the box number and location, but I only got a number for the box. So I tried again and this time saw two street signs at an intersection. This didn't ring a bell, so next I had to ask what town or city the bank was in—it took three days to get this one, but the bonus came as a slightly different use of my uncle's name for identification.
>
> By now I seemed to have enough to make a phone call to the bank. I told the safe deposit clerk that my uncle had died and I had reason to believe that he had a box in this bank under the name I got in the one session. Next I had to come up with a death certificate and affidavit that I was his closest living relative, but finally the box was opened, and in it were government bonds amounting to $25,000 all in his name but also on the face was the "payable on death to Joan W." I don't know which is honestly the nicer, the money and satisfaction that Uncle J. meant what he said or the thrill of knowing that the body alignment-sleep exercise worked so well for me—because I know I can use it to win many more victories.

Ways to Make the Body Alignment/Dream Exercise Even More Effective

If you try the exercise, but nothing happens for three nights in a row, you need a bit of a booster to get it started. Here knowledge of your personal idiosyncrasies can be quite helpful. For instance, does eating certain special foods seem to cause extra "dreaming" that night? Does a nightcap of brandy, burgundy or a hot toddy relax you enough to aid the dream-communication process? Have you tried your favorite perfume oil on your solar plexus and brow chakras at bedtime? Or how about a big tiger eye gemstone on your brow chakra with the written question underneath—perhaps reinforced by a powerful stone on your solar plexus? One or a combination of these suggestions, combined with a more careful alignment of the bodies to clearly see the Light, will break the block and get the system working for you.

J.N. gave us this happy report on how the "extras" made it all come together for him:

> I tried the body alignment/dream/astral help exercise for a full week with absolutely no observable results. So I got myself a tiger eye, some power oil, and a piece of marble. The brandy sounded good to me too, so I took a good-sized snifter to my altar at bedtime, and enjoyed it as I put the tiger eye on my brow chakra, the marble on my solar plexus and the power oil sort of dabbed at all the other chakras. The body alignment exercise seemed to go better, and I quickly slipped into a very relaxing sleep. Within an hour I was awake! And very busily writing down a formula and extremely simple chemical process. It turned out to be a real "stroke of genius." It is a simple way to convert a very bothersome waste product from our regular manufacturing process into a high grade commercial fertilizer. The result is changing a total loss on the waste of about ½% of sales, into a cost-free new product that now brings in about 6% of our total revenue. Since our pre-tax net before was about 12%, it is conservative to say that that one "dream" experience increased my company's profit by just over 50%! You were so right when you said we can do our best work while "asleep"!

W.T. has a "routine" job that is secure but "not very challenging." He also has a hobby of playing the horse races. He felt that consistently winning at the track would be a more interesting goal than "promotion to a pressure-packed job." So he worked with the body alignment exercise with this to report:

> I tried the body alignment exercise with the taping of a request to be shown the winning horses at my local track. I go on Saturdays, so perform the exercise on Friday night. The first two Fridays produced nothing, so I decided that your "extra" suggestions must be in order. I'm fond of a good red wine, so this came to my altar star quite naturally. Also, I have noted that a couple of tomatoes in place of my salad at dinner often seemed to induce dreaming, so I set a pattern of tomatoes on Friday night. Then I got a tiger eye to put over the written request on my brow center. The first night of the full system produced only three horse names, BUT THEY *ALL* WON! Now I regularly get five or six winners that way and I am making just about as much from my fun visits to the track as I do on my job. What a wonderful way to double your income and enjoy every minute of it!

CHAPTER POINTS TO REMEMBER

1. Since we are told by psychologists that we normally use only about 10% of our potential, it should be easy to harness enough more to become a "super you."

2. The "super you" will happen as you understand the functions of the four bodies (or four major aspects or your beingness) and teach them to align properly.

3. Use the body alignment exercise until you see the "Light" through the top of your head with your eyes closed.

4. Make the body alignment a habit and by itself it will bring enough improvement to create a "super you."

5. Super creativity and inspiration come to you easily as you align the bodies and get your Spirit Lover's help in "courting the muse," or bringing spirit experts to help and inspire you.

6. You can use the periods of "sleep" to do your best problem solving and creative work. Use the written question on the brow chakra technique at bedtime and get your answers easily.

7. If the regular technique does not bring the answers fast enough, use the booster technique of gemstones, brandy, perfume oil, etc. It *will* work for *you*.

CHAPTER 9

Generate Financial Windfalls and Win at Gambling and Contests— with Ishtar Energy

You may often hear it said that if you use your psychic ability for gambling or other personal gain you will lose it. And if you BELIEVE it, it is undoubtedly true. Beware of such negative suggestions, they are simply traps to hold you down. It's all based on the old metaphysical truism, "If you think you can, or you think you can't, your're right." The subtle appeal of a negative suggestion is to your feelings of *unworthiness*. The process of becoming "super you" from our last chapter should have almost completely cleared away any blocks of unworthy feelings, but if we are to be successful in gambling, lotteries or in generating big financial windfalls, the worthiness thing must be faced squarely and won for all time.

Overcoming the "Worthiness Block"

On a subtle but very practical level, most of the world's teaching institutions program the individual to feel his (or her) inferiority or unworthiness and accept it as a fact of life. It is true that the young child is inferior to his adult teacher in both physical and intellectual development, but this is NOT a permanent condition. Our tradition of "Hero Worship" in sports, science, politics and the like solidly reinforces the "I'm not as good as. ." syndrome and literally "sets us up" to accept any old defeatist suggestion that is tossed our way. And even our major religious institutions all too often bang away on the theme that we are unworthy "sinners." Some may say that it is a vast conspiracy to "keep the masses in their place" by constant psychological manipulation, but it is better understood as a critical point in the human evolutionary process that must be surmounted. We must deliberately re-program ourselves to accept WORTHINESS instead of unworthiness as our way of life.

But BALANCE is important here to avoid being exploited as an egotist. The snob appeal theme of "If you have to ask the price, you can't afford it" is equally self defeating. There is only one answer to that sort of appeal, "I KNOW that I am worth it, the only question is—is YOUR product worth the price you are asking for it?" Thus we must also avoid the necessity to wear our worthiness as a badge, and find the quiet acceptance of self that knows it is worthy and no longer has to *prove* it to others.

We can best use the combination of body alignment and the sleep programming of our last chapter for this very important purpose. For the written request, ask for a "report card" type dream or astral experience which will point out any areas of negative opinion of self that require work. If the dream response shows you receiving riches and honors, accepting them graciously and using them with joy, you have worked out a good personal worthiness feeling. But if instead you have dreams where you come up short or have something like a "nightmare," you know that lots of work is required. The follow-up should be to ask the dream technique for specifics of how you must improve to be fully worthy. Then work with the responses until you know that you have accepted yourself on the "subconscious" (or should I really say emotional?) level as well as intellectually. As a practical matter, recognize that it is your emotional body which is the block to worthiness, but when it has accepted its complete organism as GOOD, the winning should be easy.

How to Become a Consistent Winner

The habit and attitude of winning is a created mental/emotional state that will bring you more good than any other approach to life. Think of the patterns involved—the loser invariably shoots for the "biggie" and stays a loser, while the winner builds his expertise and habit of winning by knocking off the "easy ones" to get the hang of the "how to." Thus we can say that the next step after breaking the unworthiness block is to start with the "easy ones" and develop our effectiveness by tasting what it feels like to win.

The first principle is to understand the *odds* and the *potential that you have to shift them in your favor*. Let's relate to the game of roulette for instance. Here the red/black or odd/even bet is almost a 50/50 chance of a win for you—the house works on the very small advantage of the zero and double zero. But as you go to the sets of numbers or individual numbers where you might win faster, the odds in favor of the house are materially improved. The loser will invariably buck the odds in hopes of making a "killing" but winds up "broke." The winner's attitude will be, "I think I have developed my E.S.P. enough to be able to skew the law of averages in my favor and predict the red or black coming out right a goodly number of times more than I'm wrong. But I will still test it with nominal bets, stepping up the bet if I get a good feeling and see that it's working for me." Then try it just that way. Of course, carrying a contact with Ishtar and asking for his help on each play should improve your performance even more, but we must be working intelligently to deserve this sort of help from an energy transformer personality.

It is excellent to seek the application of your growing ability to contact spirit beings and the energy transformer personalities in your gambling—as a way of improving your "occult" abilities while you win. But it is important to know *your* psychic limitations as well as the qualifications and expertise of the spirit being(s) guiding you. One of my favorite old jokes illustrates this better than any discourse I can imagine. It goes like this:

> A man had been in Las Vegas gambling and had lost all his money. Then he sold his car and lost that money, too, trying to get even. He was trudging along the highway out of town hoping to hitch a ride home when he spotted a silver dollar on the ground. As he picked it up he heard a spirit voice say, "Take it to Harvey's Club and walk to the roulette table." Of course the man obeyed, and as he approached the table, the little voice said, "Bet it on number 62." Again the man obeyed and the number won. Next the little voice said, "Put it all on

the black." The man obeyed and won again. This went on for some time and now the man had recouped all his losses and was reaching for the chips to cash in and head for home. But the little voice said, "One more time, put it all on the red." The man obeyed and this time lost. The little voice said, "Damn!"

Of course the point is to learn a balance between the practical and the ideal. Remember that each *individual decision* carries with it the full consequences of the act and *YOU* are the one who benefits or suffers on the material level from the result. And as the stakes get higher, your growing anxiety may get in the way of your contact, thus producing an erroneous input that you act upon as spirit guidance—then when you lose, you materially hurt your confidence in your spirit people. Or the spirit being may earnestly want to help you, but not have developed the ability to do so. Either situation produces a net negative result for you that can be avoided only with patience and conservative practice.

The "Monopoly Money" Technique

The ancient truism, "Them as has, gets," is perhaps most true in the area of gambling. We have all heard the old ideas that "scared money loses," or "you can't play poker from hunger." The reason is clearly occult in nature. When you "have" to win, the anxiety factor is so high that the emotional (or astral) body freezes up and breaks the body alignment, thus leaving you in worse shape than mere chance because it spills over into the mental body and clouds your reason. To be an effective gambler you must "fake out" this part of your beingness and maintain the comfortable body alignment that allows for intuitive accuracy as well as good spirit contact. This can be done by using what I generally call the "Monopoly Money Technique". We have all played the "big money" game of "Monopoly" at some time—remember you start out with a "stake" of phony money, then by a combination of luck and skill you multiply it by investment in "real estate" and "buildings" (also fictitious). It's easy to keep your anxiety level low while playing the game because you know you're not spending "real money." Thus you can maintain a good level of psychic effectiveness.

In effective gambling, the situation must appear the same to you. The technique is to set aside a comfortable (to you) amount that you consider a reasonable price for an evening of exciting entertainment. Then turn it into chips, script or something else that you can easily look upon as "Monopoly Money." Now play for fun and psychic exercise as if the chips were points on a scoreboard, not that cash you sweat so hard to earn. Then the theme is win for the fun of winning and the emotional/mental body set up stays relaxed and in the effective alignment. Then watch yourself! As soon as the pile of chips gets so big that you start translating it mentally into a new car, a Hawaiian vacation (or whatever pushes your anxiety button), cash in and relax until you can again produce the comfortable body alignment.

E.K. reported on this one:

> For about two years now, my wife and I have set aside one weekend a month to drive to Las Vegas for a bit of gambling. During the whole time I only had three winning week-ends and they were nothing to write home about. Then I encountered your "Monopoly Money" technique and realized that you were right, I had been too anxious and out of tune. So I prepared carefully. I invited my Spirit Lover to help and made a small Ishtar Star on a piece of paper and wrote under it, "Ishtar, please help me win." I carried the star in my shirt pocket and touched it before I made any bet, while mentally asking for help again. To get into the Monopoly Money mood, I turned my whole stake into dollar chips which I dubbed candy mints. Then I played the whole weekend to win candy mints and cashed in 385 more of them than I had bought. I just got back from my fourth consecutive weekend of winning, and I'm close to being even for all time! But what's best is that with the help of Ishtar and my Spirit Lover, I'm confident that I can win a bunch of extra "candy mints" every time I go!

Margaret G. reported:

> I just love the horse races, and after studying your body alignment idea, I found that I was able to feel my program at the track and get a buzz from the winning horse's name. This would work for two or three races, then I'd be overcome by the excitement of the thing and start missing or getting nothing but confusion. I realized that the process of cashing a ticket and holding that nice money was breaking the spell. So I asked my boyfriend to take me to the track and handle the betting and ticket cashing so I could stay tuned in. I'd tell him

to bet three points or five points or ten points or two points across the board, etc. Before each race I took a deep breath, closed my eyes and looked up for the Light. When it was bright, I ran my finger along the program for the next race and marked the one or two that buzzed. This time I got seven straight winners including two exactas! After the first two races my boyfriend started betting with me, but he didn't tell me until afterwards. I came home over a thousand dollars winner and he won't tell me exactly how much he won, but he sure is eager to take me back to the races any time I ask.

How to Win in Contests and Lotteries

It takes more discipline and understanding to win at contests and lotteries than in the forms of gambling with lesser odds. Picture it this way: Let's say you have one of a million lottery tickets. Thus the odds against you winning are a million to one. So you go to work with magic, seeking help from Ishtar and your spirit band, do good thoughtform work and visualization of winning—and you are quite effective, in fact you cut the odds all the way from a million to one down to 100 to one. But if you still don't win, there is no way of knowing how powerful your work really was.

Thus the secret of good lottery work is to keep it strictly on a fun basis. The approach at your altar star is to joke with your spirit friends and the energy transformer personalities, saying, "Hey friends, wouldn't it be fun to win this lottery?" Then put your ticket on the altar star between the dollar bill and your picture, and ask Ishtar to give you the feeling of victory. It's quite reasonable and proper to joke with your friends at your regular morning and evening session at the altar star, reminding them in a fun way that the lottery ticket(s) is there and a subject of interest (but *not* compulsion or anxiety).

Let's examine this report from R.D. to see some refinements:

> After I got used to the energy transformer personality work, I decided to take your "make it fun" approach to the lottery to heart and apply it in our state lottery. Naturally I bought just one ticket for each drawing, and enjoyed a bit of banter with my Spirit Lover at the altar star as I said especially to Ishtar, "Let's you and I find out if Al's fun approach makes any sense." Now I won a $40 prize, then a $10 prize, then a $50 prize! It's not exactly the $25,000 or more I was thinking about, but indeed it is a good feeling to be a winner.

This time I wrote back a suggestion, "Perhaps you should ask your spirit friends how much of the prize money is their share, and what they would like you to do with it."

And in a short time R.D. wrote us the sequel to the first letter:

> Al, you were right on target! When I asked about spirit's share of the money, I got a loud and clear urge to spend about $30 of the winnings in a special act of kindness to an aging friend. Then last week I hit one for $10,000! It pleases me to include a donation to our E.S.P. Lab as part of my instructions on what to do with spirit's share of this win.

The Ishtar Permanent Thoughtform for Continuing Financial Windfalls

It is important to take one's natural personality into account in all of the magical and Ishtar Power work. I'm sure you have noted my basically conservative nature showing through clearly in the foregoing discussion of gambling and lottery techniques. Admittedly I am just not the type to "go for broke" in a gambling situation, but I also planned this section to show why I don't feel it necessary. To me, the real comfort and satisfaction of the financial side of life comes from presiding over the steady and orderly increase of your net worth, then spicing up the progress with many happy "windfalls." A minor modification and addition to the Ishtar Money/Fertility Rite of Chapter 3 can be used with great effectiveness.

You will remember that we used my favorite size Ishtar Altar Star, one that is just about seven inches in diameter, and put a dollar (or larger) bill on the star with the head of the picture facing Isis (north). For the windfall thoughtform/ritual, next cut a piece of plain paper (white or green is just right) to a size that is just about 1/8 of an inch smaller than the dollar bill, but the same rectangular shape. On this piece of paper write: "Let there be a glorious abundance of financial windfalls and general good fortune manifesting in my life from this day forward. Thank you, Ishtar and all who help." Then sign your normal signature on the paper and put it face up on top of the dollar bill. Cover that with your picture and add a small piece of marble (or one of the other Ishtar gemstones) on top. Then go through the Ishtar/Money/Fertility

FINANCIAL WINDFALLS WITH ISHTAR ENERGY

Rite, lifting the energies as love offerings to the appropriate energy transformer personalities as before, and with your receiving hand on the star and your sending hand moving from chakra to chakra use this version of the chant:

> "Nergal, Ishtar, Marduk, Bast, our living union's here at last.
> Ishtar, Marduk, Bast, Nergal, feel the power drawing circle
> Do its work so wonderfully, and bring big windfalls straight to me.
> Marduk, Bast, Nergal, Ishtar, I'm now a point in your great star.
> Bast, Nergal, Ishtar, Marduk, together now great plums we'll pluck
> And share the joy of winning, we, then use it, oh so wondrously!"

If at all possible, leave the altar star set up permanently (even if you have to hide it in a drawer), and use the chant over it at least one time, preferably two or three times to start and end each day. A little ingenuity and Scotch Tape will make your setup portable so in case of a trip it can come with you in a briefcase or suitcase.

We presented this method in our experimental class at E.S.P. Lab the first time without using the written reqest or the gemstone, and quickly got this report from a lovely lady, J.Y.:

> One of the experiments Al gave us to do in our Ishtar Class; we were to take the seven-inch Ishtar Star Symbol he passed out to the class and place it on our altar facing north. We were then to put a dollar bill across it and a picture of ourself on top of the dollar with our head facing north. After doing this and the ritual work as it was related to us, I really got results. Right off my Dad came home from a meeting and gave me two dollars (he won five dollars as a prize and split it with me). I then put two dollars in place of the one, and a few days later I was given two two-dollar bills, double again. I put one of the two-dollar bills with the two single bills and within the week I received eight hundred dollars and two days later another one hundred and seventy-five dollars. I have not removed the two singles and the one two-dollar bill. I have left them as they were. Two weeks have gone by and today I

received another two hundred and forty dollars. I continue to use this ritual every day and my good keeps coming to me multiplied. Thank you, Ishtar.

With the addition of the written request for windfalls and the Ishtar gemstone, it worked even better for B.H. Here is his report:

So you can fully appreciate the magnitude of my enthusiasm for the Ishtar Permanent Windfall Thoughtform/Ritual, let me tell you that my salary is a bare $20,000/year and until now I had little in the way of savings or investments. I set up my seven-inch altar star with the windfall request, my picture and a small piece of onyx that I happened to have saved for years, wondering what to do with it. The ritual and chanting work was fun, and I enjoyed tiny breezes on my cheek and various goose-pimply feelings as the Energy Transformer Personalities seemed to enjoy it, too. Let me say first that it is not a chore to do this morning and evening. It always gives my spirits a lift.

On the third day of the ritual work, the manifestations started! I received a check for just over $5,000 from a source so unbelievable I won't stretch your credibility to mention it! Nothing exciting manifested for another two weeks, but it all stayed fun. Then a friend dropped into my office and told me he was buying a strange form of security and there was a commission involved for someone who would represent him. He said I had done many favors for him and he wanted me to have this. In short, I made an extra $3,000 for about 20 minutes work! Next another friend received a substantial inheritance and out of a clear blue sky wrote me a check for $3,000 and gave it to me with the comment that he just had to share his good fortune with someone and I was the chosen someone! A week later I got a totally unexpected $200/month raise! And there have been many, many smaller things like winning $90 at a charity bingo party.

Out of curiosity I stopped to add it all up this afternoon, and that is what prompted this feedback report. I can account for just about $25,000 extra that I have received in just under six months of using the ritual, and well over half of it was completely tax free! Now I have no debts, a substantial savings program and a totally different outlook on life. I thank Ishtar and friends every day, and you can be sure that this ritual is a PERMANENT part of my daily life.

How to Consolidate and Multiply Your Gains

I have seen good-sized fortunes won and lost by many people over my years of experience in this work—but I'm sure you have, too. So you need a nice technique to help you *keep* and multiply your gains. There is an old bromide that goes, "A fool and his money are soon parted." And we must take care not to earn that appellation "fool" by having the same thing happen to us. A major factor in preservation of one's wealth is the continuing attention to the factor of worthiness—as your wealth accumulates, your worthiness must grow to keep pace or there will be inner stress that will indeed "cost you." And of course there must be a growing compassion and empathy for one's fellow man, but it is also essential to balance compassion with insight and the ability to say NO to unreasonable demands on your resources that so often come as pleas to the compassionate side of your nature.

The rule of thumb is simple: *Never Give People Anything While They Are Subjecting You to Psychological Pressure.* Set a tone about you so all will know that to push on you is to be refused, but that a reasonable request made in a calm and relaxed manner will receive fair and fast attention. Now if there are business requests, there is another extremely important rule of thumb—as a whole professional men are "noted" for their generally poor choice of investments. They make "good" money and have a generally high set of ethics, but they all too often step far outside of their field of expertise in making investments. Unless you are buying the stock or bonds of an old and successful company with excellent management, be expecially careful. The rule is again simple: *Make Your Investments Only Within the Field of Your Own Marketing and Technical Expertise.*

I could give you literally thousands of negative examples here, but they are not in point. Let's see YOU be a positive example, growing in worthiness, wealth, happiness and good humor, in an ever more effective partnership with Ishtar, the other energy transformer personalities, and your own spirit band.

CHAPTER POINTS TO REMEMBER

1. It is perfectly reasonable and appropriate to apply your

growing psychic ability and Ishtar Power to gambling—as long as you BELIEVE it is proper.

2. To successfully apply your new power to gambling, you must first insure that you have a well developed sense of personal worth. Do what is necessary to re-program yourself to *know* that you are indeed a wonderful person and so entitled to riches, comfort and all the good things of life.

3. Develop the habit and attitude of a winner by consistently winning the "easy ones." Know the odds and the available psychic inputs or strengths that can turn them in your favor. In other words, play as the "house," not as the patron who, on the average, must lose.

4. Work with your spirit helpers to determine their areas of effectiveness in gambling—it's better to "qualify" the spirit than be bitterly disappointed.

5. Practice the "Monopoly Money" technique to keep the anxiety level down and your naturally psychic ability up—and win.

6. Keep your lottery work on the "oh, wouldn't it be fun to win" level and you will have the best chance to win with the minimum of disappointment.

7. Set up your Ishtar Permanent Thoughtform for Continuing Financial Windfalls—if you have won the worthiness thing, this is bound to work real "miracles" for you.

8. Heed the rules of reason to preserve and multiply your personal fortune in happy partnership with all of your unseen help.

CHAPTER **10**

How to Draw on Ishtar Power for Special Help in Business or to Get a New Job or Promotion

Since we have regularly found Ishtar to be a source of special effectiveness, the area of business is a "natural" for the application of his help. After our first few "seance type" contacts with Ishtar at E.S.P. Lab, he began regularly bringing our local class people the very special energy he calls THE POWER TO ACHIEVE. Next we put a paragraph in our E.S.P. Laboratory Newsletter (at Ishtar's request) inviting our members all over the world to touch the paragraph as a point of contact with this special energy of effectiveness—I must admit I was personally a bit skeptical, but it worked! And we still keep the same point of contact in our monthly newsletter, by popular demand! Though your Ishtar Altar Star is a wonderful multi-purpose device for tuning in with the Energy Transformer Personalities, Ishtar has again asked for this opening paragraph (of this chapter) as his special way of helping YOU right now. Whenever you need a boost of sheer effectiveness, turn to this page and touch this paragraph. FEEL your aura being especially charged with THE POWER TO ACHIEVE, then USE IT to bring your fondest hopes into magnificent manifestation.

How to Use Ishtar's Gift of the Power to Achieve to Get Ahead in Business

Whether you have a business of your own, are in a managerial capacity, or even "low man on the totem pole," the principles of success are the same. The best rule to recognize is the simple truth that THE MORE EFFECTIVE YOU ARE, THE FASTER YOU WILL GET AHEAD IN BUSINESS. Note the carefully chosen words here, I certainly did not mean to imply that the harder you work, the faster you get ahead. As you get used to using Ishtar's special effectiveness you will begin to realize the big difference—often you will honestly think you are playing at a task, but will accomplish it in much less time than if you "worked hard at it." As I sat at my typewriter "working" on this section, I was called away by the whistle of the tea kettle to make my cup of coffee. As I sat back down and was looking over the beginning of this paragraph I remarked to myself, "It's just a matter of getting me out of the way and letting it take the direction it wants." I thought I was talking about my working on this book, but then the "penny dropped" and I realized it was Ishtar speaking through me the idea that he wants expressed in this section.

Regardless of the relative importance to the enterprise of your particular position, you have a series of tasks to perform each day. Many of these tasks seem like what I call "monkey jobs," meaning jobs that you almost feel a well-trained monkey could do as well (or better?) as you. In my previous books I have stressed the basic ideas of Karma Yoga for handling such things—focus all of your faculties on the task at hand and work for the sheer joy of a job well done. This is certainly part of the secret of success, but Ishtar now gives us a different slant. Each task you have is like a living entity and it WANTS TO BE DONE IN THE BEST POSSIBLE WAY. Now when you get "plugged into the Ishtar power to achieve", (e.g., by touching the opening paragraph of this chapter) the *task* can take over and use the Ishtar Energy to perform itself (yes, through you, but indeed in the higher sense on its own). And who but the task could know how best to perform it?

My editors generally frown on my using myself for an example, but this worked so well for me recently that I think I can get away with sharing it here. We had been planning a little vacation trip for a weekend and I wanted to get far enough ahead so that I could really enjoy the time off. I began the week by making a special contact with Ishtar exactly like the contact we provided in the opening paragraph of this chapter, with a request to make me super effective. The result was astounding even to me. Here are the week's highlights.

I wrote 536 personal letters answering people who had written to me, sat at my typewriter and brought through Chapter 9 of this book complete, rested on my couch and brought through (by dictating to a tape recorder) the complete set of predictions which appeared in Warren Smith's book, *Predictions for 1977*, under my name, similarly dictated an article that had been requested by a science fiction magazine, turned out a big corporate tax return for a tax client, made a financial statement and assisted in a major bid effort for another accounting client, taped three 15-minute radio programs for the Lab, got in several hours of good work in our stock market research program, conducted our normal Tuesday and Thursday evening classes, handled my routine work at the Lab including many telephone calls, and still had time for my swim before watching a couple of hours of television each evening. The impressive part to me was I felt better rested at the end of this week than I have after other weeks when I accomplished less than half as much! AND I ENJOYED EVERY MINUTE OF THE WORK.

The "trick" to doubling your output, then doubling it again and again is to touch your Ishtar contact to start each day, touch it again whenever something seems to hang up momentarily, and guide the tasks to their own completion, but basically *let them do themselves.* I fully expect to be able to do twice as much work in a week next year as I can now, and ENJOY IT TWICE AS MUCH, TOO. And so can YOU. There can be no denying that productiveness is the secret of personal business success—if you can easily do two jobs, you're *worth* both salaries to your company. A better way to put that is: as you become more and more valuable, you will without doubt be rewarded by financial success, either within your present company or by the happy event of being "pirated" by another organization which does appreciate your value. Here I sense many "frustrated type" questions, so let's take a shot at answering them in our next section.

The Ishtar Business Fertility Rite for Super Business Improvement

One typical response to a discourse on effectiveness such as the one just concluded is: "I'd love to need to work harder, but my business is dying on the vine. How can I get my sales up so I'll need your super effectiveness to handle the workload?" Just like facing a small task, we must now recognize your whole business as a living entity whose natural desire is to grow and prosper. Have you ever talked to your business? All of the thought, emotion, struggle and fun from its inception has gone to create and evolve that entity. If you have been too discouraged lately, the entity may indeed appear sluggish or "sick," but it can be very quickly revitalized—just as soon as you rebuild your own hope and determination.

The best beginning is to invite the entity (the "imaginary" spirit of your business, if this helps your intellect "swallow" the approach) to join you in a fertility rite. Picture the business entity seated just in front of you and go through the Ishtar Money/Fertility Rite as we gave it in Chapter 3, but use this modification of the chant:

"Nergal, Ishtar, Marduk, Bast, our loving union's here at last.
Ishtar, Marduk, Bast, Nergal, feel the power-circle
Manifest effectively, and bring good business straight to me.
Marduk, Bast, Nergal, Ishtar, my business comes from near and far.
Bast, Nergal, Ishtar, Marduk, together now great things we'll do.
With orders piled so high you see, that we can fill them happily.
Our business grows each passing day, my loving thanks to you I say."

Continue the chanting and lifting the energy from center to center until you feel your own enthusiasm growing and literally infecting the spirit or entity of your business. Then comes the special moment of practical communication. ASK THE ENTITY OF

YOUR BUSINESS HOW YOU CAN HELP IT INCREASE ITS SALES AND PROFITS. Just as we become more effective by learning to let a task perform itself, so we become more prosperous by letting the business build itself in the directions of its own enthusiasm. Accept the communication from the spirit of your business as new ideas and urges—anything from a new counter or window display to a new product, different advertising, or what have you. Adopt the attitude of a challenging, open mind on the personal level and let the new ideas flow through you to bolster and prosper the business.

Mary K. had a beautiful little three-station beauty shop. As she describes it:

> It was just gorgeous—it had everything but customers. I had let all my help go and was down to doing just one or two customers a day myself. Boy, was I ready for that Ishtar Business Fertility Rite! I brought my Ishtar Altar Star down to the shop, and at closing time I simply locked the doors, lit my incense, greeted the power personalities and started the rite. After about 10 minutes of chanting, I sort of wondered out loud, "Is there really a spirit of this shop?" And I got an answering set of goose bumps all up and down both of my arms. So I said, "Hi, there! I'd sure like to help you become something very special—any ideas?" I thought at first that the response was just more goose bumps, but I also felt a glimmer of an idea. I got a piece of paper and sort of let a flyer doodle itself—LET THE NEW, EXCITING YOU bring enrichment to all your surroundings was the basic theme. I boldly offered "A NEW YOU, WITH SATISFACTION GUARANTEED OR YOUR MONEY BACK," I got a thousand printed for $12.00 and paid a neighborhood kid another $5.00 to distribute them around the neighborhood (except for the ones I pasted up in the windows). All this took only two days, and I got my first new customer on the morning of the 3rd day. This is when the rapport with the spirit of the shop really started to work! I did an absolutely magnificent job on her. It was so good that three of her friends called for appointments the next day! Within one week I was so busy I had to find a girl for the second station. The next week I hired another girl to fill the shop.
>
> By keeping up the ritual and slightly involving my help in it we continued to grow MAGNIFICENTLY. Now just a scant year from those desperate days I have four (count 'em, four!) shops all doing unbelievably well. I guess I'm married to that

ritual and the spirit of the shops, but it is a wonderfully happy life, and the extra money has helped me do almost ALL of the things I've dreamed about for years.

Or as Jack D. summarizes it:

I had a good *little* business when I decided to try your Ishtar Business Fertility Rite. I was amazed at the response from the thoughtform of my business. It was so strong that I dubbed him my "Business Spook!" And "Spook's" ideas and guidance have been so good that we have better than doubled our volume (and better than tripled our profits) every year for the last four. Now I have a good medium-sized business that is well on its way to becoming a good big business!

Job Hunting Is Easy with the Ishtar Job-Attracting Fertility Rite

If it's a job you need, a few minor modifications of the Ishtar Business Fertility Rite should have you set up with a wonderful job in almost no time. First we must recognize that there is an entity or spirit of the just right job for you, which is totally real AND IS SEEKING YOU WITH THE SAME POWERFUL URGE THAT YOU ARE SEEKING IT. So the real purpose of the Ishtar Job Attracting Ritual is to help YOUR JOB FIND YOU. The best approach is to use the rite, as we will give it, first just before bedtime. This gives you a chance to "meet and talk with" the job entity and let it work to get through to your conscious mind with instructions during the night. Then repeat the rite early the next morning, and "sally forth" with confidence to win.

For the rite itself, candles and incense are helpful (preferably green candles and love/prosperity incense). Sit at your altar star and greet the energy transformer personalities as usual, and invite the members of your spirit band to help, too. Now picture the "just right job entity" seated in front of you, actually going through the fertility rite with you. Use it just as we did in Chapter 3, but with this modification of the chant:

"Nergal, Ishtar, Marduk, Bast, our loving union's here at last.
Ishtar, Marduk, Bast, Nergal, I feel the power drawing circle

Forming most effectively, to bring my good job straight to me.
Marduk, Bast, Nergal, Ishtar, do lead me there with your bright star.
Bast, Nergal, Ishtar, Marduk, together to my job we scoot,
And with your help, the world will see that I perform effectively."

Keep up the chanting and moving of the energy until you feel the enthusiastic presence of your just right job entity (at least vividly in your imagination). Then talk to it, asking for guidance to help you get together in the material world. Follow up on all your "hunches" and "crazy ideas," and by all means use the root center breathing exercise on the way to all interviews or even application-filling-out opportunities. This will put maximum power in your aura to get you the special attention it takes to win.

Jon V. was so enthusiastic about this bit of feedback that it just has to be included here:

> I am 66 and have been retired for over a year. My nephew was staying with us temporarily while he looked for a job, and we had been talking about occult things so I suggested that I help him with the Ishtar Job-Attracting Fertility Rite. We enjoyed performing the rite evening and mornings as directed for three days. Of course I was overjoyed when he came home on the third day to say he got a job for almost $200.00 a month more than he had hoped. But the capper came the next morning when I received a panic call from my old employer. They asked me to come back on a consulting basis for about three months to clean up a mess in my old department. I was so thankful for the help for my nephew that I just couldn't disappoint the job entity, so I accepted. And I must admit it's a good feeling to be really needed again! But honestly, I had no thought of a job for myself when I suggested helping my nephew with the fertility rite. You just have to say that we got two for the price of one!

George C. had this to report:

> I suddenly realized that even with the extensions I had only one more unemployment check coming. I guess I must have been enjoying my enforced vacation, but the realization that there would be no more money coming in spurred me to more serious job seeking. I used the Ishtar Job-Hunting Fer-

tility Rite Monday night and Tuesday morning. After the morning rite I had an urge to go back to a company where I had applied about six months ago. When the personnel man found my old application, he said my timing was perfect and asked if I could start on the night shift THAT NIGHT. I'm now working for a wage as good as the job I got laid off from, but this one is 60 hours a week with time and a half for all hours over 40. So I'm making lots more than before. It sure is nice to have real money coming again!

Open Your Doors of Opportunity with the Ishtar Job-Expanding and Promotion Rite

Once you're on the job, you have an excellent regular opportunity to demonstrate Ishtar's magnificent POWER TO ACHIEVE. Part of your morning's getting ready to go to work ceremony should invariably include touching the opening paragraph of this chapter to charge your aura with fresh POWER TO ACHIEVE. And if possible, carry the book with you so you can touch the paragraph again whenever you need an extra shot of effectiveness to get through a tough task. Keep your focus on ever increasing *effectiveness* with the natural expectation that your growing productivity will be regularly rewarded with raises and promotions. Most employers are fair and really appreciate effectiveness, so this may be all that is necessary to build your career. But if the promotions and raises don't seem to be coming fast enough, or if you're just plain in a hurry, you can make great strides by using the Ishtar Job-Expanding and Promotion Rite.

It's a good idea first to consider the normal requirements for promotion: 1) That you are doing a really excellent job in your present position; 2) That you *feel* honestly worthy of being promoted; 3) That you handle your human relations well, with those above, below and equal to you in the hierarchy; 4) That within the limits of the situation you are already training your replacement; 5). That your aura exudes so much competence that it broadcasts the truth, "THIS PERSON IS PROMOTABLE." Take a good look at yourself and use Ishtar's *Power to Achieve* to quickly correct any lack in one or more of the five requirements. Then re-check your attitude to be sure that you are not resenting your lack of speedy progress. You might be completely justified in resentment, but

DRAW ON ISHTAR POWER FOR HELP IN BUSINESS

you still cannot afford such an expensive luxury—resentment will not only hold you back but will most likely make you physically sick as one of its side effects. When you have met the five requirements and can come to the altar star with a happily positive attitude, you are ready for the Ishtar Job-Expanding and Promotion Rite.

Let's begin with a bit of consideration of the entity of your job. When you take a job, it is much like a marriage to the job entity. For the marriage to last, it must be fulfilling to each partner and the partners must grow together at roughly the same rate, otherwise they will grow apart and eventually separate. But it is also true of a good marriage that each of the partners wants the highest and best for the other. Thus, your running discussion with the entity or spirit of your job is some form of, "Let's be about our happy business of growing, together," and there can be no question of cooperation—it will be there for you!

To begin the Job-Expanding and Promotion Rite, invite the job entity to sit at your altar star in front of you. Again green candles and a good incense will help as you turn to the expansive modifications of the basic fertility rite. Greet the energy transformer personalities as always and invite your spirit friends to help, too. Then begin the energy lifting and moving as in the Chapter 3 fertility rite using this modification of the chant:

> "Nergal, Ishtar, Marduk, Bast, our loving union's here at last.
> Ishtar, Marduk, Bast, Nergal, I feel the power drawing circle
> Forming most effectively, to bring promotion straight to me.
> Marduk, Bast, Nergal, Ishtar, expand my job with your bright star.
> Bast, Nergal, Ishtar, Marduk, it's all the marbles up we'll scoop,
> Promotions, raises all for me, together so effective we."

When it feels really well done, conclude with a sort of "rah-rah" pep talk to the job entity. Say something like, "Come on old buddy, let's get promoted together. How can I best help you?" Then relax and pay attention to the suggestions from the entity or your own spirit guides.

Jose G. is young with a minimum of education but tremendous drive and ambition. He found the job expansion rite especially helpful, as he reported:

I am now the only minority person and the only one without a college degree at my management level in the company. Last year I was told by everybody that I should look for a new company because this one does not promote minority people past the level I had attained, and also it required a college degree for the next spot. Rather than quit, I took the challenge to my Ishtar Altar Star and worked with the job entity which I'm sure had done so well for me in the past (even if in those days it was without my direct knowledge). We did the job expansion-promotion rite, and my job entity seemed to be really stimulated by it.

On the morning of the fourth day of using the rite, I ran into the division president in the hall, and told him I wanted to be considered for the next level opening. He looked a bit startled, but said, "OK, I'll put your name on the list." Now my job entity and I worked with greater enthusiasm both at our work and at the job expansion and promotion ritual. The suspense dragged on for over two weeks, but the job entity and I decided to believe that no news meant they were still seriously considering us for the spot. We kept at it and regularly made our contact with Ishtar's power to achieve. I'm writing you today to let you know that we won! It's a $3,000.00/year increase in salary for starters and lots of prestige in the company. Now watch the job entity and me do so well in this position that we get promoted again in less than 18 months!

Gene T. had been in the same job for seven years. During that time four different people who were junior to him in the department had been promoted right past him. Gene approached the Ishtar Job Expanding and Promotion Rite almost out of desperation, but he was careful to work hard on the five requirements for promotion as well as his positive attitude. After the chanting, with the energy still flowing powerfully, Gene said to his job entity, "Good Buddy, I must have been holding you back these seven long years. Now I want to pick up the ball and really run with it for us. Any suggestions?" The only thing that came to him was a gentle prod to use the Ishtar Power to Achieve energy contact several times a day, and to tease around the office about the "new Gene." In three weeks he got his first promotion in seven years, but he didn't stop there. He kept right on with the job expansion and promotion ritual, and four months later got a second promotion. The score at the end of one year: "An unbelievable three promotions which brought raises that more than doubled my income over the year before.

Retired or Handicapped, but Need Extra Income?

Never let age, lack of related experience, education or the like stand as a block between you and your fulfillment. Let's say you are retired but inflation has put a squeeze on you and you would like to make a little money "on the side." Use the Ishtar Job Attracting Fertility Rite knowing that it is already programmed to attract the job or situation that is just right for YOU. Or for any apparent handicap—know that you'll get the just right job and then use Ishtar's Power to Achieve so well you are completely promotable in spite of ANY old handicap. Victory comes only to those who dare to try. Dive in and win!

CHAPTER POINTS TO REMEMBER

1. Ishtar set up the opening paragraph of this chapter as a special personal point of contact for you. Touch it often and let your aura soak up the POWER TO ACHIEVE, then use it to assure you success by being ever more effective

2. The first rule of business success is THE MORE EFFECTIVE YOU ARE, THE FASTER YOU GET AHEAD.

3. Approach each task as a living entity and let it work itself out through you in the most effective manner.

4. Join the spirit or entity of your business in the Ishtar Business Fertility Rite to generate super business improvement, increased sales, and expansion opportunities.

5. When you need a job, recognize that the spirit or entity of the job you need is also seeking you. Invite the entity to join you in the Ishtar Job-Attracting Fertility Rite, and be joined to your just right job in short order.

6. It is never too late to start being regularly promoted up the ladder of success. Help your job entity grow with you as you open ever more doors of opportunity with the Ishtar Job-Expanding and Promotion Rite.

7. Accept no handicap as a limit to your career progress. Dare to use the Ishtar power and rites, and success is yours.

CHAPTER **11**

Ishtar Magic for Special Help in Stubborn Health Problems

If you have applied even a little of Chapter 4, you should be feeling much more vital and full of life. All of your minor health problems should be simply falling away as you practice the Ishtar Renewal Rite and keep your chakras clean to bring your body the life-giving energy. Now, to get ready for the "biggies," I urge you to take a fresh look at the table of mental/emotional poisons and their symptoms in the early part of Chapter 4 and let the correlations sink deeper into your working understanding. Let us stress as the theme of this chapter the basic truth that YOUR BODY IS A SELF-RENEWING SYSTEM; it can and will heal itself of anything if you but help it by providing the proper conditions.

The Ishtar Unifying Rite for Health

A combination of the Alignment exercise for the spiritual, emotional, mental and physical bodies as we gave it in Chapter 8 plus the Ishtar Renewal Rite from Chapter 4 will provide you with the best possible set of conditions to help the body heal itself. Begin with the body alignment exercise, then go through the renewal rite, then back to the body alignment, then the renewal rite, etc. Keep alternating the two exercises for at least three, and up to nine complete cycles. Check the flow of energy through all of your chakras after the third cycle, and repeat the process, with emphasis on any sluggish chakra, until you feel a truly balanced energy flow.

This exercise can be done to assist any regimen given by your medical doctor, and should result in your doctor's expression of utter amazement at the speed of your recovery. It is important that you adopt the attitude of helping your doctor effect a complete cure—if the situation had been one you could control by yourself, you would never have gone to the doctor in the first place, so don't get cocky too soon. You are well when your doctor agrees that you are well—don't give the occult a bad name by going off on your own and winding up in more trouble! But there are many more things you can do to help yourself that do not interfere with the more conventional forms of treatment. For instance:

Special Gemstone Applications to Heal or Eliminate Stubborn Problems

1. Pain that your doctor can't help, as migraine headaches

In my *Miracle Spiritology,* I suggested wearing a bloodstone in the center of your forehead to keep away the migraine tendency, and it is still and excellent tool. But most people don't want to look "weird" to the people who see them in public and this, therefore, has not been a totally satisfactory approach. However, the power of the bloodstone to reduce or eliminate pain is a simple fact: we only need a better method of application to make it the completely useful tool it should be.

If you are still a migraine sufferer, let me suggest that you make yourself a tool. Borrow a drawing compass (or buy one for about 50¢ at the stationery section of your local department drugstore). Set the compass for about a 5½ inch radius and draw something just more than a half circle (by setting the point of the compass 1 inch above the edge of a piece of 8½ by 11 writing paper). Cut out your part of a circle and use rubber cement to glue it to a similar-size piece of aluminum foil with the shiniest side showing. Next bend the paper to form a cone with the shiny aluminum foil on the inside. Then glue about 15 small bloodstones inside the cone and you have produced a really super pain reliever device.

To use the device, lie down and put the open part of the cone over the area of greatest pain. Breathe slowly and deeply, using the lower diaphragm as much as possible and direct the life energy of the breath to assist the bloodstone energy of the cone in eliminating the pain AND ITS CAUSE. I have many letters from people who have controlled or completely eliminated their migraine problem this way—to quote one or two seems unnecessary here; I simply suggest that you try it for yourself and write to tell me YOUR results.

2. Gemstones for hypertension

An aluminum foil-lined cone similar to the one we just described, but this time loaded with 15 or so carnelian (agate) stones, should work wonders for overcoming hypertension and helping you to stay permanently relaxed. When you recognize that the tension is upon you (or better, when you sense the first signs of tension), lie down and cover your solar plexus with the mouth of the cone. Use the deep diaphragmatic breathing as you send the life energy of the breath to the solar plexus to assist the carnelian energy in bringing comfort and relaxation to your emotional body, and thus down through the mind to relax the physical.

3. Gemstones to stimulate a sluggish organ

An aluminum foil-lined cone with 15 or more tourmaline stones is excellent for stimulating a sluggish organ. For a greater concentration of the energy, make this cone more nearly in the shape of an old fashioned ice cream cone. To specialize it for one particular organ, make the open end just slightly bigger than the imagined size of the organ itself. Then put the mouth of the cone over the skin area nearest to the organ or gland you need to stimulate, and lie quietly, using the deep breathing and mentally directing the life energy of the breath to assist in the organ stimulation. 15 minutes to ½ hour, twice a day, spent in this manner should make a big difference. And if it can be done without discomfort or embarrassment, also wear one tourmaline taped to the skin area all the time until the organ returns to its normal state of full function.

4. Gemstones to stimulate healing of open sores, etc.

Red jasper emits the greatest amount of sheer healing or regenerative energy. Thus, an aluminum foil-lined cone with 15 or more pieces of red jasper is excellent to promote the healing of any

ISHTAR MAGIC FOR STUBBORN HEALTH PROBLEMS

sore or wound. If the doctor has put a dressing on the wound, do not remove it for the application of the energy. Make the mouth of your cone big enough to touch the skin outside of the wound area, and just put it over the wound, dressing and all, while you do the breathing and mental direction of the life energy to speed the healing. Again 15 minutes to ½ hour a day should bring a significant improvement of the healing rate.

5. A special gemstone set to stimulate weak eyes

As we grow older, we traditionally need longer and longer arms to hold our reading matter in easy focus for the eyes—or we resort to the never too convenient crutch of eye glasses. For the special eye-stimulating energy we need a slight modification of the cone shape we have been using for the other gemstone applications. Make your aluminum foil-lined cone as for any of the other projects, then flatten it to go across your eyes and cut away the round part that would otherwise rock on your forehead or the bridge of your nose. Cut away the material until your flattened cone will stand up easily on a table. Then put in three rows of six stones each, alternating tourmaline and red jasper. When your gemstone cone is complete, use it for 15 minutes to ½ hour twice a day. Cover your eyes with the mouth of the flattened cone (eyes open or closed, which ever seems most comfortable to you) and use the deep breathing and mental direction of the life force to the renewing of your eyes.

How to Make Ishtar Amulets for Healing

The tradition of carrying amulets for health, good luck and the like comes down to us from the ancients simply because when used with the proper magical attitude they worked—and still work. Vile smelling and fierce-looking concoctions and devices have been used over the years, but Ishtar is a devotee of loveliness and beauty, so it is natural that his health and healing amulet be pleasant to both sight and smell. The items needed to make the good general purpose Ishtar Health Amulet are: 1) a nice-size piece of John the Conqueror root, 2) some carnation perfume oil (it will take much less than a dram), 3) one yard each of red, yellow and blue yarn (wool or a synthetic equivalent is OK), 4) a small piece of paper on which you have drawn an eight-pointed star about 1 inch across and written beside the star, "Let there be perfect health, vitality and zest for life for (your name)."

When all of your materials are assembled, plan to put them together into your amulet on the first Friday after a new moon, beginning the 8th or 15th hour after sunrise. Begin by taking your materials to your altar star and greeting all the energy transformer personalities as by now should be your regular custom. Then begin the following chant and repeat it over and over again in a lighthearted manner until the amulet is complete. The chant is:

"Ishtar's mighty yellow makes the contact true.
Marduk clears the way with his slashing, healing blue
Nergal adds his red, my body to renew.
In perfect health I'll live. My loving thanks to you."

As you begin the chant, pick up the John the Conqueror root and anoint it all over with the perfume oil. Then wrap the root in the paper with the star and writing facing the root. Lay down the root and paper and begin to braid the three pieces of yarn into one colorful strand. When this is complete except for enough to tie it all up at the end, wrap your braided yarn around the root and paper, so that only the yarn shows, and tie it all up neatly with the ends of the yarn. The completed amulet should be small enough to carry with you in a convenient pocket or purse. When it is finished, go through the chant one more full time with emphasis on the "loving thanks" part, and carry it regularly. If the yarn unravels or gets dirty, get new yarn and renew the amulet with the perfume oil and chanting as before. We will sugggest special purpose variations of this very powerful amulet in the sections and examples that follow.

Putting It All Together to Win the Big Ones

Whether it be health-related or any other major problem, it is both reasonable and natural to work to solve it with ALL of the tools and techniques at hand. I avoided giving specific examples in the early part of this chapter to save room to illustrate how the devices and techniques work to reinforce each other and bring victory together where any one alone may have failed. This report from Zelma D. is typical of what I want to get across here. She tells us:

ISHTAR MAGIC FOR STUBBORN HEALTH PROBLEMS

I'm using a whole group of your methods and I'm really not sure which one is helping me the most. But having found complete respite from 20 long years of migraine suffering, I'm not at all inclined to cut out one to see that's it! Over my 20 years of suffering, I'm sure I must have tried every medicine and kind of doctor known to man. But nothing worked more than once the whole time. When I got involved in your Ishtar program I meant it to be for business, and I'm more than pleased with that part, but it's the migraine thing I want to tell you about.

I started practicing the renewal exercise then quickly added the body alignment exercise to add power.

Next I made the Ishtar Healing Amulet with a special written request in it, "please eliminate my migraines." By this point I was getting some help, down to about one bad headache a week instead of the usual devastating three. Then I got to thinking about the cones with the gemstones, so I made one with 18 bloodstones for the head another with 18 carnelians for reducing tension. Now I make a nightly practice of watching the 11 o'clock news with the bloodstone cone on my head and the carnelian cone on my solar plexus, while lying on the couch. Before this I always had to do more unwinding before I could get to sleep, but now I tend to drift off before the news is over and just barely make it to bed before I'm snoring up a storm.

Just the more relaxed sleep would be worth something more than the trouble of using the cones, but I have to tell you—It has been NINE WHOLE WEEKS since my last migraine, and that was before I got into the whole bit. Before this I never went two whole weeks without at least one bad migraine for the whole past 20 years. I can't tell you what it means to expect to get up in the morning pain free! Thank you seems so inadequate, but that will have to do until Ishtar answers my question of what I can do for him and you in return.

Joe D. had this happy report:

As you know, I'm 68 years old and when my wife passed on two years ago, I guess I pretty well retired from life. When I tried to get back into the swing of things, I had a most distressing problem of impotence. I went to the doctor and he said, "Face it, Joe, you're just over the hill." That I didn't buy, so I started with your root center breathing exercise, thinking that it would help, but it seemed mostly to generate lots more opportunities—which I tried to put off without turning off the ladies, while I kept looking for my physical help. Next I began regular use of the combination of the body alignment and renewal rite exercises, and I felt that this was bringing progress, but still needed more help. So I made the foil-lined cone and added the 15 tourmaline stones plus five red jaspers just for good measure. I used the cone morning and evening for a week (it was completely convenient to rest the cone in my lap while watching television, for instance), and this one seemed to be the capper—I felt LIFE down there again. To be safe, I kept up the whole process for another week before I dared to try it out. Then I arranged a very romantic date with the lady who interested and stimulated me most, and it all went wonderfully! We were married last week after a short but wonderful courtship. And I'm proud to say that our sex life has been magnificent!

Terry S. had his leg shattered in military action. When he was released from the service, he was put on permanent partial disability because he would have to wear the heavy brace on his leg and walk slowly and awkwardly for the rest of his life. "Two years of that stuff was all I could take," was Terry's comment as he turned to the "occult" for help. He quickly agreed that his mental and emotional (astral) legs are not crippled, so the body alignment exercise became the first step, seeking to bring the wholeness straight through from the spiritual/emotional/mental levels to restore the perfection of the physical. Next he added the Ishtar Renewal Rite, "With some extra chiding of Ishtar that I want to manifest his *effectiveness* through *two* good legs." Next he added the root center breathing exercise and mental direction of the root center energy to the restoration of the leg to its original perfection.

After about three weeks of spending half an hour twice a day on the project, Terry reported that he felt some "tiny" indications of improvement, but it was not nearly fast enough. Because the leg was still somewhat painful, too, we decided on a special purpose set of cones for Terry. He made three cones to be sure he could cover the whole area of the leg. In each one he put six tourmalines, six red jaspers and six bloodstones. He rigged the cones so that they could be tied lightly to his leg at bedtime, and arranged the bed so that he could sleep all night with the cones in place along his leg. He put the cones back on his leg for the half-hour twice-a-day sessions of the body alignment/root center breathing/renewal rite, too. After about 10 days he reported that the pain was almost completely gone, which encouraged him to keep up the program. In a month he tried his first halting steps without the brace. By the end of the second month, he was walking unaided with only a slight limp. At the end of the third month he reported: "My leg is not quite as good as new yet, but it is completely serviceable, and I *know* that just a little more perserverance will bring total victory!"

I have many more examples in my files, some of which are much more startling, but I don't want to stretch your credibility too much here. Let's just say that if you have an "impossible" problem and are crazy enough to try, and stubborn enough to hang in there, you can lick it.

How to Build a Perfect Figure—
the Ishtar Body-Shaping Program

Let's assume that your are comfortable with the state of your health, but would like to improve the shape and beauty of your body. The Ishtar Unifying Rite combining the body alignment and renewal exercises (just as we gave it to open this chapter) should be the beginning of your campaign. Work on this for 15 minutes or more twice a day, and conclude each session by praising your body for its improving shape and beauty. The basic technique of praise will by itself work many small miracles—any part of your body that you praise will respond by eagerly trying to earn more praise. Then a little extra help from breathing and gemstone power can really turn the trick. Let's illustrate with a few specifics:

1. Bust Development (or for you men, if you want bigger pectoral muscles to make you look better at the beach). The technique of praise here is to regularly pause to lovingly fondle the breasts while you tell them how lovely they are and how much more beautiful they are becoming as they grow. Take care to mean it! Weed out and burn away all feeling that nature somehow "gyped" you by not making them bigger in the first place—just recognize that nature meant well, but needs a little help. To go fully into this program, make three foil-lined cones. In two of them put 15 or more red jasper stones, and in the third cone, put 15 or more tourmalines. For the basic exercise, lie on your back and cover each breast with one of the red jasper cones. Put the tourmaline cone over your waist area. Then practice the basic root center breathing exercise, with this new mental image. See the life energy MOVING the cells from your waist area into your breasts, slimming the waist for lovely emphasis as you build up the breasts. Try to always do this exercise at bedtime so you can drift off to sleep with this picture as the last set of impressions in your mind. The trick to success is to understand that you are *not* trying to perform an impossible task, that you are simply assisting and directing the life force in its natural urge to produce beauty in the world. Be lavish in your praise of the body and of the life force for bringing the new beauty—and be regular in the application of the program.

Typical statistics for the ladies run like from 34-A bra to 36-C bra in six months with a one- or two-inch reduction in waist size. For the men, typically, a two-inch larger chest measurement in four to six months with an inch or so reduction in the waist. When this work is combined with the figure control work from my previous book, *Miracle Spiritology*,, it should work even more effectively for you.

2. Warts, Moles and Blemishes. Because this book is meant to be as practical as possible, let me digress here to share a personal experience. When I get carried away with the use of underarm deodorants, I sometimes get a tiny, but painful mole-like growth under my arm. There is an over-the-counter drug product called Vitamin A & D Ointment that was recommended to me years ago for relief of skin soreness. When I used this on the mole-type growth under my arm at bedtime, then showered the next morning, the process of drying under my arm knocked the growth right off. The first time, I shrugged and said, "Isn't that nice." But the same thing has happened for me at least six times over a 12-year period. I offer this not as medical advice, but as a clue that may help you with small growths.

To use the Ishtar Program, a special shape of foil-lined cone works best. We generally want to focus the energy on quite a small area, so I use the traditional old ice cream cone shape as a model. Again the tourmaline stones are the strongest for this part of the work. Combine the Unifying Rite with the root center breathing, cover the offending wart, mole or blemish with your tourmaline cone and picture the life force gently but firmly dissolving the unsightly part and replacing it with your normal lovely skin.

Typical reports on this process vary from overnight victory to significant improvement in three or four weeks. As usual, the big thing is to get yourself motivated enough to try, and then stick with it to victory.

3. Hair—Typically the complaint is too much in one place and/or not enough somewhere else. For this purpose, red jasper in your foil cone tends to be a hair grower, while tourmaline in your foil tends to be a hair remover. Again, use the Ishtar Unifying Rite and the root center breathing exercise with the cones in place over the areas to be affected. Picture the life force moving the hair from where you don't need it to the place it is needed. Keep at it until you have a nice bushy new crop IN THE RIGHT PLACE.

One more aside here. Diet and pills often have a major effect on hair growing. Overdoses of vitamins A and D will often cause loss of hair, particularly on the head. Eating liver, brains, and bananas is a help in the growth process. At least take care to have a well-balanced diet, and avoid excess vitamin pills to promote health hair growth.

4. Other Cases—If you have a unique problem, be creative in seeking help. Quiet meditation, asking what will help this, right after the Unifying Rite, will generally put you on the right track. If you feel stuck, I'll be glad to make a few personal suggestions. Just write to me, referencing this chapter of the book—tell me your problem and I'll do my best to make a useful suggestion. I'll give you my address in the next section.

A Note About Where to Get Your Gemstones

You may feel that all this sounds terribly expensive, and it could well be if we had to have jewelry-quality gemstones. But happily this is not the case. Tumbled or even raw stones, such as one finds at the local lapidary or rock hound shop, will produce the energy just as well as the more expensive variety. In 1977 prices, we are talking about a range of from 50¢ to no more than $2.00 per stone. If your local lapidary or rock shop can't help you, I'm quite sure that I can. Right now I have a full stock here at E.S.P. Lab for instance, and we are in touch with many suppliers all over the country. If you need help, write me, Al Manning, ℅ E.S.P. Laboratory, 7559 Santa Monica Blvd., Los Angeles, Calif. 90046. I will definitely answer your note, and will do my best to help you.

CHAPTER POINTS TO REMEMBER

1. Your body was designed as a self-renewing system. You have only to provide the proper conditions for it to restore its own perfect health.

2. Use the Ishtar Unifying Rite as the first step in your return to perfect health. It is often enough all by itself.

3. Study the special gemstone applications and use the ones you need. This can supply the missing energy to speed your body's recovery.

4. Make your Ishtar Healing Amulet in general or special purpose variety, and enjoy its constant efforts to renew your body's perfection.

5. When you have a really major problem, use *everything* you know to help. Remember that your medical doctor means well, so don't dump him, but use the other techniques (knowing that they are such that they will not interfere with his treatment) to assist your body's healing. Perseverance will win for YOU.

6. Use the Ishtar Body Shaping Program to re-shape and beautify your body, to remove blemishes or even add hair. Application and perseverance will do it for you.

7. If you have special problems or need help in finding your inexpensive gemstones, write me at the address above. I will answer and do my best to help you.

CHAPTER 12

Let Ishtar Power Overcome the Toughest Cases of Loneliness, Lack of Love, or Lack of Respect and Prestige

Let's open with an overgeneralization: if you feel a serious lack of companionship, love, respect or prestige, it is because you are not relating properly to your fellow beings. Man is a gregarious animal. It is his basic nature to be friendly to his fellow beings at least on a one-for-one basis, and to timidly, but eagerly, reach out for friendship and companionship. If you are not getting your share of companionship, it's time to take a look at yourself as the world sees you, for the purpose of making you more attractive and less forbidding as an individual.

A Look at Yourself Through the Eyes of the World

The first major consideration is trite, but most necessary: NOBODY LIKES A GROUCH OR COMPLAINER. People would much rather tell you their troubles than listen to yours, but if instead you can get them talking about pleasant things, you will be sought after as a wonderful companion. It's a very good idea to monitor your conversations regularly to be sure there is no flavor of grouch or complainer in your talk that will lose you friends and companions faster than all the work we may do to get you new ones.

Next, pause to take a good look at yourself in the mirror. Do you give the impression of an age gone by, or of something weird yet to come? If you saw someone with a hair style like yours and dressed like that, would you be attracted to him (her) or want to make a hasty escape? It doesn't matter how old or inexpensive your clothes are, the question concerns the way it all goes together to make an initial impression. NEAT still counts a lot—even very long hair and a long beard on a man can still be NEAT and clean, to create a positive impression on those who would be of interest to you.

With conversation and physical appearance properly disposed of, we can turn to the meat of the thing. What is your aura broadcasting to the world about you? The energy field that is more nearly the real YOU, extends for several feet (at least) on all sides of you and offers the information of your true feelings about yourself to all who come close enough to sense it. This is what prompted the famous saying of the philosopher and mystic, Ralph Waldo Emerson, "What you are speaks so loud, I can't hear what you say." But the key factor is your real and honest opinion and feelings about yourself. We're back to the classic mirror exercise that you find somewhere in most of my books. At some point you have to smile at the lovely face in your mirror and, thinking of it as the inner you, say to it, "You are a really wonderful person and obviously deserving of all of the finer things of life," and get COMPLETE agreement. If there are valid objections, correct them at once. And do take the trouble to convince your inner self of the invalidity of the spurious or taunting objections. Remember it is this *inner you* that projects its opinion of you out into your aura for all to sense. It must be a wholesome opinion to earn you respect and companionship. Do whatever is necessary to convince your inner self before you bother to try any of the other techniques of this chapter.

How to Use the Ishtar Attract-Friendship Program

We have just discussed the first step in the Ishtar Attract-Friendship Program—it is to take that good look at yourself to be sure that your physical appearance, conversation and the opinion of yourself being broadcast by your aura are all positive and interesting.

The second step involves a slight modification of the special root center breathing exercise as we used it in Chapter 5. You will recall that on each exhale, we spoke aloud the words, "I am infinitely attractive and desirable to all beings," while picturing this message being broadcast by the root center in bright red waves of energy. From the standpoint of attracting a passionate lover, this is the just right approach, but now we are interested in friendship more than passion, so the spoken words should be: "I am infinitely attractive and desirable to, and respected by, all beings." Fill your aura with this message in bright red Light Energy every morning before you leave your house, and always again just before you go into any group of people.

Step three is to make your Ishtar Friendship-Attracting Amulet. Begin with a piece of paper about two inches by three inches in size. Draw a small eight-pointed star in the upper left hand corner of the paper, then on the remaining space write: "I, *(your name)*, am infinitely attractive and desirable to, and respected by, all beings. And I am attracting many wonderful friends now and forevermore. So mote it be, and I thank you." To go with your amulet paper, gather a nice piece of John the Conqueror root, some carnation perfume oil, and about a yard each of red, yellow and green yarn. Work at your altar star with candles and incense if possible. After lighting the candles and incense, salute the various energy transformer personalities on your star, and begin to make your amulet. First rub plenty of the perfume oil into your John the Conqueror root. Then wrap the root in your amulet paper, and braid your yarn into one strand, all the time using the root center breathing and the chant: "I am infinitely attractive and desirable to, and respected by all beings." When the braiding is finished, wrap the paper and root with the braided yarn, continuing the chant and root center breathing, until you finish and tie off the completed amulet. Carry it in your pocket or purse and touch it often. When the yarn becomes too dirty, renew the amulet by repeating the whole process with fresh yarn.

Step four is to open up your horizons—strive to learn something new and interesting every day. Go to new places and do different things as often as opportunity knocks. *Be* the exciting and interesting character that has always been the inner you, but now let it out to enjoy itself in your growing circle of good friends.

A typical result of this program was reported by Dorothy C.:

> I had lived in this town for a full year without making even one casual friend. People always seemed too busy or preoccupied to pay any attention to me at all. To say I was lonely would be a major understatement, and though I had my six-year-old in the evenings, he was no substitute for adult companionship. Then I got your note suggesting the Ishtar Attract-Friendship Program and the friendship thoughtform with your letter. Just that thoughtform and my decision to try seemed to make a big difference. I suddenly noticed people smiling and holding doors for me where they had ignored me completely before—same people, too, I swear it! This encouraged me to launch into the full project with enthusiasm. I went all the way with the special root center breathing exercise, the amulet and the whole bit. And the whole town seemed to warm up to me. I've had a wonderful three months of unbelieveable popularity, invitations to join clubs that had been denied me before, parties, and all manner of warmth and friendship. I soaked it all up at first, but then I realized I was neglecting my son. So now I'm more selective in what invitations I accept, but it's wonderful to say that the Ishtar program really made my life full and happy.

Your Right to Loving Companionship

It is important to keep a comfortable perspective about your love life. Recognize that all human beings are born to love and be loved, and that *you* are indeed entitled by birth to give and receive plenty of love and loving companionship. But it is equally true that you are not entitled to deliberately break up someone else's romance just so you can have that particular partner. Most of life's suffering of the lovelorn variety stems from too quickly focusing one's desires to the "I can't live without Laura (or Jim)" stage, but Laura (or Jim) just can't see you for sour apples. Similarly, we must be extremely cautious about the "soul mate" concept—the idea that there is only *one* perfect mate for you. Let's say you are just 20 years old and have met and recognized your "soul mate," but the next day that one is killed in an automobile accident. Are you going to spend the next 60 years in seclusion and mourning? It would surely be a terrible waste!

ISHTAR POWER OVERCOMES LACK OF LOVE

All of this leads us to the only healthy and practical approach to exercising your natural right to love and companionship. That is to recognize that there is an ideal lover longing for and seeking YOU right now—and the trick, as always, is to help the good that is seeking you find you swiftly and surely. Forget about all the odds against you and all your hang-ups on other "dream lovers," and concentrate on super attractiveness and availability to the wonderful lover who is free and ready for YOU right now. Then use the Ishtar Mating Call Rite which I will present next, and find your wonderful love and companionship right away.

The Ishtar Mating Call Rite

There is an old Polynesian tradition whereby you can tell a young girl's romantic status by the position of the flower she wears in her hair. It is quite a handy idea—one's availability must be known or at least suspected before a potential lover will be motivated to show interest—unless, of course, the attraction is so great that the would-be lover abandons all caution (and perhaps even the veneer of civilization). It is the purpose of the Ishtar Mating Call Rite to put such an attractive force into your aura that truly suitable and desirable mates will be virtually tearing down your doors to get to see you.

To prepare for the Rite, assemble the following few ingredients: a red flannel sachet bag (or small red envelope will do), a dram or less of frankincense oil, and small amounts of myrtle, basil and cinnamon. A frankincense-type incense is helpful, but not necessary, and tapered candles of red, yellow or green will help to create the right atmosphere. The key energy transformer personalities for this rite are Ishtar, Osiris, and Nergal. Consider them represented by the basil (Ishtar), myrtle (Osiris) and cinnamon (Nergal). Plan your rite to begin the first Friday after a new moon at the 8th, 15th or 22nd hour after sunrise. Go to your altar star, light your candles and incense and salute all eight energy transformer personalities as usual. Warm up with some root center breathing to get in the mood for being especially attractive, then open your sachet bag (or envelope) and put in a tiny pinch of each item as you speak the activating words:

"With Ishtar's basil we establish the contact strong.
Osiris' myrtle touches my love with song.
Nergal's cinnamon adds spice and zest.
Now a drop of frankincense to perfume our nest.
This potion's power is great, you see.
It brings my true love straight to me."

Repeat the words three times, adding small amounts of each herb and the oil each time. When you are finished, speak the concluding words:

The work is done, true love must come.
My love must come now straight to me, my hearty thanks I
  give to thee.

A woman then carries the sachet in her bosom, a man in his pants pocket. Go about your normal routine, but be alert to hunches or urges to "kick over the traces" in some way that will bring you into the proximity of your new lover—and know that nature and the Rite must take its course and bring the love and fulfillment you so naturally desire.

The Rite can be successful regardless of your age or other apparent handicaps. Typical of the reported results is this one from Sally S.:

> I am 64 years old and was widowed three years ago. Since that time the only new friends I seemed able to make were other widows. But this was too lonely a life for me, and I longed for the intimacies and companionship I enjoyed during my 32 years of marriage. When I encountered the Ishtar Mating Call Rite, I was more than ready to try almost anything. It took all my patience to wait for a Friday after the new moon, but I wanted to play by the rules so to speak, and wow, was I rewarded! Within two weeks, I was being courted by four (count 'em, FOUR!) interesting gentlemen. In three more weeks, I had narrowed my field down to two, then a week later I accepted Harold's proposal of marriage. We just got back from our honeymoon, and it was delightful. I feel safe in saying that this marriage is every bit as wonderful as my first. Do give my very special thanks to Ishtar and Co.

Developing the Bearing and Attitude that Command Respect

It is especially pleasant to know that you are genuinely liked and respected. This is the antithesis of both the pushy, crass "blowhard" and the mousy "Casper Milquetoast" types. Indeed it is the area of happy balance between the two sets of socially destructive tendencies. We opened this chapter with the suggestion that you take a good look at yourself as others see you, and that theme fits here as well. How often are you too loud? How many times do you utterly dominate a conversation? Or how many times do you sit quietly intimidated by the pushy people around you? Do you HAVE to keep telling people how good you are because you don't really believe it yourself? While you're looking in that mirror, try a re-run of the classic mirror exercise—tell that handsome reflection that you are a wonderful person, entitled to the love, friendship and respect of the world and all its inhabitants. And don't quit until it HONESTLY agrees with you. You must build your external confidence on the solid base of a quiet inner feeling of personal WORTH.

When you are really comfortable with yourself, this feeling will permeate your aura and transmit itself to all who are around you, and it is the first step toward being respected and admired. But you can do even more by paying attention to yourself through the eyes of others. Take a good look at your mannerisms and speech patterns—most of us get lazy and completely overwork one or two pet phrases. For example the "Would you believe....," made far too popular by "Control Agent Maxwell Smart," or perhaps the classic four letter words that we all use in place of taxing our vocabulary. The timeworn wall sign that says, "Please don't cuss in here. Not that we give a damn, but it sounds like hell to strangers," sets a tone for careful thought. It's meant to be a joke, but how much of your (and all to often my) talk and actions sound and look like hell to strangers?

But to overdo this part would be equally disastrous—we must relax and avoid self-conscousness, simply remembering to pay occasional attention to the overall impression you are making for the purpose of self improvement. As you pay objective attention, you will naturally weed out the things that detract from your bearing and so find the world treating you with more respect. We are about to go into some powerful occult work to enhance your effect on the world, but without the "common sense" of the practical basics, you would undoubtedly be disappointed in your results. Regardless of our backgrounds, finishing schools, etc.—we ALL tend to develop sloppy habits—take a look and clean up your act as the most practical beginning of your rich, new life.

How to Charge Your Aura with the Energy that Commands Respect

Just like chickens establishing a pecking order, there is a regular round of auric activity within any group of people that subliminally establishes an order of deference and respect. A little retrospection will clearly remind you that you regularly give a high degree of deference and often even obeisance to a few people who rightly or otherwise have established their psychic and psychological superiority over you. For a less personal example, you must have known 40- and 50-year-old men who were still totally dominated by a mother or wife who was a good hundred pounds lighter and physically totally inferior to the poor "Casper Milquetoast." I have often written of the psychic struggle for mood dominance whenever two or more people come together in the same room. This is an extension of that idea, and when you understand the mechanism thoroughly, it becomes a simple matter to take charge and literally move to the top of the pecking order.

Whenever people gather together, their auras are in constant contact, feeding emotions and data into the consciousness of the various individuals through the subliminal or subconscious channels. You might think of this as a functioning analog computer which effectively measures the feelings of personal worth of each individual and balances it with his knowledge and opinions of the others present, then takes into account financial or business organizational ratings (such as the fact that Charlie is your boss), and finally brings you the feelings and "natural inclination" to assert your dominance over some and accept your subservience (however grudgingly) to others. I like to dream of an ideal state where all beings treat each other as perfect equals, but on the practical level there is no hope for that in our lifetimes, so let's make the best of the world AS IT IS—and play to win!

Obviously, the place to start is with your own feelings of worthiness. When you fully realize that your honest opinion of your worth is literally being broadcast by your aura as a major part of establishing your value in the hearts and minds of others, you should rush right back to your mirror and work some more to convince the smiling face in there that you are indeed a worthy, deserving, competent and respectable person. This time you KNOW that you MUST win at your mirror—your standing and respect, both socially and professionally, quite literally depend on it. You must *KNOW*, deep inside where it counts, that you are a completely worthy individual, and so entitled to the enthusiastic help of Ishtar and all the other energy transformer personalities.

When you have won the battle of worthiness, you are ready to look at the rest of the mechanism of commanding respect. The next consideration of our allegorical analog computer is the strength and balance of the energy flowing through your seven chakras or psychic centers. Here it is a good idea to regularly check the energy flow with your receiving hand, and if a chakra feels deficient, use one of our recommended gemstones to enhance its energy output to convince the world (or the "analog computer") that you are strong and well balanced. To expect respect from others when their psychic beingness is receiving a weak output from one or more of your chakras is to flirt with disaster. When your worthiness is established and your chakras are putting through a balanced high energy, you are ready to apply the "take charge rite."

The Ishtar Take-Charge Rite to Control Any Life Situation

The full power to take charge of any situation naturally involves all of the energy transformer personalities operating through all of your psychic centers. To set your thinking, this is something in the nature of a reversal of the root center breathing process. There the raw red power of Nergal is broadcast into your aura directly from your root center to put the hint of sheer animal pleasure where it will make all people warm and friendly toward you. But when you seek a very special respect, the reverse process is called for.

Begin the rite at your altar star with candles and incense burning if possible. Salute the energy transformer personality on each point of your star, then coordinate your breathing with the exercise of the rite. Take your first deep breath while focusing on Nergal's root center. Hold the breath for about 15 seconds to get maximum power in the center, then lift the energy to your spleen center as you say aloud, "Nergal's Red lifted to Ra's Orange, combined in power now."

Finish exhaling, then take a new deep breath focused on your spleen chakra, hold it for about 15 seconds, then lift the energy to your solar plexus and say: "Red and Orange lifted to Ishtar's Yellow now, the combination grows in power."

The next deep breath focuses on your solar plexus with the 15-second hold, then lift it all to your heart chakra as you say: "Red, Orange and Yellow rise to join Osiris' Green, the power grows stronger as it reaches each chakra in turn."

Focus the fourth deep breath on your heart chakra, and after the 15 seconds of holding for maximum power, lift it all to your throat chakra and say: "Four strong colors lifted to join Marduk's Blue, the power is almost omnipotent now."

Focus the fifth deep breath on your throat chakra, hold it as before, then lift it all to your brow chakra and say: "Five great colors lifted to join Thoth's Indigo, the power grows so strong that no one can stand against it."

Focus the sixth deep breath on your brow chakra, hold it as before, then lift it all to your crown chakra and say: "Six tremendous colors lifted to join Bast's Violet now, we are ready to set my invincible sphere of respect."

Now focus the seventh deep breath on your crown center, hold it as before, then lift it all right out the top of your head to Isis as you say: "And now the completed rainbow flows up to touch Isis above me and flow back in a great sphere of power and respect to re-enter my body through Nergal's center. Anyone who comes near to this sphere of power is irresistibly impelled to show me great respect and consider my statements those of a well qualified expert."

Set your sphere of power and respect before you leave the house on any day that you may need it. Then if you are about to go into an important meeting, take a few minutes in the nearest restroom to set it again to be sure it is working well. Use your imagination in any part of the rite that is necessary at first—practice will make it more and more real and stronger and stronger for you.

A typical report of success with the Ishtar Take Charge Rite comes from an advertising executive, A.D.:

> For three years I had tried to land this one big account. I sweated bullets over my presentation every time I got a chance at it, but all to no avail. Then last week, I got another chance. This time I did the full Take Charge Rite at home, and again at 11 o'clock at my office, just before I left to give the presentation. And this time I was accepted! I landed the account—and it will just about DOUBLE my annual income!

Arlene E. used the rite in quite a different way. Here is her report:

> Somehow, my boyfriend never seemed to take me seriously. We had been going together for almost four years, but every time I brought up the subject of marriage, he just laughed and changed the subject. Then just before our date last night, I did the Ishtar Take Charge Rite. And oh, miracle of miracles, I didn't have to mention marriage, because HE DID! We have set the date for early next month and we're BOTH ecstatic about it!

CHAPTER POINTS TO REMEMBER

1. A look at yourself through the eyes of the world will help point out the things in your personality and mannerisms that have been restricting your social life and/or damaging your prestige. Take a good look, then set about to deliberately change for the better.

2. Use the Ishtar Attract Friendship Program to quickly and easily add many good people to your circle of friends.

3. You are entitled to a satisfying love relationship. If you are presently without a lover, use the Ishtar Mating Call Rite to attract a person who is just right for you. The results should be swift and satisfying.

4. Another look at yourself as others see you will help you assume the bearing and attitude that naturally command respect.

5. Add a fresh dimension of the feeling of personal worth and you are well on your way to being admired and respected by all beings.

6. Understand the psychic mechanism that establishes the "pecking order" in any group of people. When you recognize how it works, it will be easy to move up the ladder of prestige and respect.

7. Use the Ishtar Take Charge Rite to fill your aura with the power to handle and control ANY life situation.

CHAPTER **13**

How to Use Ishtar Power to Bring Yourself Good Luck and the "Charmed Life"

Do you know somebody you call "Lucky" or "Mr. Success"? Isn't it time your friends started to call YOU something like that—because your life looks like one stroke of good fortune after another? You have all the tools to make it so RIGHT NOW. Let's get right into a solid program to make YOU the "luckiest person" any of your friends knows!

Psychic Magnetism—a Small Force Operating
Constantly Can Move the Highest Mountain—
(How to Set Your "Good Fortune" Magnetism Effectively)

When I was a teenager, I visited a friend at a plumbing supply house and my mouth flew open in awe when I saw 50 tons of steel pipe being lifted by a mere ¼ horsepower motor! Of course I expressed astonishment, and the friend replied, "When you gear it right, a very small force operating persistently can accomplish just about anything."

He may as well have been speaking of "occult work" because the same principle is true—when measured on the physical level, the forces we use seem quite puny, but when you gear them right and let them work constantly, nothing is impossible of accomplishment. In fact, recent experiments in PK (the process of affecting the material world through mind and will with no "physical" agency) have clearly demonstrated that even events which have already "happened" but are unknown to the PK operator can be altered. The trick is to so focus and control your auric emanations that they work constantly for the same good purpose.

Any program to enhance your general good fortune must logically begin right back in front of your mirror. Tell your inner self that you are striving to become an ever better being and so are fully entitled to lead a "lucky" and "charmed" life RIGHT NOW. Stay right with it and handle any and all of the objections that may still crop up. With the agreement of your own high self expressed by good feelings at your mirror, nothing can hold you back.

But how shall you get this good feeling from your high self translated into the powerful psychic magnetism you need to assure yourself of your charmed life? A slight variation of the Ishtar Take Charge Rite we used near the end of our last chapter will do it quite easily for you. Lift the energy from center to center with the breathing exercise just as we did in the Take Charge Rite. Then after the seventh breath, as you lift the whole rainbow out the top of your head, say:

"And now the completed rainbow flows up to touch Isis above me and flow back in a great sphere of power to re-enter my body through Nergal's center. This flowing power will constantly magnetize my aura to attract over increasing good fortune and lucky breaks while it repels everything that would be unpleasant to me. I now accept my new title of Mr. (or Ms.) *Good Fortune* and I know that it must manifest as ever increasing GOOD in my life now and forever. So mote it be, and I thank you."

Renew your sphere of good fortune every morning at your altar (streamline the Rite if you are short of time, but take at least a few moments to FEEL it working for you), and at any other time you feel an urge to do so. And begin each day by thanking your spirit friends and the energy transformer personalities for the as yet unknown good fortune that is on its way to manifest today.

Feedback on this part of the work is fun and often reads almost like a fairy tale. A.F. reported it this way:

For many years people had been much more apt to call me Calamity Joe than Mr. Success. I have to admit that I was a bit skeptical about the Good Fortune Magnetism Rite, but I decided to give it a good try. I felt better even the first day, but there was little to note in the way of change for about a week. Then one evening just after dusk I was hurrying to a meeting and sort of stumbled, but didn't fall. I looked down right then and sure enough, I picked up a twenty-dollar bill! Then I went into the meeting and won TWO door prizes—not bad considering I had never won anything like that before in my life.

That night I had lots of nice thank you's to say at my altar for the feeling of being a winner and the knowledge that that winning feeling would help strengthen the magnetism in my aura to bring more. Next day the mail brought me a $732.00 check from my insurance company with a note of explanation that I had been overcharged for three years and this was my refund. Then there was a totally unexpected check from Internal Revenue for $385.00 with the explanation that their computer noted an error in my tax return computation and here was the refund due me. Next, I let some friends talk me into a day at the races and I hit the first exacta for $860.00 and just betting hunches wound up way over $1,100.00 ahead for my day's fun. All of this has happened within three weeks of finding that first $20 bill that almost tripped me! To tell you that I intend to keep that sphere of good magnetism around me forever would be a gross understatement!

Martha U. reported:

After one week of using the Ishtar Take Charge Rite, modified to make me a magnet for good fortune, I feel I owe you a report. I used the exercise each morning, and sometime during each day an especially nice extra something happened. The first day I used a pay telephone, but didn't get my party. When I hung up, the telephone thought it was a slot machine and returned $2.90 for my dime. I laughed as I said thank you to my spirit people and the energy transformer personalities for the good omen. Next day I found a just right apartment to move to—and that was a real stroke of luck because I had been looking for six months. On the third day it was my Bingo night and I won four times! I've never won more than once in a night before, and the extra $80.00 was nice, too. Next day I got a totally unexpected promotion on my job and a nice raise. On the fifth day I got a call from one of those radio quiz shows and won $500.00. The sixth day was Saturday and the mail brought my tax refund check for $100.00 more than I had expected. Then, since Sunday was a day I had planned for quiet rest, I really didn't expect anything, but I was rummaging through some old papers and found the diamond ring I had lost three months ago and had given up hopes of ever getting it back. I can hardly wait for next week to start!

Timing—How to Make It Work for You
(The Chakra Check for Acceptance)

Timing is the essence of good comedy, but it is also one of the key ingredients of the charmed life. When your timing is right, you buy and sell your stocks at the right prices, you avoid unpleasant situations, and all manner of wonderful opportunities for profit and advancement are regularly with you. If ever there is a totally practical application of your extra sensory faculties, it is in developing the sense of timing that not only puts you in the right place at the right time, but has you saying the right thing to the right people at the right time.

When your sphere of magnetic good fortune is operating well for you, the feeling of being a real winner should be enough to help you relax enough to let in even the subtle psychic inputs to guide your timing to sheer perfection. By now you KNOW that the psychic data is available to your chakras and you are gaining the habit of paying attention. There remains only the idea of "finetuning" your chakras to pick up the inputs of special interest to you at any given moment. Let's begin with the easy ones. Perhaps there is a favor you would like from a particular friend or loved one—timing in making the request is the essence of both success and good human relations. Check out your subject's response in this manner: mentally and emotionally focus your attention on your subject's personality. Then ask each of your own chakras what kind of vibes it is receiving from that person. Next, mentally and emotionally ask your object to do your request. Give the idea a full minute to reach the person psychically, then again interrogate your chakras for changes in the vibes to see how your request would hit your friend. If you feel a warm response through your chakras, it's OK to bring up the request verbally—but if you feel

HOW TO USE ISHTAR POWER FOR THE "CHARMED LIFE"

negativity on the psychic levels, it is much better to wait for a more propitious time. And of course, the more important the request is to you, the more help you will get by using the chakra test for your timing.

Cathy D.'s report will help us to get a more complete picture of the technique:

> When I started to think about checking my chakras to improve my timing, I suddenly realized that most of my fights with my husband came up when something I asked him to do didn't sit right with him. So I decided to experiment with some of the routine requests around the house, like asking him to set the table, take out the garbage or something. The first thing I learned (and I guess I should have known it anyway, but somehow hadn't thought of it) was to wait for a commercial on TV before asking Jim to do something for me. By itself this has probably cut our domestic tiffs in half! But it's even better with the big things. When I want something special, I check his response through my chakras several times a day until it feels just right. Now we not only don't fight, but he has NEVER turned me down on anything since I have been working this way—and for three months it's been really heaven around here.

Walter T. combined the timing idea with the Ishtar Take Charge Ritual modified to attract good fortune, and this is his set of results:

> I'm interested in the Stock Market and wondered if checking my chakras for timing would help. I tried thinking of buying or selling a particular stock and found that it seemed to register in my solar plexus—a good feeling for yes, and an up-tight feeling for no. After six months of buying at the low and selling at the high (I was trading in only eight stocks that were cheap enough to get me in and out without a major investment), I have my broker calling me for market tips! After the first couple of weeks I used the magnet for good modification of the Ishtar Take Charge Rite before each time I asked my solar plexus about a stock. And not only have I made marvelous profits on the short-term swings (averaging about 13% net profit a month on my money), but all manner of lucky happenings seem to be around me constantly. The financial highlight was when I won $5,000.00 in a lottery!

The Ishtar Metaphysics of the Charmed Life

There is an ancient metaphysical truism which says: "That which you *willingly* share with others is multiplied in your life." The negative side of this is clearly seen in the lives of those who seek to share their troubles with their friends and acquaintances—naturally they manufacture much more trouble for themselves. Let's simply remember that this is one more good reason not to rush around telling everybody about your real or expected misfortunes, and consider the deliberate positive application of this bit of natural law in your life.

The first practical application is itself a negative: never be jealous of the good fortune of another person—even one you consider your enemy! We must KNOW that there is plenty of good to go around, and REJOICE whenever we see or hear of another person's lucky break. At every opportunity, get close to someone who has just launched a streak of good luck so that the positive vibrations from his (or her) aura can literally rub off on you. By rejoicing sincerely with another about his (or her) good, you help to charge BOTH your auras with the positive power that attracts more good. You will recognize that here we are carrying the ideas of Psychic Ecology we have discussed in our earlier work a giant step forward—not only are we avoiding generating any negative thought/reaction energy, but we are also actively seeking out even temporary sources of enthusiasm and good luck. In this process, the idea of checking out the chakras as we did in the timing section can be an excellent safeguard. If there is a choice to be near someone or to absent yourself, focus momentarily on that person and check the reaction of your chakras. Then make your decision on the positive or negative reaction that you receive.

Or when you know you are on the way to meet someone, focus on the person and check out the reaction of your chakras to sense his mood and prepare in advance to enjoy or handle it. If you do sense negativity in a chakra check, send extra positive energy ahead of you, with special emphasis on directing the sparkling throat center blue to cleanse the spleen center of the negative or upset person. These extra precautions, together with consciously entering into the normal struggle for mood dominance, will make you much more than welcome ANYWHERE. Then as you build a personal reputation of being a walking good luck charm for others, too, you will find yourself indeed living a positively charmed life.

How to Earn a Reputation of Being Lucky for Yourself and Others by Your Very Presence

As you develop the habit of encouraging others to talk about their good fortune, and so help to charge all of your auras with more good fortune, there will be a completely natural tendency for your personal presence to trigger new lucky breaks for all those you come near. Thus it is a simple matter to add a "good luck for others" thoughtform in your aura and become such a consistent trigger of good for people that you quickly get called "my walking good luck charm" by a host of friends and well-wishers. You need simply make one tiny addition to the Mr. Good Fortune ritual we used to open this chapter. Just at the end where you have said, "I now accept my new title of Mr. Good Fortune and I know that it must manifest as ever increasing good in my life now and forever," add, "And I gladly share my good by decreeing myself to be a bearer of good luck and good fortune to all who come near me. My aura is charged with good luck for others now, and it manifests in happy profusion wherever I go." Then close with the normal, "So mote it be. And I thank you." Make it a habit to renew this each morning and think of it whenever you are going into a group of people or making any kind of a visit or call.

Arthur G. sent us this piece of feedback which because of my own accounting background is one of my favorites:

> I am a CPA in a small practice for myself. I have always been friendly with my clients, but the nature of the auditor/accountant is to be poking into things and asking semi-embarrassing questions—so you get a nickname based on CPA that generally (and modestly) translates it as something like Chronic Posterior Aggravation. Your idea of becoming a walking good luck charm naturally had an extra appeal to me, so I tried it. My accounting training has taught me to be conservative, but also to spot trends quickly. The first time this happened, I was pleasantly amused, the second time quite interested, but today was the third time in the space of the last two weeks that a client has said to me something like this: "Arthur, I wish you'd drop around more often just for lunch or something—every time you come into my offices, the telephone starts ringing and we write more business that day than in an average week." Indeed I am gladly trading the title, Chronic Posterior Aggravation, for my new

one, Walking Good Luck Charm. I might add that my own business is growing very nicely as one of the obvious results, but I assure you my enjoyment of life is growing even faster.

How to Make Sure that Your Good Fortune Will Continue Forever

A good farmer knows that you don't just take from the soil, you care for it and give it balanced fertilizers, and even rotate the crops with plants that put back what last year's crop took out. Clearly the fertilizer of our work is giving of ourselves to others along with some form of tithing or regular gifts to churches, colleges and perhaps occult research or other "off beat" but worthy groups. Whenever things seem to be slowing down for you, immediate response should be a look at your patterns of giving with the idea of increasing the giving where it seems it would do the world the most good. That the concept of tithing WORKS is such a truism we need not belabor it here, but we should have a momentary look at the psychic or psychological equivalent of crop rotation.

The idea of a vacation quickly comes to mind, but that is more in the nature of letting the soil lie fallow for a period of time. In our sense, crop rotation would be the experimentation with different forms of occult and spiritual practices to keep learning, but more important to keep your work ever fresh and new. This is why I didn't write just one book and stop. In each of my books I have tried to present a complete system that has worked well for many people. And I urge you to try one of my other books just as soon as you have mastered the techniques you find in this one. But don't stop there either—examine the works of many authors and keep adding to your ability to rotate your psychic crops to take the fullest advantage of your own psychic soil. Be a good eclectic and build your personal system out of the best that is available from all sources. But in a year or so, come back to this book, read it carefully again and see how your personal growth has made these techniques much more useful and powerful to you. And as you grow, I assure you that you will gain more and more respect for the special work of this chapter. Becoming a walking good luck charm is one of the most powerful techniques you will ever encounter.

CHAPTER POINTS TO REMEMBER

1. Given a bit of time, a small force operating constantly can indeed accomplish ANY task.

2. Begin your charmed life by totally winning the confidence and acceptance of your inner self right there in your mirror.

3. Use the Mr. Good Fortune ritual each morning and enjoy watching your life become a veritable fairy tale of good fortune and lucky breaks.

4. Be aware of timing constantly. Use the chakra checking technique to be sure of your timing in any major presentation or personal encounter.

5. The chakra checking technique will work for investments and stock purchase/sales: make it a positive habit and stay in the win column.

6. Stay aware of the Ishtar Metaphysics of the Charmed Life—share your good fortune willingly in as many ways as possible and watch it multiply.

7. Add to the Mr. Good Fortune ritual the extra bit that makes you a Walking Good Luck Charm, then enjoy the special appreciation of your friends as your good and theirs are regularly multiplied.

8. Insure that your good fortune will continue forever by using the techniques of tithing and regular psychic crop rotation. Your growth will ensure you good forevermore.

CHAPTER 14

Summon Ishtar Power to See Into and Control the Future

If you are a confirmed fatalist, please skip this chapter and go on to the work of the next one—I can imagine nothing more frustrating than to see clearly into the future but feel powerless to change it! Fortunately our modern society has spawned very few real fatalists, so the rest of us must already accept some degree of responsibility for our futures, and it is our purpose now to give you *full responsibility* for your personal future along with the *full power* to direct and control it.

A Working Picture of What Makes Your Future

What is reality, and when does it become an unchangeable part of the thing we call the past? Modern Quantum Physics gives us much in the way of a good understanding when its basic experimentation demonstrates that an event is not a reality and still keeps open all its options UNTIL IT IS OBSERVED (by a human being?). The critical difference in the approach of quantum physics is that THE OBSERVER IS AN INTEGRAL PART OF THE EVENT—we might say no event is complete and unchangeable until observed. Recent parapsychological experiments in PK (psychokinesis) have involved pre-recorded magnetic types being influenced (changed) by the PK practitioner with what we might call retroactive effect. Even when the magnetic tape was reinforced by being duplicated on punched paper tape in advance, the PK effect has altered BOTH. But what do quantum physics and PK experiments have to do with your use of the Ishtar Power? Plenty! Now we can understand more of the meaning of *reality* and *future* in order to enter positively into the mechanism and assert our control.

Let's look at the critical factor in quantum physics: it is to *observe*. But if we contemplate what is really meant by the term we might properly say it implies both to *note* and to ACCEPT as fact. There are many records of a patient on the operating table being clinically dead, but the valiant doctor has not accepted this as fact and his persistent efforts revive the patient in spite of the clinical "reality." And of course the Biblical story of Jesus ordering Lazurus to come forth from the tomb remains the ultimate. On the other hand, we have seen many a wife refuse to accept the condition of death for her husband and literally try to pull him back out of the coffin quite without success. Why does one fail while the other succeeds? By the time the wife's futile efforts come to naught, far too many people have observed and *accepted* the fact that life has permanently left the victim's body.

It is precisely for reasons like this that we find the principle of *secrecy* so important to metaphysics and ceremonial magic. We must not subject a potential event to the critical scrutiny of others until they will observe and accept as fact the desired outcome! And let me remind you that the same is true of all of your work with the Ishtar Power.

Let's proceed to expand our understanding to a working view of what makes YOUR future. We must look at the part of your life and of our world that has NOT YET BEEN OBSERVED AND ACCEPTED—and it will appear as an infinite number of tendencies, a myriad of forces working themselves out according to "chance" and natural law, but constantly modified by changing attitudes and metaphysical and magical efforts by you and others close to you. Picture broad marches of history so powerfully built into a country's or the world's consciousness that one person can have little effect on them. These are the things often called "group karma" such as wars, crop failures and other natural disasters. But the closer we get to the individual level, the more nearly we reach full control over the direction and outcome of the working forces. And even where we seem to touch the "group karma," there are ways to control its effect on us as individuals. Let this sink in well, because until you understand it, a look into the future is certain to be frightening at best.

The Ishtar Future Viewing Rite—for a Look Ahead

The realm of seeing into the future belongs to the solar plexus and brow chakras, and so to Ishtar and Thoth. Think of it as having Thoth bring you the pictures while Ishtar adds the intuitive understanding, and the combination gives enough accurate data to help you chart a safe and profitable course ahead in time.

Before you try to look ahead, it is important to be relaxed with *all* of your chakras functioning normally and well. A weak chakra will influence the inputs negatively and tend to bring frightening rather than useful and accurate inputs. So the regular chakra check, as we used it for timing in our last chapter, should be your first step. If a chakra is sluggish, get it turned on well or reinforce it with a strong gemstone before you begin the actual Rite.

As usual, candles and incense are useful in setting the mood. Begin the Rite by touching the points of your altar star as you salute each energy transformer personality in turn. Then put your middle finger on the Ishtar point and your thumb on the Thoth point of your star, and say aloud: "Ishtar and Thoth, please give me a look at the future as it relates to (the reason you seek to look at the future)." Repeat the request three times, then relax, close your eyes and roll them up as if to look out through the center of your forehead. This is a stimulant for seeing pictures on the little TV screen inside your head, but take care not to ignore a simple intuitive input that can be equally useful and accurate.

As part of the development or unfolding process, I generally recommend working for a few minutes each day on relatively unimportant questions about the near future which can be verified soon, preferably the next day. For this purpose, some of my students work with the local horse races, using the rite to pick the winners of five or six races from the listing in their daily newspaper, then verifying their accuracy with the next day's paper. Of course the ones who get good at it invariably manage a few "field trips" to the track. R.T. was one of these, and here is his report:

> As you know, I spent several weeks practicing the Ishtar Future Viewing Rite on my local racetrack. At first the results

were pretty sporadic, but I stuck with it and slowly learned to get an intuitive flash of a number or set of numbers. Last Wednesday I decided I was doing well enough to drop out to the track and put my money where Ishtar and Thoth's mouths were. I bet very conservatively so the results were not spectacular, but I hit the first exacta and had five out of six winners to come home $593.00 ahead. That's a lovely way to work on one's psychic development!

Mary B. used the rite in quite a different way. This is what she had to say about it:

> I had been out of a job for four long months and seemed to have no prospects. Then I got the idea to try the Ishtar Future Seeing Rite. My request was, "Ishtar and Thoth, please give me a look at my future and help me improve it by showing me where to apply for a job." I was about to be disappointed because I didn't see anything, but I realized I seemed to be thinking about a particular intersection—streets that I don't normally travel. So next morning, I drove over that way. I used the root center breathing and the Ishtar Take Charge Rite as I was driving, and I felt almost pushed into a particular door when I got there. Sure enough, the owner said, "Gee, I'm glad you dropped in. I was about to put a help wanted ad in the paper, but you've just saved me the time and expense." I've been on my new job for a week and it's WONDERFUL!

When You See a Big Hole in the Road—Steer Around It

As you develop a good working relationship with Ishtar and Thoth, you should notice that you are regularly getting spontaneous inputs of bits of helpful information, but it is a good idea to use the Future Viewing Rite at least once a week with the request, "Please show me anything in the near future that you feel I should know about." Be sure that you are relaxed and your chakras are clear on this one to avoid confusing or erroneous inputs, but the help that is available here is beyond price.

A.F. gives us his very useful application:

> I knew that the wife and I were not exactly in a honeymoon period, but I stay pretty busy in my business and hadn't thought much about home one way or the other. When I did my Future Viewing Rite and asked for anything I should

know about, I got a bit of a shock. I seemed to hear a voice say, "Your wife will run off with an acquaintance of hers whom you do not know in about three weeks. Better be prepared." The next day I moved some funds out of the joint checking account and did a few other bits of discreet defensive maneuvering. When my wife asked for a new tire for her car, I could tell that she was thinking as an outsider—before she would have just said she was about to buy a tire, or even just bought it since I had never badgered her about money.

By this point I had decided it would be a good idea for her to go and the next 16 days I lived more as a spectator than a participant. She had cut me off sexually a couple of months before, using a trumped up health excuse, so there was no intimacy, just my interested watching of the developments. I came home from the office on the 17th day to find on my table her wedding ring and a terse note saying she had left me. Because I was prepared, it came more as a relief than a blow. I went to dinner with some friends and had a good night's sleep. I can tell the story now that the divorce is over. With the divorce laws what they are in this state, my conservative estimate of what that warning saved me in money is $15,000.00, not to mention avoiding a major depression or loss of ego if it had just been sprung on me. You can be sure that I have regular Ishtar Future Viewing Rites and no doubt will for the rest of my life. Nobody should be dumb enough to fly blind when there is this kind of help so readily available.

Miriam G. used it this way:

I was planning a junket from my home in Norwalk to San Diego to look at a piece of property. In my regular weekly Ishtar Future Viewing Rite, I got a crazy feeling that I should postpone the trip for one day. I have had lots of help from this rite, so I decided to follow the input. Sure enough my newspaper carried a report of a 21-car pile up on the freeway that happened just about the time I would have been there. I made the trip with no problems the next day. I'm not sure whether to credit Isthar and Thoth with saving my life or just with helping me avoid a messed up car, but I KNOW I owe them thanks for saving me from some sort of a big mess.

Group Karma (War, Depression, Natural Disasters, etc.) and How to Turn Its Effects to Your Advantage

Before we talk about changing the future it is well to consider the massive flow of human fortune, often called group karma, that one being can expect to have little or no effect upon by magical means. For instance, another world war is the sort of thing one would certainly work against with prayer and magic, but prudence would dictate also a strong measure of action to protect YOU on the personal level. Stop to think about it—even in the tragedy of war some people get happily ahead. And an earthquake may well destroy the houses on either side of you without touching yours at all. We are a step past steering around a rut in the road at this stage, but it is important to recognize this sort of input from your Ishtar Future Viewing sessions and plan your best course of action.

One of the better examples of making do with a group karma situation is this one reported by J.Y.:

> The first time the Dow Jones Average broke 1050, I was asking Ishtar for a broad view of the future and got a feeling of bad trouble in the Middle East which would have a depressing effect on the stock market. My investments were modest, but I decided to cash out for the profit I had in it. The check from my broker came to just over $8,000.00 which I promptly put into a savings account. It was a matter of days before the Arab oil boycott hit and the market went into that big tailspin. The money stayed in my savings account for just over a year, then I bought back twice as much of the same stocks I had sold and had some change left out of the $8,000.00. I tell you this now because the DJ average hit 1,000 again and my stocks are worth well over $16,000.00 now. I at least doubled my money while avoiding the potential losses by paying attention to the input from Ishtar.

Sophia N. feels that the future viewing saved her at least a lot of inconvenience:

I was planning a trip to visit my family in northern Italy when there came a sudden urgency for the trip in my Ishtar Future Viewing Rite. I didn't quite understand, but I rescheduled for two months earlier than I had planned originally. It was a glorious trip with many happy re-unions, but all the while I didn't understand the reason for the urgency of doing it two months early. Then when I would otherwise have been there, a major earthquake hit northern Italy with the greatest devastation in the very town I had used as my headquarters for the trip. I had the joy of seeing it whole as well as the safety of being in my own home here in the United States when the catastrope happened. Ishtar saved my life or at least helped me avoid a lot of inconvenience.

Harnessing the Ishtar Vector Rite to Change the Future

We will begin by remembering the idea from our last chapter of a small force working constantly being able to accomplish ANYTHING! The future is a bunch of tendencies or forces which are gradually working themselves out to more or less solidify into an agreed-upon set of facts we call history or the past. But here it is well to remember the definition of History that is attributed to that interesting philosopher, George Bernard Shaw—he is supposed to have defined history as an agreed-upon set of lies. And we are learning from quantum physics and PK that in this sense those two words, *facts* and *lies* may very well be interchangeable. The point to be aware of is that until you have noted and *accepted* an event as fact, it remains somehow susceptible to change by magical or psychic means—so we must learn to strive on not just until the time an event is scheduled to occur, but indeed until we have had full opportunity to note and accept the outcome.

The practical application we want to explore first is changing the potential event as it may be revealed to you in your Ishtar Future Viewing Rite. Let's say you have completed your rite, but don't like what you saw. It is important not to merely accept it and bemoan your coming fate, but rather to dive in with all the magic and means at hand to change the outcome BEFORE it has a chance to be noted and accepted as historical *fact*. The classic metaphysical method for this is to mentally take charge of the picture and by force of will *change it* to the desired outcome. For many minor events, this should be all that is necessary. But if the event is of special importance to you, you will find it best to follow up with the Ishtar Vector Rite to Change the Future.

Begin with blue candles and a good incense at your altar star. Salute all the energy transformer personalities as usual. Then if you have in any way experienced a negative vision of the potential event it is necessary to destroy the picture. Put your middle finger on the Ishtar point of your star and your thumb on the Marduk point (with the palm of your left hand over the center of the star). Visualize a stream of slashing blue energy flowing to the negative picture as you ask aloud: "Ishtar and Marduk, please help me deliver the full power of Marduk's slashing blue to completely destroy this erroneous picture." Repeat the request three or more times as you visualize the slashing energy completely obliterating the offending mental picture.

Then, leaving the middle finger and thumb in place, put your little finger on the Nergal point of your star as you build a fresh mental picture of the event as you desire it to take place. Fill in all the details very lovingly as you decree aloud: "The power of Marduk and Ishtar protects this proper picture as the strong energy of Nergal brings it to enthusiastic life." Repeat your decree at least nine times as you bring the mental picture to glorious completion. When it feels finished, decree: "My proper and positive picture has now become a permanent vector force field which works ceaselessly and inevitably to bring itself into happy physical manifestation." Repeat this at least three times and until you feel that it is finished. Conclude with: "My loving thanks to Ishtar, Marduk and Nergal. The manifestation is assured. So mote it be."

Arthur G. used the Ishtar Future Viewing Rite and was quite disturbed at what he saw. Let him tell it:

> In my weekly future viewing rite, I got quite a shock. I have a night class once a week and come home by way of a signal that lets me on the main road home by a big curve where much of the traffic comes onto the street I'm turning off from. The picture was of a blue and white Dodge coming too fast around the curve and ploughing right into the driver's side of my car as I waited for the signal. It was so vivid and unnerving that I immediately used the slashing Marduk blue energy to break it up, but I was still shaken. So I did the Ishtar Vector Rite to see that car go safely on around the curve. Just to be sure, I did the rite every night for the four nights before the next class. Even so I was a bit nervous on the way home. And

sure enough I was stopped at that signal when along came a blue and white Dodge exactly as I had seen it in the vision—of course it was coming much too fast as it made the turn. I swear to you it missed my car by less than half an inch, BUT IT DID MISS! I KNOW that the vision and the Ishtar Vector Rite literally saved my life. Just a few more inches and I would surely be a dead man! You can be sure that my thank you to Ishtar and company was profuse and heartfelt that night.

The vector rite can be used to improve your chances in lotteries and drawings, too, but let's share this one from a mother who picked up a picture of danger for her son:

When I performed my Future Viewing Rite, I got an awful picture of a small plane hitting a commercial airliner with a resutling major crash—and somehow I knew my son was on that plane. He was scheduled to fly from New York to Los Angeles next week, and I knew I couldn't talk him into going by train. So I set out to erase the picture with the powerful Marduk blue energy, and to do the vector rite for perfect safety for my son's plane trip. When I finished I felt good about it and promptly forgot the incident in the bustle of daily living. But I remembered it quickly enough when I talked to my son on the phone a few minutes ago. He called to tell me of the near miss of an aerial collision. Everybody on his side of the plane had screamed in terror as a small twin-engine craft came out of a cloud and just missed the airliner. I went straight to my altar to thank Marduk, Ishtar and Nergal, then to my desk to write this to you. My thanks to all for the help that saved my son.

Using the Ishtar Vector Rite to Increase the Price of a Stock in the Market

The Ishtar Vector Rite can be used for many applications other than avoiding tragedy. It is ideally suited to situations where a steady pressure in a positive direction can skew the curve of chance in your favor. The stock market is a favorite application—for horse races for instance, the action is too fast for the vector to take maximum effect, thus we discussed letting the future viewing rite show you the winner rather than trying to enter into and change the outcome. But the stock market is an ongoing thing where a vector can have plenty of time to take effect.

SUMMON ISHTAR POWER TO CONTROL THE FUTURE

One word of caution is in order. Many of my students (as well as my personal dealings) have had really excellent success with stocks, but prudence and the future viewing should be applied also. The vector can cause your selected stock or stocks to outperform the DJ industrial Average by 10% to 20%, but in a rapidly dropping market this would not always be enough to avoid short-term losses. My own experience has clearly demonstrated that the vector rite shows up best in a flat market—when the rest of the market stays still while your selected stocks go up, you have a marvelous feeling of special effectiveness to go with your profits. But all the while you maintain a position, there should be weekly future viewing sessions to ask the buy/sell/hold question for each stock in your portfolio.

Samuel B. had this to report on his stock market work:

> Until I combined the future viewing and vector rites to help my investment activities, I had performed way less than average. But now things are really different. In the last flat market period that lasted about six months, the three "cheapie" stocks I picked up to work on with the vector rite gained an average of just over 50%! Then I got a picture of a down market so I sold all three. Sure enough, I bought them again yesterday at an average price less than I paid the first time. I have the vectors working again and already they are starting to respond. It's not a get rich quick scheme, but it appears that I can at least double my money in a year's time—and that is just about 10 times better than anything I've been able to do before. One of the real tricks is to keep up the future viewing bit and have the courage to sell when you get that sinking vision. Before the year is out I will just about have matched my salary with stock profits!

The potential for application of the Ishtar Vector Rite is as broad as your own imagination. Again let me suggest that very fast-moving games like the commodity market or horse races are extremely tricky and lend themselves better to acceptance of the future viewing exercise. But the stock market, improving the size of your own business, getting ahead on your job, general health, attracting a "perfect" lover, and even healing "incurable" diseases are all prime subjects for the vector rite. I could give you many spectacular examples right here, but the best ones read too much like science fiction. Instead I will close this section with a simple challenge: the limit to what you can accomplish by using the complete set of tools we have given you this far is your own daring and willingness to try. What belongs here is YOUR success story, far more spectacular than any example I have given you. Apply your new knowledge with discipline and perseverance and success is YOURS.

CHAPTER POINTS TO REMEMBER

1. The future can be changed right up until the point where you note and accept an event as fact. Modern PK experiments have demonstrated that even after signals have been mechanically recorded, the content can be affected—so long as there has been no observation of the pre-recorded results.

2. When working to control an event, keep up the work not just until the time the event is to occur, but until you have noted the outcome personally.

3. The Ishtar Future Viewing Rite can give you a glimpse of the way the existing forces will work out in the future if you do not interfere in some powerful way.

4. Practice the future viewing rite regularly—something easy to keep up with, like the local horse race card, is good for building up your accuracy and proficiency. A little practice every day will soon make you good at it.

5. When you see danger ahead, take reasonable steps to avoid it.

6. Major tides of human events (called group karmas) can be sensed, and the advance knowledge will help you to turn an otherwise negative situation into progress and good for you.

7. The Ishtar Vector Rite can give you powerful control of future events. Practice this one regularly to change things you don't like as they are presented by the future viewing rite.

8. As you get good at the vector rite, NOTHING is impossible to you. Dare to try, and win!

CHAPTER 15

Let Ishtar and Thoth Help You Achieve Controlled Out-of-the-Body Experiences

Students of the occult have been intrigued with the out-of-the-body experience for centuries, and though science has yet to really recognize even the possibility, it is becoming a much more common practice here in the late 20th century. Let's begin our discussion by dispelling some of the confusion that so often surrounds the subject. First, the out-of-the-body experience, or astral travel as it is most often called in occult circles, is no more dangerous than driving a car. And acquiring at least an elementary proficiency at astral projection requires about as much developed skill and conditioned reflexes as learning to be a good automobile driver. The process itself is a completely normal one, indeed young children do it quite naturally—spending much of their night's sleep in happy play in the astral realms. We will set the scene for your own projection work by first looking at something you do every day.

The Natural Separation from Your Physical Body— Usually Called Sleep

As your physical body relaxes its grip on the real you, you are accustomed to dropping off into a state called sleep. The occult version of the technical process is simply that there is a degree of separation of "you" from your physical body in order that it may more readily absorb the universal energy necessary to its revitalization and rejuvenation processes. We think of going to sleep as a losing of consciousness. but this is quite untrue; what we really do is slip into a different state that is focused outside the physical body—then the materially-oriented person knows that the sensory apparatus and objective reasoning functions of the physical body are greatly reduced, and since to him the physical body is "me," he feels that he has "lost" consciousness. This may be a bit cumbersome in English, but only because the language itself is used to describe primarily materially-oriented situations and things. In the body-unifying work from Chapter 11 on, you have learned that your physical body is essentially like a horse or other conveyance for you—and if your horse goes to sleep or you turn off the motor in your car, you know full well that YOU have not "lost consciousness!"

Indeed, as your basic orientation to "you" leaves the physical and begins to reside in the mental or emotional body, you will find yourself dropping off to sleep as usual, but soon waking up outside the physical body and participating to some degree in the mental/astral activities around you. The beginning student seldom wakes up into full control of his out-of-the-body faculties, but the vividness of the astral colors and the nature of the experience itself are still enough to set the experience apart as far more than a simple dream.

Some of us may try to say that we never even dream, much less wake up wandering around on the astral levels, but this is now quite thoroughly refuted by scientific "dream research" which asserts that everyone has several periods of *rem* (rapid eye movement) activity during any reasonably long period of sleep. Since the rem activity has been proved to come with dreaming (or astral experiences), your only possible statement now remains, "I don't remember my dreams." Thus, the first new skill or conditioned reflex we need for your astral or out of the body work is to regularly remember your "dreams." From these memories, you can get much data on your progress and learn to differentiate quickly between a simple dream and an unplanned out-of-the-body trip.

How to Program Yourself to Remember Your Dreams and Unplanned Out-of-the-Body Excursions

Aside from your altar star, you will need a tiny eight-pointed star for this exercise. Cut one out of a piece of writing paper—it can be drawn and cut without being perfectly even, your best effort and the eight points will suffice. Keep your small star down to a size no bigger than an inch from point to opposite point. I like to think that by now you are in the habit of visiting your altar star and chatting with the energy transformer personalities at or near bedtime, so I will suggest that you just tack this small exercise on the end of your nightly visit, as a way of entering more fully into the fellowship. When your thank you's and bits of encouragement or simple discussions with the spirits and personalities at your altar star are finished, pick up the tiny paper star and touch it first to the Ishtar, then the Thoth points of your altar star as you ask: "Ishtar and Thoth, please help me to fully remember any important dreams and all of my out-of-the-body experiences tonight." Then with something of a flourish, tape the tiny star to the center of your forehead over your brow center (Scotch Tape or regular adhesive tape will be fine), and say: "This small star I place on my forehead as a covenant with Ishtar and Thoth and a reminder to my own inner beingness to cooperate in bringing my night's experiences into full conscious memory in the morning. So mote it be." Then go on to bed in happy anticipation of more fully enjoying your night's activities.

It is very good practice to keep paper and pencil on your nightstand. If you should wake up during the night, take a couple of moments to jot down notes on what you remember already, and always make notes in the morning before you leave the bed to help you remember more. Without the notes, some things may fade from memory before you have a chance to fully digest or appreciate them. If the results are not completely satisfactory the first night, keep up the work—encourage your own inner beingness and KNOW that perseverance will win.

Agnes N. has this to report on her dream work:

As I told you, I fully believed that I am a non-dreamer because in my 35 years of life I remember having only three dreams. I was pretty skeptical about your tiny star exercise, but it seemed important to my progress so I gave it a try. On the morning after the first night's exercise, I was a bit frustrated but also encouraged. I remembered nothing specifically, but there was a hazy recollection that I had been busy as all get out out there. So at least I knew I should try again. The hazy memories were the best I could do for about 10 days, but I kept feeling that they would suddenly clear up. No such luck, but on the 11th morning I did remember two clear scenes, and after a full month I am doing very well. Sometimes I only remember that I was in a class-like situation most of the night, but other times a whole set of experiences come back quite clearly. And I feel that I can now distinguish easily between a dream and a real out-of-the-body experience. The big difference seems to be that I am a spectator in the dreams, rather like going to a strange movie, but in the out-of-the-body trips I am definitely an actor—experiencing and feeling just as if it were happening to me in my physical body. You're right that this is a necessary way of getting familiar with the out-of-the-body realms before one would have the courage or serenity to try to leave the body consciously.

Steve W. already knew he "dreamed" regularly, so his response came faster:

The first night I tried the tiny star on my forehead to remember my out-of-the-body experiences, I brought back a wonderful memory! I was out there in the presence of my spirit teacher and received some special instructions of a very personal nature that I feel have given my overall growth and progress a really big boost. I have been aware of helpful spirit activity around me for several years, but THIS is the first time I got a chance to visit my teacher and REMEMBER it!

Degrees of Projection, Astral and Mental—the Shortcut Ishtar Exercise for Mental Projection

We might best look upon the whole area of dreams, visualizations, visions and projection of the consciousness outside the physical body as a continuum with each type of experience we speak of blending or shading into the other with no clear lines

ACHIEVE CONTROLLED OUT-OF-THE BODY EXPERIENCES

between. And the practical approach need not always care exactly which phenomenon is occurring so long as you are able to bring back accurate and useful information. We should be able to quickly agree that a "good" projection is one that accomplishes the purpose for which you attempted it, and particularly during your learning period just let it go at that.

This leads us to the immediate use of an elementary waking technique for quick projection, useful particularly in viewing actions taking place at a distance from you at the time of your projection. Again the key energy transformer personalities are Ishtar and Thoth. The exercise should begin at your altar star, moved to a place where you can use it while sitting in an especially comfortable chair. As always, candles and incense help in setting the mood. When they are lit, greet all eight energy transformer personalities, then spend a few moments in the basic body alignment exercise we have used so frequently in our other work together. When you feel the bodies aligned well enough to bring in some Light, ask aloud: "Ishtar and Thoth, please help me in the projection of my mental body to (name of the place you want to see)."

Then begin the exercise itself by imagining that your mental body is shrinking to become a tiny dot of concentrated consciousness right in the center of your Brow Chakra. As you "imagine" you feel the mental body shrinking, say: "My mental body shrinks now to become one with Thoth in his chakra."

After 10 seconds or so, when you feel as tiny as possible, will the mental body to expand until it includes the place (or person) you want to see. While you are "imagining" the expansion, say: "As Thoth, I expand this mental body to see (your chosen target)."

If you tune in with a clear picture the first time, sit there and enjoy it as long as you wish. If there seem to be little or no results, don't be discouraged. Repeat first the shrinking, then the expansion process again and again until it works for you. I have deliberately used the word "imagination" in this process to avoid any argument from your materially oriented thinking processes. Time will prove to you that you are doing much more than simple imagining, then you can vary the words as it seems most suitable to you.

When you have seen (and heard) as much as you want, shrink your mental body back to the dot in your Brow Chakra once more, then will it to return to its normal size and place within the greater system called "you." And of course conclude with special thanks to Thoth and Ishtar.

The results of this elementary exercise can be dramatic as this report from Marie S. tends to show:

> My husband had been working late at his office once or twice a week for several weeks. On this particular night he seemed to be very late about it. Always before, he got home by 11:30 anyway, but now it was close to 1:00 A.M. and I was uneasy. I had tried the Ishtar/Thoth mental projection with some success twice before on trivial things, so I decided to look in on John to be sure he was all right. I used the exercise with the request, "please help me project my mental body to see John right now," and on the third or fourth expansion attempt I got a scene, but not in his office. It might have been a bigger shock if I had tuned in a few minutes before. As it was I saw John and a woman I did not know in what was obviously a motel room. They were in their underwear and seemed to be dressing. I held the picture while I tried to focus on the conversation. It wasn't easy, but I was sure I heard him call her Barbara. When the exercise was complete, I did a bit of soul searching and decided to be asleep when he came home and approach the subject over breakfast in the morning.
>
> As I poured John's coffee and sat down to breakfast I tried it this way: "John, if you would be as loving to me as you were to Barbara last night, I'm sure I could keep you satisfied and happy. Can't we talk about it?" The expression on his face was that of a little boy caught with his hand in the cookie jar. He swore that it was the first time and that it would never happen again. And somehow he has managed to get his work done at the office and be home with me every night since—and the attention is wonderful, like a second honeymoon. My special thanks to Ishtar and Thoth.

How to Generate a Fully Conscious Astral (or Out-of-the-Body) Projection

Before we begin the work of this section, let me remind you that in each of my six previously published books I have given one or more different methods or approaches to conscious astral projection. At the moment I like the method I am about to give you here better than others, but that could change again—and my reason for mentioning it is to help you keep trying, in the off

ACHIEVE CONTROLLED OUT-OF-THE BODY EXPERIENCES

chance that this method doesn't feel comfortable to you. For specific references to my other works on this subject I suggest particularly my *Miracle of Universal Psychic Power*, and/or *Miracle Spiritology*. With that out of the way, let's get down to our serious business.

The work of the mental projection exercise from our last section will have you well prepared to combine the mental and emotional bodies for a true and complete out-of-the-body experience. In addition to Ishtar and Thoth, Bast becomes the other key figure in your controlled projection. Without mentioning it before, we took the mental body which we would most closely associate with Ra out of the higher chakra counterpart of Ra, which is Thoth's Brow Chakra. Similarly, we will be using the higher chakra counterpart of Ishtar's emotional body for our launching pad for safe and effective out-of-the-body projection. Of course you know that this is Bast's Crown Chakra.

Many methods suggest that you lay your physical body down on a couch or bed for this work, but that creates a condition which your inner mind all too often associates with sleep, with the result that you go to sleep instead of making your desired astral grip. So let us suggest here that you pick a comfortable chair with arms on it so your physical body will not tend to fall over while you are out of it, but still try to be sufficiently upright that there is a greatly reduced tendency to nap. Otherwise, prepare as we suggested for the mental projection exercise. When you finish greeting all eight energy transformer personalities, ask aloud for special help from Ishtar, Thoth and Bast this way: "Ishtar, Thoth, Bast, please help me produce a fully conscious separation of my emotional and mental bodies from the physical so that I may grow and learn from the experience. I ask also that my spirit teacher be close by to meet me as I make the successful separation."

Check the body alignment to be sure you are getting plenty of Light through the system, then begin by shrinking your mental body to a tiny point in your brow chakra. When this is complete, shrink (or imagine the shrinking if necessary) your emotional body to a tiny point inside your crown chakra, while you say aloud: "My mental body shrinks to become one with Thoth in his chakra, while my astral body shrinks to perfect oneness with Bast in her crown chakra."

When the shrinking is complete and you feel the oneness, expand both bodies to a focus roughly three feet behind your physical body as you say: "As Bast and Thoth, I expand my bodies and transfer my waking consciousness to the freshly assembled astral/mental vehicle behind my physical body." Expect to find yourself fully awake behind your physical body at that point, but if you do not feel a complete transfer, repeat first the shrinking process, then the expansion, decreeing the transfer of consciousness. If you should not succeed within 18 or so cycles, thank your energy transformer personalities for their help, promise to try with them again tomorrow and conclude the session. It takes the average student a week to 10 days to get a working handle on the system and produce a conscious separation at least sporadically.

We will give you several helpful trouble-shooting tips in our next section, so don't despair if you seem to have a slight block on this one. But before we trouble-shoot, let's enjoy some reports of special help from successful use of the exercise.

Here is a report from Harold R.:

What a wonderful feeling! I use the Ishtar/Thoth/Bast astral projection exercise at least once a week now to renew it. As you know, I work in transportation and handling of very touchy high explosives and I was near the point of having to quit this exceptionally well-paying job because of my nerves. Let's face it, I had progressed from scared to death to completely petrified. Then I had my first successful out-of-the-body experience which included the special pleasure of meeting my spirit teacher face to face. There was a special calming effect just from the experience—and of course it was easy not be be afraid of separating from my body this way, *knowing I could get back.*

The new perspective and sense of spirit guidance and help have made me a new man, with plenty of caution but *no fear* on my job. The ulcer is healed, my skin rashes are gone and I feel wonderful. Now I know I can keep my job and honestly enjoy it! But the best part is my whole new outlook on life. I often wondered why you so casually refer to your physical body as your "horse," but now I KNOW. You were right, I now own eternal life and need not listen to someone trying to convince me I have it—nor do I need to convince anyone else. I am serene and growing ever more wonderfully in the Light.

Werner V. gives us his account of this very useful application:

When we divorced, my wife took the children to another city several hundred miles away. Because I have to work harder than ever to keep up the alimony and child support payments, the visiting privileges quickly proved to be meaningless. But I love my children and I miss them. So I decided to try at least an out-of-the-body visit to them. It took three nights of using the exercise with Ishtar, Thoth and Bast (even in a chair I fell asleep the first night) to get out of my body, and two more nights to get enough control to will myself to the children and make it stick. Then what a wonderful surprise! I "accidentally" projected into my youngest son's bedroom, and his body was apparently asleep on the bed, but he was awake in the room playing, and recognized me at once! He exclaimed, "Daddy, I hoped you would come! I had a feeling you could do it." I won't go into a lot more detail, but let me say that this is a real lifesaver for a lonely man. And my young son has taught me a lot about understanding and really enjoying life. Had I known it sooner I would most likely still have my family. But I know how now, and I'll have another family, but I'll also enjoy the fellowship with my young son—at least until the world convinces him that my visits are all in his imagination.

The potential value of controlled out-of-the-body projection staggers the imagination. We know that the Iron Curtain countries are working hard on the facility for espionage and other military applications, but the greatest uses will always be positive ones. You can learn new physical skills, study philosophy while your body sleeps, make wonderful love (yes, astral sex is possible and wonderful in spite of what you may have heard to the contrary), visit loved ones, or be about fully serious psychic missions in cooperation with your spirit band. And of course you owe yourself ONE fully conscious out-of-body trip just to KNOW that YOU own eternal life, that this physical body is indeed just a horse and you can grow a brand new one when this one wears out or is destroyed. All this and fresh experiences that it seems best not to tax your credibility with at this point are waiting for you. Give it a solid try. But should you feel still stuck in the physical body, come back to this chapter and work with the trouble-shooting points we will give you next.

Troubleshooting Your Astral Projection Exercise
(What to Do if You Seem Unable to Get Out)

There are normally only two things that will block your getting out of your body, and both are forms of fear. First is the normal fear of the unknown. This naturally makes you afraid to get out of your body—you don't know exactly why, but it's a frightening prospect. This fear is overcome by knowledge and experience. Go back to your practice of mental projection, and while the mind is out, teach it to imagine your full mental and emotional consciousness out there with it. Read more about astral projection and experiment with other techniques (such as the ones I mentioned in *Miracle Spiritology* and *The Miracle of Universal Psychic Power*). Perseverance and growing knowledge and experience will very soon reduce this type of fear to a minimum that will not stand in the way of your successful projection.

But just about the time the student overcomes the fear of the unknown, he (or she) is struck with awe at the magnificence of the prospect of his own out-of-body experience, and a brand new fear develops. Our psychologist friends would probably call this one an anxiety—in other words, the student becomes over-anxious to get out, and again the tension works just like bars in a cage to keep you in. I call this another fear because a bit of analysis will show you that this time it is fear that you cannot get out. This is overcome with patience and perseverance, or much more quickly with a touch of Zen. In Zen we learn by contemplating a paradox until we receive enlightenment by perceiving the higher truth which makes both of the conflicting statements true. In this case the paradox is simple. You can achieve your projection at will just as soon as you satisfy these two conditions: 1) You must want to leave your body with all of your beingness; 2) You must not care one whit whether you succeed in projecting. Meditate on this paradox as a way to grow around ANY obstacle. When you fully understand this, NOTHING can stand in your way.

CHAPTER POINTS TO REMEMBER

1. Though it is not yet recognized by modern science, the out-of-the-body experience is a natural phenomenon relatively easy for anyone to practice.

2. The process we call *sleep* is normally accompanied by at least some separation of the mental and astral bodies from the physical. The separation allows a more rapid renewal of the body's energies.

3. Use the tiny star ritual to program yourself to remember your dreams and out-of-body experiences when you awake from your normal night's sleep.

4. As you remember more of your sleeping night's activities, you will begin to readily distinguish the difference between a dream and a full out-of-the-body experience.

5. There is a continuum of experience from dreams and visions through simple mental projections to complete out-of-the-body experience.

6. Practice the Ishtar/Thoth mental projection exercise. It has many good uses of itself and it will help to prepare you for full out-of-the-body projections later.

7. The Ishtar/Thoth/Bast astral projection exercise should bring you easy and complete out-of-the-body ability with a few week's practice. You might also try alternate methods as suggested particularly in my two other books mentioned in this chapter.

8. If a month's practice has not yielded a good projection, follow the trouble-shooting suggestions, overcome the blocks of fear, and strive on to complete success.

CHAPTER 16

Troubleshooting with Ishtar—
the Power of Positive Stupidity

There is frequently a magnificent "honeymoon" period when the student first seriously encounters metaphysics or a good occult system—the initial enthusiasm overcomes all manner of ignorance, sloppy technique, doubt and even fear to bring success after success. Then one day the honeymoon ends and as the student is picking himself up off the floor, you hear his plaintive wail, "Why doesn't it work for me anymore?" We are all dreamers, hoping to make each honeymoon last forever. I hope this one does last for you, but if the time comes when you feel that the power has gone out of your work, do remember this chapter and dive right into its work to get a complete and *permanent* handle that in time should earn you your own title of MASTER.

When we stop to analyze the magical process, it is easy to understand the honeymoon period. I have a pet name for it, "The Power of Positive Stupidity." As a beginning student you don't realize the complexity and all the fine points of magical operation, so your enthusiasm at finding something that "really works" generates enough power to make up for all your technical deficiencies—we all know the power of enthusiasm to literally bowl over everything that tries to stand in its way. This is the quality of which Jesus spoke so highly when he said, "Except ye become as a little child. . . . " The joker comes as your enthusiasm demands more knowledge and expertise, so you learn about all the things you were doing wrong and your doubts grow in power as your enthusiasm wanes. The inevitable result is the feeling of having fallen off your lovely pink cloud right back into a mud puddle. When this happens to you, it is NOT a time for despair, but for rejoicing! Now you can go back to the old drawing board and become a MASTER of the system who no longer needs to depend on "beginner's luck." This takes us right back to the fundamentals—like back to tackling dummies in football.

Your Master's View of the Fundamentals

When we fully understand and apply the fundamentals, we are assured of reasonably good results, then by adding a few fine points we can indeed be consistent winners. Your Master's view of the fundamentals should look upon the magical process as a simple three-step operation. First there is the basic contact which puts you in tune with the energies of accomplishment, next is the psychic ecology, the washing away of all doubt, fear and limiting thought-forms, then comes the positive work that wins. We may find it useful to add a few ideas of *timing* as part of our fine points, but the fundamentals are the key—without them, all your pseudo-sophisticated work will come to naught. Let's apply it now, step-by-step to your *certain* victory.

Step 1: Apply the Power of Positive Stupidity to improve your basic contact with Ishtar and the other energy transformer personalities

If you get no results at first, or any time your results begin to tail off, the first thing to check is your "front mind's" attitude. At some point it will begin to question: "How can touching a piece of paper or a medallion put me in contact with all this omnipotent energy?" And if this attitude is allowed to continue unchanged, it will indeed reduce your altar star or medallion to a worthless piece of paper or metal. First, counter the doubt logically with this argument: There is indeed an energy of shape and form, and though it is weak by comparison to normal physical forces, it is still strong enough to act as a focal point for the magnificent energy of the Infinite as directed to me by God's wonderful Ambassadors whom I know as the energy transformer personalities.

Then go to your altar star and devote 10 minutes or more to

renewing your *experience* (as opposed to belief or faith) of the energy. Greet the energy transformer personalities as always, then hold your receiving hand ½ inch above the center of your altar star and concentrate on *feeling* the energy flow as you chant aloud:

"I feel the energy flowing into my hand from my altar star. I rejoice in it and know that it is real. I feel it renewing my full contact with each of the great energy transformer personalities. Through this perfect contact I salute my energy transformer friends and rejoice in the wonder and beauty of it. I am filled with fresh enthusiasm which perfects my tie to all the power to achieve *any* goal. I am happily too dumb to know anything but success and I give my heartfelt thanks for the joy of ever more glorious victory."

Feel your enthusiasm grow with each repetition of the chant, and do it at least nine times, or more if it takes more to feel personally fully omnipotent. Then take your fresh, omnipotent enthusiasm with you into Step 2.

Step 2: Apply the Power of Positive Stupidity to a complete cleansing of your psychic atmosphere—perfect your psychic ecology

With all my emphasis on psychic ecology, I am regularly amazed at how completely negative a human being's attitude can be, particularly as he screams, "Why doesn't any of this junk work for me?" Typically, the person has carefully defined an "impossible" problem and demanded a complete solution in a day or a week, with a chip on his shoulder to boot. If you should encounter people like that, give them a wide berth lest they contaminate you with their hostile negativity. But take a good look—there is some of them in each one of us!

Do your best to adopt a really positive attitude, then use the super enthusiasm you developed in Step 1 to burn away any lingering negativity. Invite all your spirit helpers and energy transformer personalities to assist as you specially salute Ra, Isis, Thoth and Osiris, then feel the swirling power cleansing you completely as you chant:

"All spells and energies sent to me by fire of Ra now purified be.
By love of Isis toward me be filled, wisdom of Thoth bends you to my will

THE POWER OF POSITIVE STUPIDITY

> With the power of Osiris you work for me, my success and health ever greater must be.
> All spells and energies now must help me, and as my will so mote it be."

You may recognize this as the Miracle Spiritology outside cone of power protection chant, but it has even extra significance for use here. Let your "positive stupidity" give it fresh power and meaning to sweep away any limiting thoughtform whether of your own creation or sent by another. The key here is to build the feeling of a completely pure psychic atmosphere that is completely conducive to the well being and manifestation of your positive work.

Step 3: Now do the positive work that wins

As you dive into the positive ritual or ceremony of your choice, bring the clear psychic atmosphere and the "little child" enthusiasm to bear with the full force of your positive stupidity. One of the really big secrets of success is to make every part of the work FUN. When you are happy and really enjoying what you are doing, the boost to your enthusiasm rubs off on all the nature spirits and entities involved and even gets more power from the energy transformer personalities. The real power of positive stupidity is the part that can forget all the limitations and pressure of your "normal" life and focus as the little child on the fun of the work itself. When you can bring this attitude to your altar, you are assured of success.

Kurt W. had this to report on the Step 3 trouble-shooting procedure:

> When you stressed the fun element in the work to me, you really hit a nerve. I suddenly realized that I had approached my magical work as something resembling a Gestapo agent. I went back to find the joy in the basic contact with the energy transformer personalities, used the Miracle Spiritology outside cone of power chant also with happiness, then launched a really fun prosperity rite. This time instead of a negative reaction, I got a promotion and $300.00 a month raise on my job. The same night I played poker with some friends and won $150.00 in a $1.00 limit friendly game. Thanks for the tip about making it fun—it works!

Applying the Principles of Timing to Your Work

We will shortly go all the way back to ancient Babylon to speak of the planetary hours system of timing your work. And it will be a magnificent help in timing tricky projects. But the personal timing we will discuss here is of even greater importance. It is human nature to get the timing all wrong. We naturally tend to do a prosperity ritual when we are feeling a great lack of money, a health ritual when we feel sick, a friendship ritual when we feel lonely, etc. And that is exactly backwards. When you try a prosperity ritual with your mind on the big batch of bills you want to pay, the odds are ten to one that your thinking about the bills while doing your positive work will backfire and bring you more bills instead of money.

Thus we can give you the primary rule for timing any positive work as: *Perform your magical rite when you feel that you already have more of what you seek to multiply than you have had in a long time.* Remember that it is your Inner Beingness (often called subconscious or unconscious mind) which participates with the energy transformer personalities to bring your magic to manifestation. And the manifestation will come through as a full reflection of your inner mood at the time of the work. We are about to examine a magnificent system of fine points for timing tricky or especially important magical work, but all the external timing in the world will be worthless unless you learn first to harness your good moods, or better, control your moods and build them up to a peak of happiness, opulence and health as a prelude to any magical work.

Audrey L. had this to report on her troubleshooting:

> Well, you finally got through to me about timing my magic to fit my mood. As you know my prosperity rituals had seemed to backfire for two full months and I was getting to where I was scared to try any more. But when you pointed out my mood and focus on the stack of bills, I realized you were quite right. So I splurged and bought myself a nice steak to fix for dinner. I did myself a really fine spread and when it was finished, along with some good Burgundy, I felt at peace with the world and quite opulent. So I dashed to my altar star before the mood had a chance to wear off. This time the prosperity rite was really fun, and I enjoyed contemplating

THE POWER OF POSITIVE STUPIDITY

nice piles of *extra* money. Sure enough, in just three days I was notified of a 50¢-an-hour raise and asked if I would mind some overtime on Saturdays for a few weeks. And the same weekend I was invited to the races with friends and won $863.00 on the first race exacta! Now that I know for sure what you mean by timing your magical work to fit your moods, I am sure I will be a very effective magician.

How to Increase the Power of Your Magical Rites by Harnessing the Babylonian Planetary Hours System

It is often truly amazing to contemplate the advanced knowledge of the "ancients." In the ancient science of Acupuncture (now finally being accepted by modern science) we find the statement of fact that the twelve meridians have cyclical periods of intense activity and relative inactivity. Similarly, throughout the ancient sciences and their modern counterparts, we find cycles of activity of great importance in treating disease, starting an ocean cruise (the tides), and most of our significant activities. The trick is to know WHERE YOU ARE in a given cycle to know if it is best to strive harder or to rest and await the more propitious time that is soon to come.

If you have ever seen a Farmer's Almanac, you know how much our old American farmers depended on their knowledge of moon cycles in the planting of their crops. And everyone naturally takes sun cycles into account—can you imagine planting pansies in Maine in December? For the typical above-ground crop (which we can take to mean a positive magical rite of major importance to you), the prudent farmer would do his planting in the fairly early spring, just shortly after a new moon while the moon is in a fertile sign (any water sign, or Capricorn, Taurus or Libra). But most of our magical work is toward relatively short-term goals—and we certainly don't want to restrict our activities just to the springtime. With this in mind we can borrow from the very ingenious system of the Ancient Babylonians, and find a good time ANY day for our magical rites.

It is always a good idea to take the moon phases and signs into account, but even this can be circumvented quite well by the device known as the Babylonian Planetary Hours System. Just as the Acupuncture Meridians are known to reach cyclical peaks of activity individually during each 24-hour period, so your chakras and their related energy transformer personalities also reach cyclical peaks at easily predictable times each day. Thus, by choosing a time when the key chakra in your rite is at a peak of effectiveness, you can materially improve the power of your work. Since you are by now well familiar with the names of the energy transformer personalities and how they relate to your chakras, we need only examine the system of planetary hours to simply and accurately pick the right time for any specific rite.

First let us note that the days of the week are named after luminaries that correspond to the energy transformer personalities we are accustomed to working with. For easy reference we will recap this for you in table form right here:

Day of the week	Luminary (or ruler)	ENERGY transformer personality	Chakra
Sunday	Sun	Ra	Spleen
Monday	Moon	Isis	Risen Kundalini
Tuesday	Mars	Nergal	Root
Wednesday	Mercury	Thoth	Brow
Thursday	Jupiter	Marduk	Throat
Friday	Venus	Ishtar	Solar Plexus
Saturday	Saturn	Bast	Crown

Note that the heart chakra, represented by Osiris (Earth) does not appear in the tabulation, but can be properly represented by his consort, Isis. Also, it is good to understand that the ancient Babylonian system of naming the days of the week has come forward into at least all of the Western World and is indeed recognized worldwide.

Now we will begin to see how to put this to use. The luminary and related energy transformer personality after whom a day has been named reaches a peak of power on that day, and so is said to be the ruler of the day. Similarly, on an hourly basis, the ruling luminary of the day reaches an extra peak of effectiveness during the first, eighth and 15th hours after sunrise, and the other luminaries reach peaks during the other hours in a magnificent never ending cycle of power. The sequence of cyclical power peaks follows the traditional pattern: Ra, Ishtar, Thoth, Isis, Bast, Marduk, Nergal, and repeats itself on toward Infinity. If you care to make a table to prove it to yourself, write the days of the week across the top of a piece of paper, then number from 1 to 24 down the left edge, and beginning with the first hour on Sunday, fill in the table: Ra, Ishtar, Thoth, Isis, Bast, Marduk, Nergal, Ra, Ishtar. . . . .until you come to the 25th hour which will "miraculously" be Isis, the ruler of the first hour of Monday, and all the way to the 25th hour from Saturday's sunrise which will again be Ra, ruler of Sunday.

Note that there are at least two, and often three, hours during any day when any one of the energy transformer personalities you desire to stress is having a period of peak power. And if you seek to stress two kinds of power (for example our work in mental projection using Ishtar and Thoth) you can pick a day ruled by one, and the hour of the other. In the case we just mentioned, you could use an Ishtar hour on Wednesday (Thoth's day), or equally effectively a Thoth hour on Friday (Ishtar's day).

The best order of preference in selecting your timing is FIRST consider your *mood*, SECOND look at the moon phase and sign, THIRD select a good day and hour. Remember if your mood is exceptionally good it is quite proper to forget everything else and dive into your rite. But if you have a good mood sustaining ability, you can go for the finer points of timing to make your magical work even more fully effective.

Combining the Power of Positive Stupidity with the Planetary Hours System for Ever More Effective Magical Work

Amelia N. was far less than satisfied with her results until she got into the timing and troubleshooting part of the work. Let her tell us how it helped:

> I was what you might call a hard core lonely person—not a loner, but just plain lonely. At 40 I realized that the world would surely call me an "old maid." But this was not by choice, there had been several romances that almost made it to the altar. When I encountered your Ishtar Mating Call Rite, it seemed tailor-made for my problem, so I used it with gusto. And I have to admit it did get me asked on several dates, but honestly not with anybody I could get interested in. I decided I needed just a bit of extra power, so I started looking at the troubleshooting procedure.

In spite of my alone condition, I had always been a basically happy person, so I decided that my mood was not the problem. There remained only the ideas of timing. I waited for a new moon, then looked for a fruitful moon sign on a Friday or Tuesday. The first one available just happened to be a Friday, so I planned my Rite to begin at Nergal's hour to add the spice. I must say the rite somehow felt better than it had when I did it before and I put plenty of positive stupidity into the fun of it. When I finished, I really felt it was accomplished, and sure enough in just three days I met a very interesting widower who was just as lonely as I. We didn't mess around with convention or preliminaries very long—in fact we were married three weeks ago (just 22 days from the completion of the ritual) and just got back from a magnificent honeymoon. Everything is indeed roses. My thanks to Ishtar, Nergal and the whole gang!

Charles S. gives us this insight inot his troubleshooting work:

My mental projections were working pretty well, but I have had a special longing for a complete out-of-the-body experience for many years—perhaps it is the yearning to own eternal life as you have described in so many of your books. Over the years I have tried just about every method of projection ever written about, but I remained STUCK in the prison of this physical body. When I tried the Ishtar/Thoth/Bast method, I met with the same trapped sensation as always. I did realize that there was a touch of anxiety because I've wanted "out" for so long, but I felt I had that down to an irreducible minimum, so I looked toward my timing.

I wanted to go all out, so I waited for a new moon, then for a fruitful sign on Wednesday or Saturday (I figured that Ishtar would be of enough help anyway). As luck would have it the next Saturday found the moon in a fruitful sign, so I scheduled two sessions (one at each of the Thoth hours). With a lot of relaxation and much help from Bast and Thoth, I actually got out of my body at the first session, but only for a few seconds. Even so, that was enough to prove to me that I could do it. I mostly said thank you to all the energy transformer personalities while I waited for the next Thoth hour (I finished the first rite about 11:30 A.M. and had to wait 'til 6:00 P.M. to try again). This time the anxiety was greatly reduced because of my mini-success before, and indeed I stood behind my body, then gleefully walked into another room and all through the house. I even got a bit of personal instruction

THE POWER OF POSITIVE STUPIDITY   195

from my spirit teacher before a noise outside startled me and I popped back into the physical body. It is a truly magnificent experience that indeed does give me a comfortable ownership of eternal life.

Let me say this to all of your students: Never give up. Perseverance and following all the rules will bring you that big manifestation of your dreams. And as Al would say, hang in there and win!

Mike T. had this to share about his troubleshooting work:

I had been a GS-9 for 11 years. It seemed to be a permanent plateau, but I was not at all satisfied with it. It tried various forms of magic over the years to assist in my promotion, but nothing seemed to work. Even the Ishtar Job Expanding and Promotion Rite seemed not to do it for me. So I had a look at your troubleshooting procedure. Since this one was a "biggie" to me, I planned for it well in advance. I picked a target time with a growing moon in Pisces that fell on a quiet Thursday. I worked to build my mood of effectiveness, worthiness and opulence to a peak (I put two whole weeks effort into this part) right at the Nergal hour on the appointed night. Somehow my job entity seemed stronger this way and I managed to impart my specially built mood with the help of the regular ritual. Of course this was all planned with a review and testing period in mind, and I'm most happy to report that today I received my notification of promotion to GS-11!

CHAPTER POINTS TO REMEMBER

1. The childlike enthusiasm of the "honeymoon period" often brings great success as one first begins to use a good magical system.

2. As you gain more knowledge, all too often the doubts creep in and your magical work begins to fade in effectiveness.

3. When you realize that the honeymoon is over, rejoice and apply the Master's view of the fundamentals to gain your permanent and lasting power.

4. Apply your power of positive stupidity to build a maximum of enthusiasm for the joy of your contact with the energy transformer personalities and the resulting power.

5. Let the "Power of Positive Stupidity" enthusiasm assist

you in a program of thorough cleansing through the psychic ecology of the Miracle Spiritology Outside Cone of Power cleansing rite.

6. Then carry your cleansed enthusiasm into the positive work and win.

7. Recognize the special value of mood and time your magical work to harness your very best moods. Work for health when you feel good, for wealth when you feel rich, etc.

8. For the really tricky and important rites, follow the moon phase and sign and the Babylonian Planetary Hours System for the extra surge of power that assures complete victory.

CHAPTER 17

Now Let Ishtar Open the Door to Your Higher Powers

When you have all the love, money, prestige, sex and health you want, what's next? From the materialistic viewpoint, we could look upon this chapter as a form of insurance policy—this is the way to be certain that you can keep all the good you have and continue to increase it. And we might add that if you feel you do not yet have enough of the material good things of life, this is the surest way to get it. In keeping with the Biblical idea, "Seek ye first the kingdom of heaven," we can say that the fresh secret weapon we offer you here might best be called SPIRITUAL GROWTH. If there is a real legacy from the early days of psychiatry, it must be the pronouncement of the great man, C. G. Jung, that he never achieved a complete healing without significantly improving the patient's relationship with God.

Now don't panic! I do not have my own special brand of religion to sell you here, and it matters not if you are a professed atheist or agnostic, we will find a path of spiritual growth that is comforable for YOU. By now you have used enough of the Universal Energy to be willing to relate to it at least so long as you can call it by your own pet name. At this point you are well embarked upon your path to becoming a master magician or occultist. To get this far you have demonstrated a degree of discipline and can be considered ready to take and pass the first tests.

Passing Your Test of Fear

Pause and play a game with me. Let's say I can introduce you to an all-seeing all knowing being who will graciously answer any three questions for you with absolute accuracy. Reflect on this for a few serious moments, then write down your three questions.

Now let's get to the joker—at least 90% of the questions people write in response to this "game" are clear indications of the questioner's most pressing set of fears and hang-ups. Be honest with yourself for a moment—did you fail to write down any questions because you have so many you couldn't decide which was most pressing? This would indicate a great need to overcome a pressing set of fears, which may not be too clear to YOU as yet. On the other hand, a single question would indicate that you are way out of balance, with the stresses and hang-ups all focused in the one direction. Or if you said, "There's nothing I really need to know," are you that serene or is it smugness, complacency or an ego trip?

This kind of self study, combined with a deliberate facing of the fears you turn up, will help prepare you for the classic *test of fear* that you MUST pass somewhere in the early stages of your magical and occult career. Let me stress that it is NOT a big deal if you fail the test the first few times—many do. Just take it as a lesson, pointing the need for more work in facing and growing above your fears. The good student will goof on many things as he learns, but always the response must be to pick up the pieces, digest the lesson, and strive on to greater victories.

If you have read much in the occult field, you have surely encountered a term like "The Terror of the Threshold." This may sound like a bit of colorful allegory, but at some point in your development process you will indeed come face to face with it IN PERSON. If you are out on the astral and not prepared for the experience, you will find yourself popped back into the body with a thud, feeling as if someone had hit you hard right in the solar plexus. But if you are ready, PASSING this test will give you a big boost along your pathway of growth. Make a habit of facing and eliminating your fears on a regular basis—it will surely help your spiritual growth, and the happy fallout of material progress will also be your natural reward.

M.A. had this to report on a series of encounters with the Terror of the Threshold:

Over a one-year period, I had three manifestations of the Terror of the Threshold, and in spite of my high desires, I flunked the test all three times. This thing is so illusory it automatically takes the form of one's greatest fear object! But each failure did bring its own lesson about my personal weaknesses, and I took each as a fresh challenge to grow and overcome. Then last night I had a real doozy! I knew I had help in slipping out of my physical body, and as I stood up in my emotional/mental body beside the couch, I saw the most grotesque and threatening creature one could possibly imagine. This time I won! I had an intuitive feeling that it was my own spirit teacher in disguise, so I extended a hand in a loving gesture and said, "Hi, Pussycat." Suddenly I felt like a little kid being patted on the head for finally learning a tough lesson. As an obvious reward, I was permitted a personal discussion with my spirit teacher that cleared up several things I have been puzzling over for months. And somehow I know that I am on a wonderful growth spree—there is and will be really wonderful progress now!

Passing Your Test of Love

At about the same time you begin your test of fear, there is another important hurdle to surmount. I like to call it the test of LOVE. Others might call it a test of compassion or of your acceptance of others. In a "dream" or astral setting you will suddenly find a complete stranger bawling you out up one side and down the other—a very frequent part of this is to refer to you as a member of the race or ethnic group you have had the most trouble accepting as worthy fellow beings. Or you may find yourself in a situation where you seem to be being treated most unfairly. I call this the test of LOVE because you will never progress far along the path of personal evolution until you develop enough love to encompass EVERY being. Part of this is getting the perspective of insight that naturally separates the offending *action* from the being itself. You must truly love the person, but you do not have to accept or condone any negative *actions*. The trick is to lovingly but firmly assert your own rights in any situation COMPLETELY WITHOUT RESENTMENT, but with enough personal power and sense of worth that you do *correct* the situation.

Perhaps an easy way to relate to this is to recall the axiom of any positively run organization: FIX THE MISTAKE, NOT THE

BLAME. But that idea of fix the mistake, not the blame, applies also to YOU—even if you should fail one of these tests. If this happens to you, take it as a "report card" type experience whose purpose was to point up another weak area for you as an aid to your growth. Let's be sure we understand the full implication of the test of love, and that it works both ways. Thus there will be NO UNPARDONABLE SIN OR MISTAKE! And surely also, *no eternal damnation*. We may be punished BY our mistakes (for instance the immediate "retribution" that comes from sticking your finger into a light socket) but never FOR them.

I hope you feel the touch of mysticism and oneness with all beings that is meant to sneak up on you right here. I could give you some wild feedback in this section, but it tends to get much too abstract to translate into understandable English. However, I can assure you that you will soon have one or more of these experiences (particularly if you have not already), and if you are preparing well, you'll come out with the good feeling and the "reward" rather than the touch of sheepishness that says, "Shot down again." Although this section is short, its import is of really infinite value to you, if you will only understand and apply it.

Now Comes Your Biggie, the Test of Power

When you have mastered the tests of fear and love, the progress comes very quickly. It is important to realize that real psychic and spiritual power grows best in an atmosphere of harmlessness and love. But it has been truly said on the material level that *"power corrupts."* And the tendency is certainly the same on the higher levels of life. We have agreed that your real purpose for being in this physical manifestation is to participate in your own evolutionary process and indeed become a Master in your own right. But you are NOT a Master until you *have* a great deal of *power*—and have accepted its corresponding responsibility.

You "Star Trek" buffs will understand part of the responsibility of power when you remember the prime directive: "Thou shalt not interfere with the natural evolution of a planet." And we are all familiar with the awesomeness of the power that came with His baptism and lead Jesus to spend the 40 days in the wilderness adjusting His consciousness to handle it.

Let me try to bring this down to a more personal level—several years ago my personal searching stumbled onto a psycho-electronic device (pictured to me in a vision) that I at first wired backwards. It was only a "lucky" interference by my son who unknowingly dismantled the thing that kept it from "killing" me (that is, from permanently depriving me of my present physical body). It became quite clear that I was in possession of the ultimate murder weapon—you could elminate any adversary and go completely unpunished by man because his laws deny the very possibility of such action. This part of the power was easy for me to handle because I have passed the test of love and know that there are NO circumstances under which I would use it. But follow along. Next I wired the gadget properly for use as a positive magical device. As part of the initial experimentation the machine demonstrated the ability to DOUBLE THE SALES VOLUME of a test product *or business* virtually overnight! And it racked up a couple of truly "miraculous" healing demonstrations for good measure. Then I sat in quiet contemplation of the RESPONSIBILITY that comes with such power, and it was nearly overwhelming. What if the world should learn of your possession of the device and beat a path to your door? You would have the power to make one man rich and keep another poor, or to heal one and deny it to another—think of the tremendous temptation to "play God".

Next one remembers the old "Millionaire" program—the mess the million dollars usually made in the lives on which it was bestowed—and combines this with the knowledge that some people cry out for healing, but subconsciously cling to their infirmity as an escape or way to avoid facing their problem—and the weight of responsibility seems to grow even heavier. Then comes the last temptation: tell no one and use the device exclusively for your own selfish purposes, but if you have passed the test of love you know that this, too, is impossible to you. Stop for a moment now to *feel* how you would handle it.

I won't leave you dangling at the end of this one, I'll "fess up" to what I did. The soul searching said, "Proceed with extreme caution, and if you reach a point of trying to play God, step completely aside and let your highest spirit guidance suggest the proper decision." Then I launched a deeper study of the device itself and "fortunately" found that it has its limitations after all. It works only with the best made thoughtforms of an accomplished ceremonial magician who is motivated by untainted love, and even then the programmed outcome can be aborted by the intervention of highly evolved spirit beings—even as they used my son to save me at the outset. But for me, the experience was at least one passing of the personal test of power—with the result being what I consider phenomenal progress for me in the few years since the encounter.

To fail THAT test and look upon all people as a set of dolls or puppets given to you for your amusement (as some almost great magicians have done) would set you back many years, if not many lifetimes, of potential progress. I had to express this on the personal level because the pressures and feelings are so intensely subjective in this whole area. But I can assure you that your growth and progress will bring you sooner or later to your test of power, and I hope that in this discussion I have helped you understand the special significance of it.

How to Pass Your Test of Power

In essence we are leading you to the position where you can ask for omnipotent power from the Infinite through the energy transformer personalities, and get it. But first you must prove that you can handle it. It's rather like the point where your young son asks for a .22 rifle or a motorcycle. If he has proved his sense of responsibility and ability to handle himself, you would have to seriously consider it, otherwise you would answer NO without hesitation. In truth the best way to earn your power is to deepen your love affair with life. Have you learned the empathy that *instinctively* considers the right to life of the fly or ant that seems intent upon annoying you? And is there yet enough love in you to invite the intruder onto your finger to be carried outside for your mutual benefit? But is that love also extended to yourself and YOUR rights so that there is a balanced give and take with the environment? Throughout all my writings I have tried to teach the ideas of well balanced growth, and never was it so important to you as it is when you near your test of power.

The time to prepare for this test is NOW! If you have the lessons of all three tests well in mind and make a habit of considering them in *all* of your routine decision making, you will be alert when the real tests come and so advance much faster. But don't think you can fool the high spirits and energy transformer personalities who will be involved in testing you. They will take great care to catch you in those unguarded moments (usually out of the body) when what you really are and feel will clearly show through. The test, even when you fail it, is a complement and an aid to growth—it shows you clearly whether you have really become the being you know you should be or are still deluding yourself with wishful thinking. Thus you know that every experience of this nature is good for you, and if you take your failures as simple but strong spurs to greater striving, your progress and achievement are assured.

The Rewards of Passing All Three Tests

Even the passing of all the tests does not excuse you from the usual problems of life, but it certainly gives you a whole new set of tools for dealing with them. You may find yourself doing all of the same things in apparently the same ways—the difference is "underneath." But what a wonderful difference it is! You will find yourself no longer a junior partner with your spirit teachers and the energy transformer personalities. At this happy point you enter into full and equal partnership. You will still enjoy the FULL range of human emotions and experience, but with a certain feeling of inner strength and power that KNOWS it can handle anything it may encounter.

This is an area for the poets, because the language itself is not capable of direct explanation of the depths and magnificence of the experience. At this stage of progress the life-long mystic finds himself also a master magician, and vice versa—we know that there are indeed an infinite number of paths to growth in spiritual terms, but as you reach this point of achievement they all merge into ONE.

This is one of those places where the feedback does not lend itself to the language. When you touch even a part of the wonder of the power and feelings that await you, you will no doubt become a poet for the moment yourself. Instead of the normal feedback, indulge me for a few lines as I share the feeling as best I can with a little of my own poetry inspired by a few moments of oneness with all that is:

> What makes the ocean's edge such a peaceful place?
> Is it waves gently tipping their caps of lace,
> Or graceful gulls gliding near the shore?
> Yes, it's both of these and so much more.
> We sense a power touching us there,
> Permeating water, sand and air.
> Then as along the beach we plod,
> We find we're very close to God.

But we know that this power and peace are not of any place, so I tried again:

> There is a peace, a quiet peace, deep in the heart of man.
> That powerful and vibrant peace dares you to say, "I can."
> Then anything you dream of is something you can do.
> The universal stream is a fount of strength for you.
> So seek that peace, that quiet peace, deep in the heart you own.
> True peace reveals the touch of God, you'll never be alone.

And of the experience itself, we might put it this way:

> In darkness deep and quite alone, I waited for I knew not what.
> The place was strange, to me unknown, but deep inside I knew my lot.
> Abruptly shone a shaft of LIGHT, engulfing me in brilliant gleam.
> A great voice lectured in the night, revealing much of God's own scheme.
> "Though some may say, 'tis best alone,' the teaching came like drops of dew,
> "You're never really on your own. The LIGHT is *real*, it's there with you."
> Still in that LIGHT, the voice spoke on, "The LIGHT is real, and as you share,
> That deeper love is never gone. Like unto God you, too, will care

>   For flower, tree, and bird on wing, and humans, grown or tiny child,
>   Forever more your heart will sing. God is with you all the while."

We'll get back to the practical in our next chapter, but this short diversion was indeed necessary. I am strongly impressed with the inability of most of us to use language to share our deepest feelings and spiritual experiences. A Whitman, Gibran or Emerson I am not, but perhaps from the very homeliness of this tiny part of the work you can find a spark that will grow up into your own deeply mystical fire, and in this way I can have shared the beauty and wonder that I so intensely wish to bring you here.

CHAPTER POINTS TO REMEMBER

1. Regardless of your religious beliefs, or lack of them, real spiritual growth is the insurance policy that guarantees that you can keep the material gains you have made and indeed gain much, much more.

2. The "Terror of the Threshold" is real. You will soon meet the test of fear. Prepare for it, win, and strive on to many more wonderful achievements.

3. At about the same time as the test of fear, you will also get the test of love.

4. It is not a major catastrophe to fail one of these tests. Digest the lessons, "fix the mistake, not the blame," and strive on to pass the same tests very soon.

5. The test of love will also teach you that there is no unpardonable sin and no eternal damnation. The law of the universe is LOVE.

6. The most difficult is the test of power—you will find that indeed you have your own personal tempter. Prepare well to pass this one.

7. The reward of passing all three tests (in your own good time) is a special new relationship to the universe. It can only be hinted at poetically, but it indeed fits the description "Pearl of Great Price." Strive on and WIN!

CHAPTER 18

Ishtar Pyramonix: Discover and Work the Glittering Gold Mine of the Past

We live in a fantastic time! Many hints of the advanced technology of long lost "ancient" civilizations went unrecognized for several thousand years until our "modern" technology advanced to the point where the investigators have something of "their own" to relate to the unsettling artifacts. Books are being written suggesting that many of the stranger remnants of the past were left by visitors from outer space, and we are not here to argue for or against the probability of such visits—but outer space or not, modern archeology is definitely finding solid proof of advanced "ancient" technology which surely adds a fresh measure of credulity to the persistent legends of Atlantis, Lemuria and the like. This would remain idle speculation and have no place in our practical approach to making *your* life richer and fuller were it not for the simple fact that you can go back and have a look for yourself and return with very profitable knowledge.

Here I often think of the period shortly after the dropping of the first atom bomb when Aldous Huxley wrote his fascinating little book, *Of Ape and Essence*. *In this fictional story we viewed a time after an atomic war had destroyed technology, and found that the principal industry of the remaining few was "cemetery mining," to recover useful articles from the lost civilization. Wouldn't it be especially exciting if I could teach you to go back

---

*Harper & Row New York, N.Y., 1972 (Paper)

and retrieve working models of the devices of the past? Even this may not be impossible, but it is beyond the scope of this work. However, I can offer you the next best thing—quick and easy two-way passage of at least your mental body to see and study the wonders of civilizations and technologies long past.

Mental Projection to View Past Events

If you have practiced the mental projection work from Chapter 15, you already have the basic discipline necessary to a useful look into past ages. You will remember that we simply decided where or what we wanted to view, then practiced the alternate shrinking and expansion of your mental body (or of your consciousness) until you were able to expand to encompass the event you wanted to see. At that time, we carefully kept it all in the present because that was enough for your materially-oriented mental processes to "buy" at the time. But now that you are an accomplished mental projector, you are ready to shed the imaginary limitation of time and examine your favorite historical events in detail—or better, go "cemetery mining" in the useful technology of the long-buried past.

The joker at first is your lack of bench marks or reference points to use as targets to get to a time and place that can reveal something really useful to you. But you can build up your confidence and expertise by exploring fairly familiar or recent historical events, and perhaps poking gently into one or more of your recent past lives.

Let's review the mental projection process and make the minor modifications which will add your history probing ability to your by now well developed present-event-viewing technique. Remember to start with the basic exercise to align the spiritual, astral, mental and physical bodies to the point where you can look up with your eyes closed and see the beautiful mystic Light. Then before you begin the shrinking/expanding of the mental body, choose a fairly recent event for a practice target. Picture it clearly for a moment, then begin the shrinking and expanding of the mental body until you can expand it to take in the target event. Your materially-oriented thinking process may fight a bit, but keep at it until you do get at least a hazy picture. Then comes the really new part of the technique—WILL the picture to run forward then backward in time so that you can pick up all the action and conversations by selective *willing* to focus and change the direction of the picture-making process.

I have suggested that you practice on a fairly recent event in order to get the least possible argument or fighting from your three-dimensional thinking habits, but in truth the only limitation to how far back you can go or how clear will be the picture is your own inner expectation. Think that it is easy, and easy it will be. The, when your practice with recent events has built you a good degree of confidence, you can have a clear look at even the events of civilizations which have been completely obliterated as far as physical traces of their existance is concerned.

Before we look into the very distant past, let's share this practical application of the practice on recent events by Artie P.:

> I have a couple of infrequently used keys that are of great importance to me on the rare occasions I do need them. I normally keep them in a special little box in my dresser drawer. But the other day when I went to get them, the little box was empty! Fortunately I have been practicing the mental projection into past events, so I didn't panic. I told myself that this was a simple challenge to use the new technique on the practical level.
>
> For a starting point, I tried to remember the last time I used the keys, and the circumstances came back clearly enough to give me a bench mark. So I sat down quietly, did the body aligning exercise, then the shrinking/expanding of my mental body until I got the picture of my last use of the keys (I was just a bit nervous at first so I must have gone through the shrinking/expanding cycle close to a dozen times to get there—usually I can make it in four or five cycles). Next I focused my attention on the keys and directed the picture to run forward until I saw me put them down somewhere. First I saw the breaking of my normal pattern. I put the keys into my shirt pocket instead of the usual place in my pants. I watched myself take off the shirt without noticing the keys, and drop the whole bit into the dirty clothes hamper. As I ran the picture forward, more clothes were added, then my wife emptied the hamper and took the clothes to the back porch by the washing machine. As she was loading the machine, the keys dropped out and she casually put them on the window ledge nearby. At this point I terminated the exercise, walked to the window ledge and THERE WERE MY KEYS! When I teased my wife about it later, she didn't remember at all. So that exercise saved me GOBS of time and frustration!

Picking Your Landmarks for a Good Look at the Wonders of the World's Distant Past

History for its own sake has always been a boring subject for me, so I'll have to ask you romantic types to bear with my perhaps overly practical approach. When you have developed your disciplines, by all means do it YOUR way, but we can learn it just as easily on the practical level—and for people like me, the "carrot" of potentially bringing back an exciting "new" invention adds enough extra mystique and fun to keep up one's enthusiasm during the sloppiness of the learning period.

The idea of picking a special landmark or target is much like selecting a station on your radio or TV. We know that ALL the signals of all your local stations are right there in the room with you all day, but you use your tuner to bring in just one at a time—otherwise you would experience only chaos instead of your favorite program. Similarly, in the realm open to your mental body's projections, all the knowledge and all past events that have occurred on this planet exist in a magnificent array of pictures, sounds and feelings. Without a target event in the past, you would be most likely to simply expand into something taking place in the present, or at random anywhere in the past. And of course the more interesting the target is to YOU, the easier it will be to hold your concentration and focus.

The trick to picking a good target is to choose something that you have a reasonable chance to understand. If you have a solid background in electronics, a target like the picture of the ancient EgyptianTV system with its coaxial cables could be excellent, or perhaps the recently discovered Babylonian battery. And naturally a target of watching the actual building of the Great Pyramid at Cheops should be a good lure for many of us. Or closer to home how about beaming in on a lecture by Plato or Aristotle! You might come back from this quickly with a desire to learn the ancient Greek language, and very little more—but how do you know unless you try? To really get the most out of this work, you may find yourself taking something like a crash course in a field that is new to you, but that, too, will serve to broaden your horizons.

Let me make one more set of suggestions, particularly for those who are interested in profiting by rediscovering useful and practical ancient inventions as part of your mental projection work. My own experience has been that one tends to project to a period that is too advanced, thus you tend to be "snowed" or utterly baffled by what you see. It is always better to start at the earlier development stages of the technology and follow its evolution forward in time. For instance, if you were looking at a modern automobile but had no background in internal combustion engines, you could learn and understand much more by back tracking to observe and digest the original invention, then follow the engine through its evolutionary stages and in effect learn just as the technology itself was developed.

Whenever or wherever you send you mental body, you will find it especially useful to be on the lookout for the smaller details—to have seen and in this age *patented* a simple device like the zipper would be of much more value to you than to puzzle for years over the theories and reasons for a magnificent "kreedoscramph refinery." Leave the magnificent "ceramic glokenfelder heterodyne ossenphephereres" for a time when you have mastered enough of the basics of the ancient technology to bring them forward on a profitable basis. Meanwhile, let's pick up the ancient equivalent of safety pins, dog collars and similarly down-to-earth devices that we could use and successfully market IN THE HERE AND NOW.

But don't let me slow you down too much. We are all aware of the stories of how Nicola Tesla (who among other small things brought us alternating current and was the genius behind the company, Westinghouse) would picture a complete device in his mind, and give drawings of the parts he required to various assistants—and invariably put the pieces together into a fully-functioning unit. Let this be your goal, but stay practical and get your share of the simple but lucrative goodies along the way.

Mining the Creative Ideas of the Ancients

Persistence and perseverance are often key ingredients in the successful tapping of the riches of long-lost technology. You may find that in your first few mental projections, you run into nothing but devices and techniques that make no sense to you. But as you continue to run the pictures backwards to find the originating ideas and principles, you will regularly find your reward.

John J. has this to share with us:

I own and operate a small metal plating shop which was bringing me a bare living, but not much more. When I bumped into the idea of using mental projection to look into the technology of the ancients, I thought immediately of metal plating technology and decided to try it. I spent the first week practicing the mental projection into just the present time. Then with a good feel for it, I projected back to the Bronze Age for a look at techniques. I didn't pick up much, but I did get a glimmer of legends of the old Atlantean civilization. So I spent a week orienting myself in Atlantis (by a week, I mean of earth time, but I only devoted about a half hour an evening to the project). When I finally got zeroed in, I was indeed amazed at the ingenuity of their plating work. I will not go into the details because it is a patentable process that I brought back—but it reduces my material cost by 40% with an even greater savings in labor. By not raising my prices when everyone else did, I have attracted about three times my former business volume and it is all highly profitable to me. My month of half-hour trips into the past is rapidly making a rich man of me.

P.R. had this to report:

As you know, I am basically a manufacturing jeweler but with a greater than normal interest in gemstones. I also have been fascinated with the legend of Atlantis for many years, so I pounced on the mental projection idea with real gusto. It took about 10 tries to get into an interesting part of Atlantis—I was watching them *manufacture* many types of precious and semi-precious stones. Each time I came back, I made copious notes for myself, and after several really fascinating "trips," I had enough data to try. So far I am able to make three varieties of "synthetic" stones by duplicating nature's process in a much compressed time framework. I have shown them to many "experts" and not one of them has even suspected that my creations are not natural. I'll not ponder the potential here, but you can be sure that my future looks much brighter.

Let's suggest a few more ideas for bench marks for YOUR mental projection into the secrets of the past. Was the Ark of the Covenant a receiver of outer space communications as has been recently suggested, or what was its real purpose? Careful reading of the scriptures of any of the older religions will turn up many passages which, when taken literally, suggest a very advanced ancient technology—how about a look to see? Or is some special problem really bugging you—then how about projecting way back to see how it was handled in the ancient technologies?

Another Popular Application—
a Look at Your Own Past Lives

We won't begin with an argument or apology for the concept of reincarnation—it's not necessary. When someone asks me if I *believe* in reincarnation or astral projection, I generally say, "No." Then I quickly add, "But I don't *believe* in breathing, either, it is a natural part of life, you don't bother to believe in it, you just do it." If the idea that you have lived in different bodies in times past makes you uncomfortable, just skip this section and use the parts of the work that do appeal to you. But if you change your mind some day, these suggestions will be here waiting for you.

Since a past life is literally something YOU have lived before, the normal requirement of a bench mark for reference is often unnecessary. Use the body aligning exercise and the mental body shrinking/expansion with the announced goal (it is good to say aloud what you seek to expand into) of touching an interesting period in your immediate past life (later you may progress backward one life at a time). Then *will* your picture back and forward to pick up details—it is particularly interesting to bring back historical data of which you had no previous knowledge, but that you verify in the library, etc. But again history for its own sake doesn't send the practical person very far, so let's look for the meat.

Mental projection into recent past lives can be quite helpful in turning up latent or hidden talents, in understanding present physical or psychological weaknesses that may have come forward with you at least as strong tendencies, and in recognizing some of your present problem-solving techniques and how much of it all came forward with you. It is often most enlightening to explore your past life relationships with people who are either especially attractive or antagonistic to you in this life. In these cases your bench mark can be the last time you were associated with that particular person. A little practice can reveal much interesting and useful data.

And there are times when you may want to use mental projection to help a friend or relative who is in, or is heading for, trouble. Mary's daughter, Sue, had been what Mary described as a "model daughter" up until six months before her 21st birthday. Then Sue started to have nightmares, to withdraw from everything and to be almost paralized with fear too much of the time. Let Mary continue:

> When the doctor said that there was no physical cause for Sue's anxiety, he suggested psychiatry as a possible help. But this would have been far too expensive and too slow for my purposes.
> I had been using the shrinking/expanding bit for some mental projection, so I decided to try a look into Sue's past lives for help. I was able to recognize her in her immediate past life, and to my dismay I saw her killed in a messy accident on the day of her 21st birthday. I felt I should probe further, so I got back one more life and saw a jealous gypsy put a "curse" on her that she would forevermore lose her life in a tragic accident on her 21st birthday. This seemed to make sense, so I talked it over with Sue. She shook as she considered it and agreed this was probably the cause of her problems. Next we assembled as much protective and spell-breaking supplies and ritual material as we could and went to work on a sort of jury-rigged, super uncrossing/exorcism project. We worked from sunset until midnight, then went to bed and Sue slept all night for the first time in weeks. So we continued our work for eight more days just to be sure. I am very happy to tell you that the critical time has past. Sue had a quiet 21st birthday celebration last week and she is back to her old light-hearted friendly self again. Getting a look at the past life cause turned the trick, and I'm sure saved Sue's life.

As J.S. turned 30, he realized that he virtually hated his job and desperately needed a new and better career. Here is his report:

> Wow, did I begin to regret being a dropout! Without that high school diploma it seemed that all the good career doors were closed to me. I couldn't think of a way around all this, so I decided to try a look, or rather a talent search, into my past lives. It took three or four tries to get the hang of it, then I began to examine the past with hope and interest. The blacksmith life seemed to be of little help—not many calls for them these days. But a ways back I saw myself hand-crafting beautiful musical instruments. Now I was intrigued and got a few books on instrument making from the library. And I found

myself thinking of ways to do it better almost from page one. So I started to make a clarinet as a hobby project. When it was finished, I took it to a local "jam session" and it played so well I let a guy buy it from me for a whole bunch of money. To shorten the tale, I now make customer woodwinds, strings and percussion instruments and I'm toying with the brass section next. A hobby inspired by a look at a past life has grown up into a fulfilling and financially rewarding new career—and the people who hear my instruments could care less about my lack of a diploma.

Can We Look Forward, Too?

In Chapter 14, we worked out our understanding of the future and gave you a good method of working with the Ishtar Power to see ahead in time. Now that you are accomplished at mental projection both into the present and the past, you should find it easy to apply the projection technique for a look ahead. Here it is important to remember that you are seeing *tendencies* picturing themselves as the working forces *would* bring them to pass, and you will notice that the further ahead in time you seek to project, the more hazy and filmy your picture becomes. But particularly close-at-hand things can be viewed with great accuracy, while there is still a chance to bring all of your magic and physical skills to bear to change an undesirable outcome.

Often these results seem spectacular only to the person who has experienced them, but they are definitely useful and important. For instance this report from Bill C.:

> It was a quiet Sunday afternoon and I got an urge to have a brief projection into the immediate future, just to help me get better at the process. And it was brief all right! Almost immediately, I saw the wife and kids in an automobile accident. Fortunately I had the presence of mind to stick with the picture to see what caused it, and I saw a broken part in the left front wheel brake system. I quickly terminated the projection and headed for the garage. I'm not the world's best mechanic, but when I pulled the wheel it was easy to spot the trouble because I had seen the exact part in my projection. This one piece was so worn I could almost bend it with my fingers, and no doubt it would have failed the first time we really needed it badly. I got the part replaced and the whole brake system checked. And I'm happy to report there have been no auto accidents or brake failures in my family.

And of course a good proficiency at mental projection into the very near future can be especially useful in the commodity market, for horse races, timing your stock purchases and sales, and especially to check out important sales presentations. I have a file full of classic feedback reports on practical applications like these, but this is the time for a challenge rather than the account of what someone else has achieved. YOUR special feedback belongs here. Dive into the basics of mental projection and practice as much as it takes to be at least reasonably good at it. Then write and tell me of *your* feedback report that belongs here!

CHAPTER POINTS TO REMEMBER

1. Modern archeology has turned up much evidence of advanced technology in civilizations long past. There are many "new" inventions waiting to be brought froward from the ancient times.

2. Mental projection can be used to go backward in time as well as to view the present events as we used it before.

3. Choose your reference points or bench marks on the basis of your individual interests and training, and use them to focus your projection on the ancient devices or events of your choice.

4. Practice to build your ability by projecting into events of the very recent past. This can be another good way of finding misplaced articles.

5. If you are projecting into the ancient world, hoping to profit by bringing back a useful invention or the like, take care to start far enough back to see the evolution of the technology. All too often we don't understand what we see because we try to start in the middle—if it happens to you, just go back deeper into the history of the process.

6. Mental projection is a good technique for viewing your own or a loved one's past lives. It can be helpful in understanding "unreasonable" fears, hatreds or especially strong attractions.

7. Look at your past lives also to discover your latent or hidden talents.

8. You can also look into the near future with great accuracy by using the mental projection process. The applications are limited only by your own creative imagination.

CHAPTER 19

Exotic Applications of Ishtar Power

When I planned this chapter, I had a fancy subtitle for it, like: "Oil from rainwater," "lead into gold," "diamonds from garbage," and countless other feats. But Ishtar hit me with one of my favorite practical questions: "If I want a loaf of bread, does it make any real difference whether the heavens open up and deposit it in front of me or I simply send my son to the grocery store—so long as I have plenty of money?" I certainly had to agree. So let's keep our focus not on parlor tricks and showmanship, but on making a richer, happier, more rewarding life for you NOW and for the rest of your long and happy life.

Another Free Gift for You—
a Source of Great Extra Power

When I first described your Ishtar Altar Star, I cautioned you not to deface your book, and offered you a free copy of an ideal-size altar star just for writing me to ask for it. Now I will add to my free offer a new development that Ishtar has brought us as a fully mobile source of extra power and help. Inspired by Ishtar, one of my class students took his big altar star to his reducing photocopy machine and began playing at shrinking it. He made two stars of the first smaller size, then four of the next, etc., until he had a page of tiny stars all reduced from the big one and so carrying the essence and all the power of the shape and symbology. We will call this the Ishtar Multi-star Sheet. And you can feel its great power quite readily with your receiving hand. The sheet can be used whole or cut into several strips of power for application to smaller or awkward places to reach. This is truly an exotic application of the Ishtar Power because it is so simple, yet effective.

Let's begin with the simplest use, the direct application of the Multi-star Sheet to a part of the body needing help. Here is a report from one of our early users, C.G.:

> The Ishtar Multi-star Sheet indeed has many wonderful uses. I just finished using it to heal an infected root of a tooth. I simply touched the sheet to my face in the vicinity of the infected area for about five minutes twice a day for thee days—now the infection is completely gone, and all is clear and healthy.

B.K. used it in a similar manner:

> For over 20 years I have suffered from the disease made famous by Richard M. Nixon, phlebitis. The problem has been in my left leg. For the last five years it was pretty much under control, until a few weeks ago when it flared up and I hurt and hobbled so badly that I was sure the doctors would put me back into the hospital for it. But the Ishtar Multi-star Sheet arrived in the nick of time. I wrapped it around the swollen part of my leg with a bit of Scotch Tape—taking it off only to bathe. And within two days, the swelling was gone and it feels like a brand new leg. I think that is what you could call fantastic!

Let's pause here to remind you that you have your Ishtar Multi-star Sheet free for the asking. I will remind you and give you the address to write me to ask for your copy at the end of this book.

More Magnificent Applications of the Ishtar Multi-star Sheet

The principles of sympathetic magic work well with the Multi-star Sheet, too. And the practice is EXOTICALLY simple. All that is necessary is to put your picture (face up with the head toward magnetic north) on the sheet and ask Ishtar for extra energy of the type you need most. This can be further enhanced by putting one or more appropriate gemstones on top of the picture, roughly covering the chakras that need the greatest boost of energy. And the real capper can be to make one of the foil-lined cones we used in Chapter 11, full of gemstones chosen for maximum effect on the desired chakras. Cover your picture with the cone as the picture rests on the Multi-star Sheet. You might also put a specific request written on a small piece of paper on top of your picture before you cover it with the cone. Let's see how well this has worked for others.

F.D. has this happy result to share:

> I felt generally run down and was having a terrible time making it through a whole day on my grueling job. Then, mercifully, your Ishtar Multi-star Sheet arrived, and I tried the obvious. I simply put my picture on it with my head facing the north as directed. The next day I made it through my day's work with energy to spare. I then discovered that I have to remove my picture from the sheet at bed time or I will have so much energy I can't get to sleep. Now my morning ritual includes putting my picture on the star sheet as I thank Ishtar for the wonderful help and energy I know I will receive throughout the day. Funny though, in just two months my new super effectiveness got me promoted to a long-sought supervisory position that is not nearly so demanding physically. Now I thank Ishtar as I put my picture on the sheet in the morning for my ever growing effectiveness as well as the extra energy. I credit this small piece of paper with my $300.00/month better income as well as the joy of having a better job and the energy left over to enjoy the extra money.

M.L. added the cone for a big business boost. Here is the report:

> My mail-order business had never quite gotten off the ground. I was covering my advertising costs, product costs and postage, but there was almost nothing left for me. Then your Ishtar Multi-star Sheet arrived and I decided to go all out to help my business. This seemed to be a heart center/Osiris-oriented project, so I made my foil-lined cone and laced the inside with 24 pieces of green adventurine. Then I made my written request, "Ishtar and Osiris, please increase and prosper my mail order business." I put my picture on the star sheet with its head to the north. On top of that I put my written request which I weighted down with a piece of turquoise

EXOTIC APPLICATIONS OF ISHTAR POWER   219

for good luck. Then I covered the whole bit with the cone of green adventurine. Within three days, my mail-order volume seemed to triple, and indeed I closed out the first full month of the system with a total volume almost three times greater than my previous best month.

I thank Ishtar and Osiris daily, and the business has continued to grow, not that rapidly, but very encouragingly. And I am making a better than good living where I was sweating just to stay in business before. I am enclosing my regular monthly tithe of Ishtar and Osiris' share of the profits. Thank them again for me.

Special Ishtar Gadgetry for Even More Power

Let's have a deeper look at those foil-lined cones powered by gemstones that we introduced in Chapter 11. Let's say that you have a project requiring maximum power from three chakras—Nergal, Marduk and Osiris—as an unbeatable business or prosperity combination. Begin by making your three cones as always. Next procure two pieces of bare wire each about four inches long—music wire (which I always called piano wire when I built model airplanes) is excellent because of its inherent stiffness. Slip one wire into your Nergal cone from the point so that about three inches of it can serve as an energy collector, and the remaining inch sticks out to act as a lead wire. Glue it in place, then do the same thing with the other wire for your Marduk cone. Now join the two cones at the big end and glue them together. Then you can cut the two ends out of a small tin can with a can opener to use as plates. And a ½-inch piece of dowel rod will do for a separator. Attach one plate to each end of the dowel rod with a small tack. Now you need just two lengths of wire, six inches or so long—attach one to the Marduk lead wire and one of your plates. Attach the other to the Nergal lead wire and to the other plate. Then your picture on top of a piece of the Ishtar Multi-star sheet goes between the plates, with the optional specific written request on top of your picture. Cover the plates, etc. with the Osiris cone and you have brought the special power of three chakras to join with the power of the Ishtar Multi-star Sheet for the blockbuster power type work.

Those who are familiar with our E.S.P. Laboratory pyramid and Atlantean Energy Generator work will recognize that this is the principle behind the Atlantean Generators Mark II & III, although these devices use a bit of extra electric-like amplification of the power. (For more background on the basic pyramid work, I refer you to my book, *Miracle of Universal Psychic Power*.)

C.R. reported on this part of the work:

> I knew I had a physical problem, and the doctors' X-rays told them I had a tumor about the size of a golf ball. The operation was scheduled for two weeks from that fateful day. I didn't come directly home from the doctor's office but stopped off to get the rest of the materials I needed to make my foil-lined gemstone cones. I made cones of blue agate, red jasper and tourmaline (one of each). I used the top and bottom of a tomato paste can for my plates, but I had no dowel. So I "borrowed" one of my husband's dice. Using the "crazy glue" I generally use to repair my fingernails, I got the plates glued to the die. Fortunately, my husband keeps a bunch of alligator clips on hand (or I would have had to try clothespins) and we had plenty of wire. From scratch I would say it took me about 2½ hours to complete the setup.
>
> I wrote my specific request, "Ishtar, Marduk and Nergal, please remove my tumor so I can avoid the planned surgery," on a small piece of paper. That, my picture and the Ishtar Multi-star Sheet went between the plates. The blue agate and red jasper cones were attached to the plates by wire and I covered the plates and picture, etc., with the tourmaline cone. I actually went so far as to go in for the operation, but I didn't have to have it. A last-minute check by the doctors turned up NO TUMOR AT ALL. I feel wonderful, and you know how often I'm saying my thank you's to Ishtar, Marduk and Nergal.

Q.J. had quite a different problem. Let's look at his report:

> I had had my house up for sale for exactly a year with absolutely NO results. I was just about at the point of moving out anyway because my new job was 35 miles each way from it. But I had a major part of my net worth tied up in that equity, so I decided to give it one more try. I made three foil-lined cones, one each for Nergal, Marduk and Osiris, exactly as you suggested. Because I'm in electronics, I had plenty of material for the wiring and plates. I made the setup with the Nergal and Marduk cones feeding the plates, put my picture on the Ishtar Multi-star Sheet and covered it with my request, "let there be a quick sale for my house at a fair price." The Osiris cone then covered the plates and I added a silent prayer

EXOTIC APPLICATIONS OF ISHTAR POWER 221

for help. Within two weeks the house was sold! Many thanks. Again RESULTS are the proof. Thanks for the guidance and help, and keep up the good work.

Need Still More Power? There Are Ways

You "electronickers" should already have realized that there are ways to bring even more power to bear on a problem. But let me share the results of our many years of research in this area. Yes, the energy generated by the foil-lined gemstone cones pretty much follows the basic rules of electricity, but the magnification of the power comes from adding extra double cones in parallel, NOT in series. In plainer language, each double cone will contain stones for two different chakras. To get maximum power from the units, connect the higher chakra leads of all of them together and the lower chakra leads together, leading the lower chakra wire to the bottom plate and the higher chakra wire to the top plate.

How many should you use for maximum power? Let me give you the feedback here from my personal stock market investment/research project. I use the buy slip from a selected stock as the "picture" to be activated, and add the specific request, "Let the market price of ____ common stock rise rapidly and steadily to $____ per share or more". Over a period of many months of trial and error, I determined the apparently most effective configuration to be the equivalent of five double cones (each double cone containing seven sets of stones, seven stones to a set, representing each of the seven chakras) in parallel with a 3 to 1 amplifier coil, and a variable capacitor for tuning to maximum effectiveness. All of this is carried to the plates and Ishtar Multi-star Sheet and covered with a six-inch marble or green gel covered pyramid.

Even with the trial and error methods of the early period, by the 18-month point of the program I had *realized* (that is sold and converted to cash) dividends and profits aggregating better than $10,500.00 on an average investment of less than $15,000.00. This breaks down to something better than $7,500.00 taxable as long-term capital gains and the balance subject to the dividend exclusion, but otherwise taxable as ordinary income on dividends and short-term capital gains. Terrible, huh? By this point in my research program, my aggregate profits far exceed my total remaining investment—so in the vernacular of the day, I'm playing on the house's money.

I have also used this special configuration to power special help for others in business and tricky human relations situations with "phenomenal" success. To go into more detail here would seem to me to be too much beating of my own drum. And since these are the most recent developments, I don't have a big file of success stories—YET. I trust that YOURS will be a success story very soon to be added to my growing feedback file. I will look forward to it.

The Most Exotic Power of All—
Back to the Fundamentals

The greater the power of gemstones and such techniques as multi-star that you bring to bear on a problem, the greater the necessity for really good fundamentals. You must constantly remember that all of the extra power comes into focus to increase and amplify the MOOD of the magician at the time of setting up the request. Thus, the greater the power, the greater the potential backfire if you are up-tight or focused on the negative when you are making the setup.

All of this "exotic" work remains subject to the basic troubleshooting work and timing of Chapter 16. Do take care to do your practice work with the allegorical tackling dummies of the Ishtar program—the FUNDAMENTALS. The more power you harness, the more important it is to use good basic fundamentals. Again, let me wind up a chapter not with feedback but with a challenge. Literally nothing is impossible to you when you harness the Ishtar Power in good nature for a truly positive purpose. The most spectacular feedback has yet to be received in my mailbox. Indeed it is programmed to come from YOU. Do dive in and use the principles and techniques that Ishtar has given you through me in these pages. Get YOUR magnificent results, then share them by writing me YOUR special feedback letter. And as I said, I'll give you my address for your feedback and/or your request for the Ishtar Altar Star and for the Ishtar Multi-star Sheet. Dive in and WIN.

CHAPTER POINTS TO REMEMBER

1. If there is something you need and it reaches you by purchase or "miraculous" means, the practical result is the same so long as you have plenty of money to pay for it. Strive for *practical* results and you will win regularly.

2. Along with your free altar star, your ownership of this book entitles you to my gift of your Ishtar Multi-star Sheet. Ask me for it at the address I will give at the end of the book.

3. The Ishtar Multi-star Sheet will bring you much extra power and energy. Use it freely and enjoy the magnificent results.

4. The foil-lined gemstone cone we presented in Chapter 11 can be used with your Multi-star Sheet for even greater power.

5. Double cones can be electrically joined to your system to bring greater and greater power as more double cones are added to your system.

6. The most exotic power of all is the careful execution of the fundamentals. Put it all together and win.

CHAPTER **20**

How to Make Ishtar a Partner in Your Permanently Victorious Life

Ishtar has given you a truly magnificent set of programs and tools in the preceding chapters. Now it's time to put it all together into a permanent overall program for healthy, happy, loving, prosperous and victorious living that you can use for the rest of your life. Let's agree on a set of key words that you can check regularly to be sure you remain on the high road of ever more wonderful progress and happiness. The big keys are MOOD, ATTITUDE, CONTACT, ACTION, EFFECTIVENESS and GROWTH. When the keys are all positive, you can be assured that you are and will remain a consistent winner.

Putting It All Together as a Super Love Affair with Life

Rudyard Kipling also had a set of six key words to keep you out of trouble—remember: WHAT, WHERE, WHEN, WHY, HOW and WHO. Think of these as neatly summed up in our one key word, EFFECTIVENESS and see how very powerful these keys must be for you. Let's see how the six big keys fit together to make your sojourn in the body a magnificent mutual, super love affair with all life.

The first key, MOOD, must always be of *love;* not the insecure being crawling and groveling in a vain attempt to buy acceptance, but a vibrant creature so full of the richness of love that you have plenty to spare for every being in the universe. Your second key, ATTITUDE, must always be positive; full of the controlled power that KNOWS "I can." The third key, CONTACT, really grows out of the first two; when your mood and attitude are right it is easy to touch your Altar Star, physically or mentally, and feel the Energy Transformer Personalities bringing you all the power you need to accomplish the task at hand with plenty of time and energy to spare. The fourth key, ACTION, is where many fall down—but the first three are worthless until YOU USE the power by taking specific action; but until the mood, attitude and contact are right, action would be premature and most likely doomed to failure. The EFFECTIVENESS assures that your action is not futile flailing around, but that even your apparent mistakes will prove to be spirit interference designed to make it all come out right—here Kipling's key words combine with Ishtar's special POWER TO ACHIEVE to bring you victory after glorious victory. And the positive by-product is the GROWTH which guarantees that you can *own* the fruits of your successes and not be owned BY them.

If the troubleshooting work of Chapter 16 does not put you immediately into the win column as soon as you apply it, take a quick look at the six big keys. An honest appraisal will tell you at once where you are falling down. Accept LIFE itself as your moment-by-moment *report card*. Expect to share a smile and loving helpfulness and cooperation with every creature or person you encounter along your happy way. And if your very presence does not uplift all those around you, clean out your chakras and check your six big keys at once. When you accept loving and victorious living as your natural life path, and put out the effort to make it a 24 hours-a-day experience, NOTHING can hold you back or rob you of your success.

What Should Ishtar Get Out of All of This?

With all of the totally dedicated and unfailing help we get from the energy transformer personalities, it is a good idea to pause here to ask: what should you expect to give Ishtar and the others in turn? Or in other words, what's in all this for Ishtar?

First you can regularly sense the satisfaction of the energy transformer personalities and their real job in helping you—just as you should find real joy in helping others. And what do YOU expect in return when you help another? I hope it's not gratitude or a return favor that is profitable for you. When you help someone from the level of spiritual orientation, your hope of "reward" is to see that other person grow in the ability to help himself—in other words, your real contribution is toward the positive evolution of the species itself by helping ONE of its number become a stronger and better person.

Thus we can flatly state that YOUR own *spiritual growth* is the best way to return the favor(s) to Ishtar. But how shall you measure your growth so you can feel sure that you are doing your best for Ishtar as well as yourself? The development of physical and even psychic skills is pretty easy to notice. You KNOW that when you can do the same tasks that were hard a few days ago with ease today, you must be growing in skill and expertise. But what of the emotional level that rests above the physical/mental complex of dexterity and physical/psychic achievement? Are you handling the stresses and emotional trials of life better than a few weeks or months ago?

I like to tease about the way to measure the emotional growth that has to be there if we are also to grow spiritually. Of course it fits into our first two big key words, mood and attitude. But in all honesty, none of us is perfect yet. There will still be those times when you will "blow your cool." My tongue-in-cheek measure of emotional growth is: ARE YOU REGULARLY RAISING THE PRICE OF YOUR ANXIETY? And I really mean, can you handle more stress and confusion without becoming anxious or frustrated now than you could a while back? Then, along with the "raising of your price," are you in your heart honestly more loving and considerate of others than you used to be? These things demonstrate the growth that amply repays your Energy Transformer Friends for their tireless efforts on your behalf.

The ultimate goal is to grow to the point where you are not simply accepted by Ishtar and the rest as an equal partner in uplifting the world, but that you are so strong and pure that you can indeed come into their presence AS AN EQUAL. If it takes more than one lifetime to achieve this, that's all right—there's plenty of time, so long as you are making honest progress.

Now, the Fertilizer for the Soil that Produces Your Good and Your Growth

We have brushed the concept of tithing as a powerful fertilizer for producing your greater good. Every farmer knows that he must in some way give back to the soil what is removed from it by the crops—otherwise the soil becomes barren and eventually produces nothing. We began by recommending the old religious tradition of giving 10% of your income to one or more churches or worthy charities. And for most of us, this will indeed act as the primer for the pump or fertilizer for the soil, bringing us ever greater crops of good. I would be remiss if I failed to mention here that our own E.S.P. Laboratory is a long established church and religious/educational organization which is worthy of receiving a portion of your tithe, if you are inclined in that direction. And the substance will be put to very good use in helping to light the way for mankind's progress. But never give because this or any other organization needs the money. Rather give because you KNOW that you need to do so, and then give with joy, happiness and love. And in this way, you will open wide the windows of heaven to pour out its many blessings on you.

But in a higher sense, the material giving should be like the top of an iceberg—far more is hidden beneath the water than shows above it. And this deeper part is the REAL tithe. It is the gift of YOURSELF. Do you go out of your way to encourage others and help them into the Light, but gently and without trying to stuff your own beliefs down their throats? When you see another creature in distress, is it your NATURAL instinct to reach out a helping hand? But do you remember, also, that you are quite like the goose that lays the golden eggs—do you have enough love to take care of YOURSELF first so that there may be a strong and powerful YOU ever ABLE to give Light, encouragement and help so needed in this world? Thus we come full circle, to say again that your goodness and personal growth are your ultimate gift of help to the world, and you will do well to understand in this way that classic statement attributed to Jesus, "I, if I be lifted up shall draw all men unto me." The same is true of you—as you lift yourself up, you do, indeed, lift the whole world with you.

The Chain Reaction of Love and Friendship

In all of our class work at E.S.P. LAB, we begin our second hour with a chakra cleansing exercise and aura brightening chant ending with the idea that "I am now an Ambassador of the Living Light, literally brightening every room I enter and uplifting every person who comes near my aura." The method of aura brightening is also a sharing of Light and Love with every creature and particle of the Universe until we feel our perfect oneness with all that is. It is this oneness which I call a beautiful spiritual "high" that we strive to take with us back into the full routine of our daily living. This really is the triumphant life. I commend it to you, also. Do what is necessary, as often as necessary, to build, rebuild and renew your oneness, but LIVE it, it is your greatest gift to yourself and the world.

But how does one live in the oneness? This is the tithing or giving of YOURSELF. Think of your presence as the trigger of a magnificent chain reaction of Light, Love and Good. Wherever you go, *BE* that Ambassador of the Living Light and *start* another chain reaction of good. You now have ALL the tools, and NOTHING IS IMPOSSIBLE TO YOU. Stick with the six big key words, strive on to make a wonderful life for yourself, and in the process you will leave the world a better place than you found it. And we might properly say, good friend, that is the meaning of life.

A Parting Word of Friendship

The closing chapter of a book is always an emotional experience for me. Somehow I feel that in our sharing of the Ishtar Power and the great truths he has brought us, we have become deep personal friends. There is a touch of nostalgia as we come to the end of this special work together, but it is mixed with happiness and enthusiasm. We learned when we graduated from high school that the ceremony is quite properly called commencement, not *end* or *graduation*. I hope that this will be the commencement of a closer friendship for us as well as a richer, fuller life for you.

You no doubt have noticed that I have sprinkled a few enticements toward my getting to know you here and there in the book. I have offered to send you a drawing of the Ishtar Altar Star and also the new Ishtar Multi-star Sheet as a specific gesture of friendship, with no obligation on your part. But of course I hope you will also share with me some happy reports of your own magnificent results, and we would love to have you as an active member of E.S.P. Laboratory. For any or all of these reasons, I invite you to contact me. Write to me, Al Manning, ℅ E.S.P. Laboratory, 7559 Santa Monica Blvd., Los Angeles, California 90046. I'll look forward to deepening our personal friendship and sharing our growth TOGETHER.

CHAPTER POINTS TO REMEMBER

1. You now have a magnificent set of tools for triumphant living. Use them effectively with the set of key words: MOOD, ATTITUDE, CONTACT, ACTION, EFFECTIVENESS and GROWTH.

2. Your effectiveness will be enhanced when you remember that it includes Kipling's famous six words: WHAT, WHERE, WHEN, WHY, HOW and WHO.

3. When you need some real trouble-shooting, check your six big key words to see how well you are using them—and most problems will be solved at once.

4. Ishtar's reward for all of his help to you is the uplifting of the whole world that comes from YOUR GROWTH.

5. Fertilize your spiritual soil by regular tithing, but keep the emphasis on the giving of YOURSELF and your Light to uplift the world.

6. Be an Ambassador of the Living Light, and start fresh chain reactions of Light, Love and Good wherever you go.

7. I want to deepen our friendship and to give you your Altar Star and Multi-star Sheets. Do write me and ask for your drawings—and, I hope, give me a good "feedback report" on YOUR wonderful progress.